DISPOSSESSED

DISPOSSESSED

Stories from India's Margins

Ashwin Parulkar • Saba Sharma • Amod Shah • Shikha Sethia
Rhea John • Anhad Imaan • Annie Baxi

SPEAKING TIGER

SPEAKING TIGER BOOK LLP
125 A, Ground Floor, Shahpur Jat, Near Asiad Village
New Delhi–110049, India

First published by Speaking Tiger 2017

ISBN: 978-93-86582-53-9
e-ISBN: 978-93-86582-54-6

10 9 8 7 6 5 4 3

Typeset in Minion Pro by SÜRYA, New Delhi
Printed at Gopsons Papers Ltd

Dedicated to the memory of
S.R. Sankaran
one of free India's most compassionate,
brave and uncompromising public servants

Contents

Preface

The essays in this volume are about encounters with people with profoundly different lives from those lived by most readers of this book. We know too little about them and, partly as a result of this, have not learnt to care. The essays are written by my fine and sensitive young colleagues in the Centre for Equity Studies, who had themselves led lives of relative privilege, but who spent many months trying to research and understand a little of the deprivation, discrimination and want which are experienced as lived realities by millions of our people. They were profoundly shaken by the stories they encountered: stories of incredible suffering, of violence from the state and community, of uncaring, hate and humiliation. But, like me, they also always found evidence of love, courage, resistance and hope.

The opening section of this volume titled 'Born Busy Dying', is an unflinching forensic account of starvation and how starving families survive denial and an uncaring state. Although famines have been erased in modern India, endemic starvation persists. But this is surrounded by both official denial and public indifference. Almost all who suffer the misfortune of dying of starvation do so unobtrusively and anonymously, creating not even a ripple outside their own mud homes. But very rarely, a few starvation deaths catch public attention, usually because of some alert local reporter and persistent local activists. I therefore suggested this research study, identifying some ten such momentarily 'celebrated' episodes of starvation which briefly entered middle-class consciousness, rocked legislatures and dominated the front pages of newspapers. The idea was to go and find the families in which these deaths occurred, and document what had happened in their lives before, during and after the brief public attention their condition attracted.

Two of my young colleagues opted for this investigation. One of them was Ashwin Parulkar, in his early thirties, raised by immigrant parents from Maharashtra in the United States. The other was Ankita Aggarwal, trained as an urban planner who switched gears early, and went instead to the UK for a post-graduate degree in development studies. She returned to India and worked for the Right to Food campaign, before joining my office in the Centre for Equity Studies (CES). Nothing they had read, studied or experienced had prepared either for the intensity of suffering, deprivation and official indifference they were to encounter in India's rural interiors. Ankita was a little more resilient, perhaps because she had been raised in India. We found that Ashwin struggled a bit more to reconcile what he had seen. The affection of his colleagues and the chance to engage with the work after the team had left the field helped to heal him. I encouraged him to write about what he saw, and *The Wall Street Journal* carried six of his stories. For this volume, I requested him to write not just about what they saw and heard, but also of what he *felt*. This is the log-book of an unusual journey of empathy by these two young people.

The next section, titled 'Engaging with Unequal India', is a collection of stories that emerged from a larger study of destitution which a team of young people undertook with me in CES for about a year. Some of these were part of the hunger and social exclusion research unit in CES which we named after S.R. Sankaran (to whom this book is also dedicated). The idea here was that while we understand a little about poverty, perhaps even about extreme or ultra-poverty, we know very little about destitution. That is a condition in which not only is dignified and self-reliant survival no longer possible, but relationships, solidarities, the agency of self, even hope, crumble. For this study, teams of two spent around a month each at sites where they expected to find numbers of destitute people, in order to observe their lives with respect and empathy. The product of this year-long study of destitution merits a book of its own. For this volume, we decided that each team would identify one story from the site they visited, and write about it.

Saba Sharma, a young researcher trained in anthropology in Belgium, opted to travel with Ankita Aggarwal to a colony of leprosy patients in Raigarh district of Chhatisgarh. I had served as a District Collector twenty years earlier in the same district, and at that time had found those diagnosed with leprosy to be among the most stigmatized people I had encountered anywhere. I developed a close bond with them, and learned about their stories of expulsion from their families and villages, their exclusion from work and their loneliness. Saba and Ankita found that much had changed in these two decades. Stigma persists, but it is not so absolute and unforgiving as it was in the past. Still, the children of leprosy patients can only marry children of other leprosy patients. Families have rebuilt bonds, but the feelings of belonging remain tenuous. The story they tell here is an observant and gently humorous tale of a visit with an old woman with leprosy to the district hospital to be treated for a cataract.

Kanchan Gandhi accompanied Ashwin Parulkar in a series of visits over several weeks to a slum in Jaipur with a high population of Bengali-speaking Muslims. Kanchan is an accomplished geographer, with a doctorate from Singapore, and she was the coordinator of the Sankaran unit at CES. Ashwin and Kanchan's evocative account works at many levels. It vividly and observantly describes life in any typical Indian urban slum. Within this, it follows the lives of three single women who are forced by circumstances into begging, and the paradox of both the humiliation and the dignity of their struggles. And finally it describes the consequences of the 2008 bomb blasts in Jaipur, which led to the profiling of the impoverished young men of the settlement as 'Bangladeshi terrorists'.

Anhad Imaan, an unusally sensitive young man, studied Sociology in Hyderabad, before joining us to study the lives of homeless men and women in Delhi for his first job. Amod Shah left his job as an asset manager in a company in Singapore and as an environment consultant to join CES for the study in destitution. They spent a lot of time with our colleagues in Aman Biradari who work with the destitute homeless men who congregate in thousands on an embankment close to the Yamuna River in Delhi, called Pushta, just adjacent to the Nigambodh Ghat. In Amod's words, 'Smoke from the ghat's funeral pyres often lends the area an inhospitable, almost ominous air. But perhaps this is also what makes it one of the few places in the city where the homeless do not compete for scarce space with the rest of Delhi's residents'. Their stories are more sombre, of ill health among destitute men, of limbs invaded by maggots, of tubercular lungs and wandering minds, and of the despair which pervades destitute men when their bodies and minds start giving up.

Kanchan and Ashwin spent a month in a settlement of Musahars in Bihar's Muzaffarpur district. The Musahars are among the country's most dispossessed and oppressed communities, considered the lowest even among Dalits. Their account is a bleak one, of landlessness, hunger, debt bondage, disease, the lack of schooling, the failure of all government programmes and the trap of a web of false criminal cases laid against them in land disputes. By contrast, you see upper-caste landowners who have made good in the city, leaving the Musahars even further behind.

Shikha Sethia, who had worked in the private sector in the Hague, Singapore and Delhi, most recently as an economist, also encountered ubiquitous despair in her site of research, the Bhagwan

Mahaveer Viklang Sahayata Samiti in Jaipur, where an average of a hundred disabled men and women converge every day from the far corners of India, without almost no money. With a group of young interns, she spent many summer days talking to the patients assembled there. Most, she found, 'appeared to have lost hope of living to see any positive transformation in their circumstances'. And yet, as she persisted, it became clear to her and the other young researchers that 'this apparent lack of hope was a conscious effort to expect as little as possible from the process, to avoid disappointment'. Each was 'part patient and part pilgrim, there to be healed and to find the strength to transform his or her life'.

We decided to try to understand in more depth what life would look for a girl or woman who is disabled and has to negotiate her life in the Indian countryside. We tried to develop a methodology for these studies that are egalitarian and democratic, based on empathy and respect. The central core of this approach was that the principal researchers into the lived experiences of rural women and girls with disability would be disabled rural women themselves. These are people who simultaneously endure and battle so many multiple life challenges—of gender, disability and rural life. For those coordinating the study in three states—Odisha, Jharkhand and Karnataka—the challenges of learning and sharing meaningfully with rural disabled women who had battled life but had uneven access to formal education and were not trained researchers, amidst so many disabilities and languages, can be imagined. It was my young colleague Rhea John who so ably led this study, with all the grace, empathy and sensitivity that it required. She was drawn to the study because of her abiding interest in understanding marginality, and she reflects in her essay here on what she learnt about life if you are challenged in so many ways at once

An idealistic young lawyer, Mohsin Alam, returned after his doctoral studies and set about trying to understand the nature of housing discrimination against Muslims in Delhi. Why do Muslims tend to live in separate settlements in the city? Is it that they are excluded from or forced out of mixed settlements, and if so, how does this actually work, as they negotiate with property dealers or house owners? Or do they opt for Muslim majority settlements because they find in these greater security or cultural affinity and acceptance? To find answers to these questions, he brought together a diverse set of young researchers who spent many weeks talking to property dealers, house owners and people seeking a house to rent. Among these was Annie Baxi, a doctoral scholar in Psychology and a counseller, deeply interested in marginality and gender. She reflects on her encounters with discrimination and sensitively uses these to reflect both on her privilege and her own identity.

The last story in the collection, again by Saba, is of a 'De-notified Tribe', the Lodhas, in rural Bihar. These were communities notified by the British colonial rulers in the nineteenth century as 'criminal tribes'. Although this designation was formally abolished after Independence, Saba and Ankita found that they continue to carry the stigma of a criminal mindset even today. Saba writes about how their upper-caste neighbours and the state administration label this impoverished landless community as one of lazy thieves and drunkards, and tells the story of a man who takes one step toward overcoming his prejudice, by becoming at least a little more thoughtful, if not caring.

HARSH MANDER
New Delhi, 2017

PART I

BORN BUSY DYING

ASHWIN PARULKAR

A field investigation of government responses to starvation deaths in Bihar, Jharkhand and Madhya Pradesh

‘I wonder how people starve to death
When God blessed the land that lacks the harvest
Their stones are quality, but their homes are poverty
And the whole world ignores the robbery.’

—Nas, ‘Blood Diamonds’ (2012)

INTRODUCTION

My colleague Ankita Aggarwal and I visited hunger-prone villages in Bihar, Madhya Pradesh and Jharkhand from September to November 2011 to chronicle government responses to the starvation deaths that had occurred between 2005 and 2010.

A decade before our travels, the Supreme Court had recognized poor people's 'rights to food' through access to food, nutrition, pension and public works programmes. In the summer of 2001, numerous starvation deaths had occurred in Rajasthan at a time when public storehouses held over 50 million tonnes of food grains. Public food and nutrition programmes were defunct.

The People's Union on Civil Liberties filed a public interest litigation on behalf of the poor that year, asking the courts to recognize the duty of officials to deliver social services as a Constitutionally backed human right of the disadvantaged. 'Article 21 of the Indian Constitution protects for every citizen a right to live with human dignity,' they wrote. 'Would the very existence of life for those families which are below the poverty line not come under danger for want of appropriate schemes and implementation...to provide aid to such families?'

The orders were historic as they interpreted the right of access to eight social protection programmes as inherent to the Constitutional right to life (Article 21), transforming the administrative duty to implement social security programmes into a Constitutionally recognized legal mandate.

In 2009, the UPA government promised to pass a National Food Security Bill upon re-election. Policymakers could no longer ignore the paradox blighting India's claim as an emerging nation. Four decades of food production surpluses and a high long-term growth rate—just over 8 per cent since the 1991 economic reforms—existed alongside the country's shameful distinction of being home to more than 200 million hungry and malnourished people.

The National Food Security Bill was therefore conceived as a human-rights law meant to ensure people's access to food vis-à-vis the social protection system. Passed in September 2013, it assures the right of 67 per cent of Indians—about 820 million people—to buy highly subsidized grains from the public distribution system (PDS), as well as other entitlements for vulnerable people, such as maternity benefits for pregnant women and lactating mothers, nutrition services for children under six years old at local anganwadi centres and free mid-day meals for students at government schools. This figure represents 75 per cent of India's rural and 50 per cent of its urban population. Poorer states have to provide access to the PDS's wheat, rice and coarse grains to a greater percentage of their population, above the national 67 per cent cut-off. Bihar, for example, has to ensure that 86 per cent of its rural population benefits from the law.

The central government had given states an October 2014 deadline to implement the Act. Only eleven states, including Bihar and Madhya Pradesh, had begun to identify beneficiaries and distribute ration cards by then. The central government has since extended the deadline three times.

According to an April 2016 audit conducted by the Comptroller and Auditor General of India (CAG), eighteen states had enacted the law by March 2015. Yet, only 51 per cent of the people in those states had been identified by officials.

Implementation of the Act has been slow, in part because states are left to devise their own methods to identify the two kinds of beneficiaries entitled to food and nutrition programmes. The first are 'priority' candidates, eligible to buy 5 kilogrammes of grains a month, paying Rs 3 per kilogramme of rice, Rs 2 for wheat and Rs 1 for millets. The second, 'Antyodaya' candidates, are considered to be the most vulnerable of poor people, such as the elderly or infirm. They are entitled to 35 kilogrammes of grain at subsidized prices. The central government had initially directed states to create their lists of beneficiaries based on the Socio-economic Caste Survey, but did not make the survey's data public by the time the Act was passed.

Critics have also identified policy and budget decisions by the central government that threaten to curtail the impact of the law. Biraj Patnaik, principle advisor to the Commissioners of the Supreme Court on the 2001 right to food case, pointed out two moves that he believes violate the law's provisions and those of previous court orders establishing access to social programmes. For one, budgets for nutrition services under the law were slashed by 50 per cent and maternity entitlements by about 30 per cent. Secondly, a March 2015 order issued by the Department of Food and Public Distribution (DFPD) directed states to eventually phase out the identification of the most vulnerable Antyodaya cardholders. In 2015, Patnaik reported in *The Hindu* that the DFPD directed officials 'not to add any new household to this category if any household drops out due to an improvement in social and economic status, death, etc.'

Some field surveys, however, show signs of progress. In their August 2015 report in the *Economic & Political Weekly*, 'Bihar on the Move,' Jean Dreze, Reetika Khera and Jessica Pudussery reported that their 2014 survey in four rural districts of Bihar—Banka, Gaya, Purnea and Sitamarhi—showed that 78 per cent of of 997 families had correct ration cards and, in the previous two months, they had received 69 per cent and 79 per cent of their grains entitlements, respectively. This was a vast improvement compared to Bihar's performance in the previous decade. They found that beneficiaries in Bihar received only 10 to 15 per cent of their grains entitlements during the 2000s.

Findings from 2011 also showed improvement in Bihar. That year, people were able to buy 76 per cent of their entitled allotment of grains.

In 2014, field researchers reported that 'in earlier surveys households complained they had been excluded from the Below Poverty Line list' and 'with expanded PDS coverage under NFSA, that problem had been largely resolved.' But Gaya district, where stories in this book take place, showed no signs of improvement during their survey. It was 'the worst by a large margin as far as the PDS is concerned. In some villages, the NFSA did not seem to have had any impact at all.'

Despite national debates on the need for rights-based approaches to tackling hunger, not much was said publicly about how starvation response should be instituted in food legislation. Debates did emerge on other critical areas of food security: whether to reform food procurement and delivery systems; whether to reform public food distribution or scrap it for cash transfers; whether and how poverty lines should be revised to properly identify the poor to provide them access to social programmes; and the extent to which related deprivations, like malnutrition and the lack of clean drinking water and sanitation, should be included in food policy and legislation.

In the draft bill of 2011, the government had incorporated a version of the National Advisory Council's recommendation defining starvation as *prolonged deprivation of food that threatens the survival of a person.* By the time the bill was passed in September 2013, the term was removed from the definitions section and from cohering sections, such as Rights of Persons Living in Starvation, which outlined systems of redressal, relief measures, methods of identification and investigation of starvation and starvation deaths.

We had set out for the field to ask how officials respond to incidents of starvation deaths. We quickly realized that the central questions were: who were these people who starved to death and how did they actually live? We visited villages segregated by caste. Tribal and Dalit people lived in destitution without adequate food, clean water, roads and proper shelter. There were also few to no nearby schools and hospitals. In conversations with people who had lost loved ones to hunger, we heard that their family members had died after enduring long periods of low food intake: a daily meal of rice or roti with salt, and sometimes local flora that grew in the village. The general pattern of demise went something like this: an economic shock—from the lack of work or the inability to access health care during an emergency—precipitated days of struggle without food.

The role social protection programmes can play in the lives of poor people was apparent. In each case, families were denied consistent access to the food, nutrition, public works and pension programmes intended for them. Diseases such as tuberculosis debilitated adults of working age, while most children, particularly infants, were visibly malnourished.

'True peace,' Martin Luther King Jr. once wrote, 'is not merely the absence of tension: it is the presence of justice.' In these villages, the silence we often encountered was not the quietude of peace. It was evidence of the injustice of death-inducing poverty. That is what these stories are about.

Note: Versions of the chapters that detail our experiences in the villages of Banwara, Heta, Hindiyankalan, Manan Bhiga and Manjhladhi were first published in *The Wall Street Journal*'s India Real Time Blog as part of a six-part series called 'Starving in India' in April 2012 (http://blogs.wsj.com/indiarealtime/tag/starving-in-india/).

Jalhi Bongia, Bihar

September and November 2011

Naresh Mandal (21, Male), Failu Bhuiya (25, Male), Vifiya Devi (60, Female), Heera Lal (32, Male), Bharti aka Aarti Kumari (5, Female), Riki aka Rinku Kumari (3, Female), Danesh Kumar (4, Male), Gulab Kumari (13, Male), Sonya Kumari (12, Female), Kalvati Kumari (12, Female), Jitendra Kumar (5, Male), Baldev Kumar (9, Male), Rakesh Kumar (8, Male), Dulari Kumari (8, Female), Sugwa Kumari (1, Female), Rajmanti Kumari (2, Female)

We had stopped visiting the villages for fieldwork in November 2011. Through April 2012, we were compiling our findings and writing about them. But something happened in May. I had to stop. I was thinking of death too much. The facts held up, but I felt like I was in a room with four walls that were about to smash together.

By October 2012, I was in Bihar again, in the villages of a district called Muzaffarpur. I was there to learn about other forms of human destruction, so when I learned that a yatra protesting the scaling back of provisions in the proposed National Food Security Bill was stopping in Muzaffarpur en route to Patna, I decided to go.

There were about 200 people gathered in a field. Rupesh was standing on the stage with a hand on the microphone like a rapper. Rupesh is the State Advisor to the Supreme Court Commissioner's Office on the Right to Food. 'Every day you read about starvation deaths in the newspapers,' he was saying. 'In Gaya there is a village called Jalhi Bongia. The Bhuiyas of this village are landless and to get their daily bread they have to migrate to cities in other states like Rajasthan to work in brick kilns and stone-crushing sites. For years now they have been coming back with silicosis or tuberculosis'. Jalhi Bongia is a village in the Mohanpur block of Bihar's Gaya district; it had the first starvation deaths that we learned about.

We had met Rupesh in the basement of his office in Patna's Panchwathi Nagar section one rainy Saturday morning. He was warm, yet intense, sometimes leaning forward while he spoke, both elbows on the table, hands together, or leaning back in his chair with his hands behind his head. The day we met, he was wearing a white v-neck t-shirt, glasses, a thick head of white hair and a beard; this youthful, boyish face. We sat on metal chairs at a long, rectangular, water-stained wood table which left little walking space in the room. His colleague, Sanjay, a thin man in his fifties with dark prescription sunglasses, joined us. Sanjay was a Champaran-born farmer turned social activist and since he is fluent in English, he writes or translates many of the primary materials that came out of the fieldwork conducted by the office.

The way Rupesh told it, I knew he had told it many times. In the drought of August 2005, the people of Jalhi had no farm work and the ration shop, angwanwadi centre and public works programme were all closed. It had been like this for years. Members of the village's Bhuiya community were leaving Jalhi in lean seasons to work in the brick kilns, coal mines or glass and plywood factories in other parts of Bihar, or in Gujarat, Maharashtra, Orissa, Rajasthan and Uttar Pradesh, to avoid hunger. The Bhuiyas are a Dalit caste—untouchables outside the Hindu caste hierarchy—that have lived in extreme poverty in Bihar for generations due, in part, to long-held cultural practices of discrimination that prevent Dalits from accessing resources reserved for higher castes—namely land, education and jobs. In 2007, the state government identified the Bhuiyas and nineteen other Dalit communities for special housing, water, food and education programmes, intended to improve their lives and redress historical wrongs. Some Bhuiya families in Jalhi Bongia owned land. But the quality was poor and it wasn't much: about 2 to 4 dishmil, a square plot of dirt the size of a home garden. There are no irrigation facilities or water harvesting sources to protect farms in times of drought. For generations, the village's lower-caste Bhuiya and Ravidas families had worked on the nearby farms owned by landed Yadav farmers.

But that year, villagers who did not migrate to other states could not find farm work because the crops had failed. None of the Bhuiya villagers owned a ration card to buy wheat and rice from the local grain shop. Villagers who did—mostly Ravidas families—were not receiving their monthly installments. Bhuiya children were suffering because the anganwadi centre was not providing cooked meals, grain supplements and health services to the village.

Each of the Bhuiya families suffered a string of hunger-struck sleepless nights. One night, a few adult Bhuiyas weighed the options: find whatever food available in any way possible, or succumb. The community lives in a cramped hamlet in a row of mud-and-wood huts tightly wedged together. There is a dirt road 7 kilometres off the National Highway that leads into the village, through hamlets segregated by caste. On the other side of the road that lines their huts is a stretch of scorched fields bordered by thickets of wild weeds. Behind the thickets are hills and forest where Bhuiya men, women and children go to collect wood to sell in the markets when local work dries up. Days before, villagers had buried one of their goats in a patch of dirt between the thickets and the hills. Four adults walked into the weeds that night and performed the sacrament. They dug up the goat, carried the carcass into the hamlet. Village men and women cooked and ate it. The next morning, they fell sick with diarrhea. Sixteen people died within days of each other. Twelve were children.

Local and national newspapers reported the deaths. When Rupesh got word, he sent a team to conduct the first of a string of investigations into reported starvation deaths in the area. 'The hope was to direct the state government's attention to the plight of those suffering drastic conditions of hunger,' he said. His team visited Jalhi and surveyed the performance of the social protection programmes deemed rights by the Supreme Court, the condition of child malnutrition and the availability of work. He found that none of the victims' families had ration cards, the anganwadi centres and the mid-day meal programmes were defunct, and no one had received employment from the public works programme.

Rupesh sent the report to district and state government officials in late 2005. He said he received no response. Reports in Hindi and English newspapers said that the people of Jalhi resorted to eating the dead goat because they were starving, which moved government officials to issue statements on the cause of the tragedy.

A joint investigation team of government officials and NGO members visited the village that September. The District Development Commissioner (DDC) on that team filed a report to then-District Magistrate, Sandip Paundrik. Officials reported that villagers had died of diarrhea. They did not mention the status of food and work programmes or the lack of public infrastructure, like a working hand pump for drinking water. Mr Paundrik told the *Times of India* in September 2005 that 'the report that the DDC submitted states that no death occurred due to hunger and all the deaths reported were due to diarrhea.' The article also stated that Mr Paundrik dispatched the civil surgeon and a medical team twice to 'affected villages' and that both teams reported that 'no further deaths occurred.'

A researcher on Rupesh's team walked into the room with a stack of reports and placed them on the table while he talked. Rupesh handed us a copy of the report his team had recently conducted and sent to the Chief Secretary of Bihar. The study listed about 100 investigations into reported starvation deaths in Bihar from 2006 to 2009. It covered six districts, including Begusarai, Muzaffarpur, Gaya, Patna, Nalanda and Jahanabad. The Chief Secretary of Bihar is the head bureaucrat identified by the Supreme Court as responsible for the implementation of all right-to-food programmes in the state. This official is charged with ensuring that the families of victims of starvation-related deaths are provided immediate access to food, work and nutrition programmes. The Chief Secretary of Bihar at the time of this field research did not respond to phone or fax requests to be interviewed for this book. The inaction that followed the Jalhi tragedy, Rupesh said, was the catalyst for the statewide survey.

'Over the next four years numerous other deaths [in Bihar] were reported in the media,' he told us. 'The state had been hit by three consecutive drought years from 2006 to 2009, which led to the deaths of many poor people.' The team found that these deaths had all occurred under similar conditions: victims were from Dalit and tribal communities who struggled to find jobs in villages where food, work and pension programmes programmes were defunct. Each of the victims also belonged to those Dalit or low-caste communities that have been historically denied equal access to natural resources, job opportunities and education. Rupesh's team tried to provide a relevant context for the conditions of 'starvation'. They cited the Supreme Court Commissioner's definition of that term from a document called the Starvation Protocol.

The Commissioners wrote the Protocol in consultation with a team of economic, medical and nutrition experts in India called the 'Hunger Watch Group'. The goal was to urge governments to consider community-wide consultations between local officials, affected and concerned citizens and doctors to respond to people afflicted with chronic hunger, malnutrition, starvation and corresponding diseases associated with undernutrition. The Protocol's definitions of 'hunger' and 'starvation' were originally devised by the Jan Swasthya Abhiyan in their 2003 'Guidelines for

Investigating Starvation Deaths' and meant to provide citizens and officials criteria for identifying the needs of people suffering discrete, yet related, stages of demise, and addressing them through social programmes and medical care. 'Hunger' was understood to be the 'denial of adequate food to ensure [an] active and healthy life' while 'starvation' was the state in which 'hunger is prolonged to an extent that it threatens survival.'

These consultations would be based on a two-part 'verbal autopsy'. Phase 1 would be held with the family of a person suffering hunger to assess their food and work conditions and the social programmes they had access to. Phase 2 would be held with the wider community—'members of the tribe, caste...to which the affected people belong'—to similarly, identify potential challenges that could be faced by larger numbers of people yet to be identified, such as being denied access to anganwadi centers, ration shops and social security benefits. The District Panchayat would be tasked with reporting the findings and coordinating with District Collectors to provide immediate relief to individuals, and long-term access to programmes for communities being excluded from benefits. The idea, the protocol says, is to approach the crisis as a public health concern and to identify people living with hunger and malnutrition-related ailments before deaths actually occurred. 'Few people die directly die of starvation,' the Protocol states. 'They live with severe food deficits for long periods, and tend to succumb to diseases that they would have survived if they were well-nourished. Starvation does not require absolutely zero food intake, but rather prolonged periods of such low food intake as to be incompatible with survival.'

In the context of this definition, Rupesh's report provided a glimpse of how each poor person, already malnourished and living in extreme poverty, lost their battle with hunger and disease when each of the eight food, work, nutrition and pension programmes meant to ensure food security under the Supreme Court's orders on the right to food did not deliver services as promised. Local and state government officials did not respond to the report.

In October 2009, the local media reported the starvation death of a woman named Murti Devi who had lived in the village of Tetua Tola. Rupesh conducted an investigation in her village and submitted his findings to the Supreme Court Commissioner's office. He reported that people were not receiving rations from the grain shop for six months, the Mahatma Gandhi National Rural Employment Guarantee Programme was defunct and, as in other drought- and hunger-prone villages, people were migrating to other areas of Bihar and various other states to find work to avoid hunger.

Rupesh decided to bring Murti Devi's case to the public's attention. He told us that the goal was to spur the action that should have followed the tragedy in Jalhi. He gave interviews to print and television outlets. 'After we brought her [Murti Devi's] case to the public's attention in light of other deaths that occurred over the last few years in the state,' he said, 'a debate emerged over how to stop the starvation deaths from happening.'

The people of Tetua Tola protested Murti Devi's unnecessary death by staging a roadblock near the village. Debates appeared in local print and television media outlets on how to address the crisis. But the rage over capricious public responses to unnecessary deaths and failed social programmes did not hasten serious and committed government action to address these woes.

***

The deaths in Jalhi were integral to the larger story of public action on starvation deaths in Bihar. The incident was so tragic that it made the state advisors aware of the importance of collecting discrete primary data on the social and economic conditions of poor villages and vulnerable communities on a regular basis. It also made local journalists more vigilant about such deaths and better prepared to cover similar cases that would occur in the future. But the long-term result of fact-finding missions, to Rupesh's frustration, was not compliance with laws. The programmes and policies in existence to prevent such travesties from happening in the first place were not implemented or followed.

Why did the media's timely reporting and the frequent investigations by right-to-food activists not translate into real pressure on the government, either to mend broken social programmes, or to recognize and enforce the rights of poor people to these programmes?

We went to the village hoping to learn about the tragedy from the viewpoint of the people who lived through those days in August 2005. We wanted to know the conditions of hunger, employment and access to public services at the time of the deaths, what action had taken place afterward, and if any changes had occurred to date which improved their food security and ability to access social programmes.

A Jesuit priest named Father Jose runs an organization called Jeevan Sangham in Bodh Gaya, about a kilometre from the site of the tree where Siddharta Gautama found enlightenment. People from all over the world come to see that tree, which no longer exists; while a short distance away, the descendents of the people that the Buddha saw have inherited their suffering. They exist and no one sees any of them. Since 1994, Jeevan Sangham has run educational outreach programmes for Dalit and tribal children in seven panchayats in Gaya district. Most of these children have never been to school. Especially the girls. They focus on girls who are vulnerable to child marriages.

Father Jose says that when they first started many of the parents of children had never even heard of a school. They had to teach the parents the concept of an education before receiving permission to provide one. Can you imagine, he asked me. And no, I literally couldn't.

He and his staff work in remote villages in the district and hold residential programmes for children at the Jeevan Sangham campus for two weeks every season. We stayed there for a couple of nights and were woken in the morning by the choir singing songs I had only ever heard before as gospel music back home.

Father Jose also works with Rupesh and several NGOs on the hunger and malnutrition crisis in the area, because many of the children they teach suffer from it. He has conducted investigations into starvation deaths with Rupesh as part of a team known as the Supreme Court Commissioner's Joint Commission of Enquiries (JCE). Since 2010, the Supreme Court Commissioner's Office has dispatched these investigation teams after advisors notify the national office of reported starvation deaths. The teams usually comprise state officials, human rights workers, researchers and bureaucrats responsible for development programmes.

Father Jose gave us a report from the JCE's September 2010 visit to Jalhi, which contained primary data on the families of fourteen of the sixteen people who died in 2005. Ten were children. According to Father Jose's survey, most people's lives had not improved five years after the deaths. Nine of the victims' families had yet to receive ration cards. Six families did not have a National Rural Employment Guarantee Act (NREGA) card. The eight that did, had yet to have their bank accounts opened at the post office to deposit the wages due when they complete any work sanctioned by the programme.

I kept Father Jose's survey in the front flap of my notebook on the motorcycle ride from Bodh Gaya to Jalhi Bongia. The village is 13 kilometres off the National Highway through a series of dirt paths that cut through numerous little villages and hamlets. About twenty-five minutes after turning off the main road, we entered a windy dirt path to the Bhuiya tola of Jalhi. We passed a woman walking with her two little girls, with a bundle of forest wood atop her head that she was carrying to the market.

We arrived at the tola where about ten children were playing a game in a dirt trench, flicking a matchbox between themselves in the circle they had formed in front of the row of mud huts. The roofs were made from trees that grow in the village—assan, shakuah and dauh. On one side of the road, a winding white pathway led through the huts to more huts in the interior. On the other side was barren land, with dead grass and a few large trees, where a group of young and middle-aged men squatted next to a charpai, their elbows draped over their knees, smoking throught their fists and speaking expressionlessly.

The children stopped playing. They stood there, blinking at us. We hopped off our bikes. 'Hello,' I said. There was only silence. We would get used to this in each of our visits. With adults you could sense the initial confusion, mistrust, fear, curiosity. With children, there seemed a kind of ambiguity that you could not locate or do anything about until you spent a little more time with them.

Some of the men sitting on the charpai under a tree stood up and walked up to us. Shivdari Manjhi stood in front, squinting through the sunlight with a hand on his hip, elbow out. 'Where are you coming from,' he asked. He was fifty-five years old. His skin glistened. I walked over, met him halfway. We'd come to learn more about the incident that occurred in August 2005 and the conditions of the village as they stand now, I explained. It never felt right to say why we had come. And it was the first thing we had to say. Inside, there was always a gnawing shame for asking them to relive the most painful event of their lives. It never went away. I had partially memorized the names on Father Jose's survey. Shivdari's son, Danesh, was one of the victims. He was four years old when he died.

'Several people have come to the village since then,' he said. He coughed while he talked. It sounded painful. Officials and journalists from Patna and Delhi had visited in the years since. We had read the reports. Father Jose had even asked other Jesuit priests and NGO workers that he knew in European countries to come to Gaya. Journalists from Ireland covered their story. Little had changed, Shivdari explained. He covered his mouth while he talked and coughed the words through a closed fist, turning his head occasionally to spit the phlegm into the dirt. His eyes were red. He was thin and frail. The skin under his neck was loose and ragged. Between coughs he said, once, that he wasn't well—he'd been diagnosed with tuberculosis five months earlier and was taking medication given to him by the doctor at the Mohanpur public health centre, about 10 kilometres away. Three tablets a day, he said. He was too weak to work. His twelve-year-old daughter, Beli Kumari, was supporting the family by selling forest wood in the market. She walks about 15 kilometres each morning into the forest interior to collect a large bundle of wood that she sells the next day for about Rs 35 to 40 in the market. She walks to the market, which is about 20 kilometres away.

'Mukesh!' he shouted. A small boy in shorts standing with the other children perked up. Shivdari Manjhi's son. He had his arm around another little boy. 'Bring out an extra charpai so we can sit.' Mukesh darted towards their hut, which was just across the dirt path behind our motorbike. A group of about fifteen men gathered.

***

The *Dainak Jagran*, the *Times of India*, the *Irish Times* and a 2011 newsletter by Oxfam International reported that fourteen people had died in the village after eating the dead goat. They also mentioned that food, nutrition and work programmes were defunct at the time of the deaths, and that local officials visited the village after the incident received media coverage to provide immediate access to the public distribution system. The Oxfam newsletter reported that in the six years after the incident, people were receiving a more regular distribution of grains, though not their full quotas on a monthly basis. Rupesh told us that, in coordination with the district government, his office had set up village courts, called Nyay Dals, made up of villagers and local officials to monitor the performance of the food, nutrition and health programmes.

The reports did not, however, detail the actual events that took place during the August 2005 calamity or describe the complex conditions of poor health, chronic hunger, physical isolation and unemployment that play a role in the frequent nutrition-related deaths that still occur in Jalhi Bongia. Our time in Jalhi Bongia revealed that endemic hunger had been—and still is—a way of life for the ninety-eight families of the Bhuiya community of this village. The story behind the deaths of sixteen villagers in August 2005 underscored the desperate circumstances in which many people still live.

In November 2011, we sat with Shivdari Manjhi and other villagers at various times while they told us what happened. Shivdari Manjhi said that the Bhuiyas of Jalhi were suffering from a combination of hunger and illness at the time of the deaths.

'There was no food in the house. People weren't eating at home, or getting it from outside because there was no work,' Lalhan Bhuiya, the father of another victim named Heera Lal, said. In normal times, people found work on land owned by Yadav farmers for 3 kilogrammes of rice a day. But that year the monsoon rains did not come until August, so farm work had dried up months before. Drought would plague the area for the next four years. In 2005, fifteen villagers migrated to Rajasthan, Uttar Pradesh and Delhi to work in brick kilns. Villagers who stayed behind survived by selling bundles of forest wood to market traders. Villagers walk to the forest 15 kilometres away in the morning and return before dark with a bundle of wood. Men, women and children as young as nine years old do this work. The next morning they walk 13 kilometres to the nearest market to sell the wood for Rs 35 to Rs 40. In times of relatively good health the wages are still not enough to feed a family of five or six. Villagers often rely on loans from the market to avoid hunger.

In August 2005, a combination of factors led to crisis. There had been months of drought and no farm work. The local ration shop a kilometre away had also been shut, so there was no way of getting cheap grains. People in the tola became too weak and sick to do physically intensive work, such as collecting and selling forest wood. Unable to leave the village, they suffered in isolation until the hunger became too great for some people, who made a desperate and fatal attempt to feed themselves.

Lalhan Bhuiya walked over to a patch of wild green plants on the ground that resembled spinach while others narrated the events. He plucked the plant, known locally as chakora, out from the roots. He tore some leaves off the base and said, 'At the time of the deaths we boiled the leaves off the chakora plant twice a day.' Chakora and another plant they called mukha would satisfy them for one to two hours. Enough to work, villagers said.

'Do you still rely on this for meals,' I asked.

'Yes. When times are desperate. What else are we going to do?'

Sometimes a neighbour can spare 1 or 2 kilogrammes of rice—enough for one day. They boil the rice to supplement the plant. But in August 2005, no one in the tola had any rice in their homes, because the fair price shop had been closed for months. The chakora, Lalhan Bhuiya said, is 'enough for one or two hours…to have enough energy in the morning to go to work and then just enough to not feel hungry when you sleep.'

The month the tragedy occurred, Mr Bhuiya's thirty-two-year-old son, Heera Lal, and three other villagers—Naresh Mandal (21), Failu Bhuiya (25), and Vifiya Devi (60)—were also relying on the chakora to survive. Nights during that summer went like this: a group of people would cook the chakora and feed themselves and other villagers. Hunger pangs would come two to three hours later. The pain would keep people awake throughout the night. This went on for weeks to months, villagers told us. By early August 2005, it was too much to bear. In the dark of night, the four villagers decided they had enough. They crossed the dirt path and walked through the thickets to dig up a goat they'd buried days ago. They brought it back to their huts, cooked it and ate the meat, hoping not only to ward off pain but to know the sensation of relief that comes from genuine satiation. The next morning they would experience violent fits of simultaneous diarrhea and vomiting.

Villagers say that they had a hard time cleaning the effluvia in the tightly cramped, unsanitary environment. Within days, children contracted illnesses from the exposed waste. The poorly constructed one-room mud huts, wedged close together, were not sufficient barriers to the spread of disease. The combination of monsoon rains and the lack of adequate cleaning utensils, or means of disposal, made it impossible to stifle contagions. Their physical isolation and lack of money or transportation made access to urgent and effective medical care difficult as well. Facilities like the local health centre are located on the National Highway, but no one in the tola owned a vehicle to travel there or a cellular phone to call anyone outside the village for help.

The community banded together and tried to help the four families by caring for the dying and cleaning up the surroundings with no facilities or assurance of help. The solidarity was remarkable and tragic. All were reeling from the same kind of hunger that prompted their four friends to eat the rotten meat. They were all together, yet each alone. We were unable to ascertain the exact time span between the deaths of the four adults. Several villagers said the first four deaths occurred within one to two days after the victims ate the rotten meat. Villagers also explained they were unable to reach a doctor in time to save these men and women, but a local quack came to the tola while the four adults were dying and gave each person water. Villagers were unsure of the name of this person but said their friends died within hours of that visit.

Mothers, fathers, brothers and sisters who had lost loved ones told me how they tried to cope. Villagers who were not sick would clean the waste from the orifices of their ailing friends and family members with their bare hands. Victims convalesced on charpais. Neighbours would scoop the fallen waste up from their dirt floors with their hands. Those floors turned into a noxious blend of mud from faeces, vomit, mucous, blood and rain. The stench was horrific. It lingered in homes days after the deaths. Many of the villagers who tried to nurse their friends and family to health were ill themselves—about thirty-five people, villagers said, were suffering from tuberculosis on our visit.

Each of the ten child deaths reported in the media occurred within the next week: Bharti Kumari (5), Riki Kumari (3), Danesh Kumar (4), Gulab Kumar (13), Sonya Kumari (12), Kalvati Kumari (3), Jitendra Kumar (5), Baldev Kumar (9), Rakesh Kumar (8) and Dulari Kumari (8). Two other child deaths happened during this time, but were not included in media reports. They were baby girls, Sugwa Kumari (1) and Rajmanti Kumari (2). They were also sisters.

'As soon as we'd bury one person,' Shivdari Manjhi said, 'another one would die.' Shivdari and his wife, Malan Devi, shared the horror with other parents of ailing children: while caring for their own son, Danesh, they witnessed and tried to prevent the deaths of other children. They cleaned the waste and tried to nurse those children. Others, including the ailing, tried to help them save their son.

Dainak Jagran journalist Amit Kumar, who accompanied us on one of our visits, said his paper covered the story after the four adults died and during the span of time that the children were dying. 'The people's condition worsened because they had no money to buy medicines,' Kumar said. He said that people sold possessions to get money to pay for medical care in other areas of the block to save their children.

***

Today, the Bhuiyas of Jalhi Bongia still battle a pernicious kind of destitution that is a constant threat to their lives. More than thirty people had died of tuberculosis in the years between the 2005 tragedy and our November 2011 visit, villagers and Father Jose said. While we were there, more than thirty people were living with the disease. A 2011 survey of the village conducted by Rupesh showed that twenty people had died of silicosis or tuberculosis that year alone. We were not able to confirm the high rates of both diseases from a medical expert, but people told us that many friends and neighbours had died of these illnesses in the year of our visit.

According to Rupesh and Father Jose, people have been contracting infectious diseases since migrating to work in other states. Until three or four years ago, Father Jose said, most people who left Jalhi ended up working in stone quarries in Rajasthan. It is a vicious cycle. People who are already chronically hungry and malnourished flee the desperate poverty of their villages, only to work under unsafe and arduous conditions in a strange place with low pay and cramped and unsanitary living quarters. In the absence of affordable and reliable medical care, these factors hasten diseases and—in many cases—premature death. People often resort to alcohol to cope with the kind of depression that is associated with the daily grip of extreme poverty, and the frequent grief that arises from the untimely deaths of loved ones.

Alcoholism is especially high among young men in the village who are forced, sometimes in their early teens, to assume head of household responsibilities after their fathers die of illnesses that they, too, are likely to suffer in the future. Listening to the tone of the voices of these young men recounting the stories of people who died reminded me of poet Robert Hayden's description of his own depression: *my dark nights of the soul,* he called it. I pictured the dark night of August 2005, as they spoke in low volumes, picking at the dead grass under the tree where we sat. It seemed, listening to them, that the only way to articulate madness was with clarity and calmness. I imagined what went through their minds witnessing so much death, disease and hunger in the very homes I was looking at as they talked. The high rates of alcoholism, chronic malnutrition, hunger and depression according to Father Jose, present a challenge—to say the least—to living healthy lives.

Villagers claim that the spread of diseases made them fearful of migrating. Some people still do leave Jalhi out of desperation, but the year we visited was the first of many that most people chose to stay home.

Some young men don't have a choice. The Mandal brothers—Anil, Gitendra and Sudeep—find various kinds of manual labour in Gujarat a few months a year to support their mother and two younger brothers. Their father died a few years before our visit. The young men are in their late teens and early twenties. Their one- and two-year-old baby sisters, Sugwa Kumari and Rajmanti Kumari, died in the 2005 tragedy. Sudeep explained their situation: 'In our house it's our mother and five brothers. We don't have land and there's little opportunity to find work on the fields. We divide up our earnings to give to the family. When we leave and the family runs out of money, we get loans from the local market. We eat when we get paid.'

Most other young men around the ages of twenty to twenty-five who migrate go to work in the brick kilns of Rajasthan. Others go to Uttar Pradesh and Delhi. A local contractor provides each person Rs 1,000 before leaving the village, with the promise that they'll get paid a larger sum when their work is complete. While away, they work from 8 a.m. to 8 p.m., get a daily wage of Rs 200, and live in one room with several other men from different parts of the country. They're able to save up to Rs 5,000 in about three months and return home to give the money to their families. Villagers in group discussions said that many of them contract illnesses in far-away sites.

Accessing health care is perhaps one of the biggest problems the community faces. The public health centres are supposed to be free, but sick people are often turned away. 'The issue,' Father Jose said, 'is that these people came back with tuberculosis and didn't find any treatment. Many of them went to the block hospital and were told that there was no medicine...and they were almost chased out of there.'

One woman named Dulari Devi narrated such a story to me. The local administration had been made aware of the tuberculosis problem in May 2011. According to Amit Kumar, forty-four people in the village had been diagnosed with the disease. Gaya's Civil Surgeon and physicians from Barachatti and Mohanpur blocks came to the village. Dulari Devi and others told me that the medical staff arranged transportation for many TB-infected patients to go to the private hospital in Gaya. Dulari Devi's husband, Sambu Bhuiya, was one of them. While there, they said, the nursing staff treated the villagers poorly. Nurses and the doctor gave them water but refused to provide them with medicines when the people of Jalhi said they had no money to pay for them. They were told to leave. In order to get a ride back to the village, they had to agree to exchange stocks of grain from their homes. Two days later, Sambu Bhuiya died.

***

In August 2005, after the deaths occurred, the serving block development officer visited Jalhi. Villagers told us that this official told the people that the primary cause of death was diarrhea. We could not contact the official because he had left that post and it has been occupied by a number of people since 2005. The District Magistrate at the time also ordered the Civil Surgeon to visit Jalhi. Villagers say that official administered a saline solution.

Meanwhile, newspaper reports highlighted the fact that people were not getting rations from the local grain shop. Orders were given to provide immediate access to the shop, but villagers only received their regular quota of 25 kilogrammes of grain at discounted rates for a few months. There was no accompanying order to give ration cards to people who qualified for but did not have them.

In September 2005, local officials told the *Times of India* that the endemic poverty was due to a labour crisis. Officials claimed that villagers were not demanding work from the NREGA programme, because they require daily wages and the programme only deposits wages once every fifteen days. But two independent surveys and data from our visit showed serious problems in the implementation of the programme. The 2010 survey conducted by the Supreme Court Commissioner's JCE showed that less than half of the victims' families had job cards and none of the villagers had their bank accounts opened at the local post office. The two activities should happen concurrently.

The larger point is that local bureaucracy had made no progress on fixing failed social programmes in the village between 2005 and 2010. This prompted the Supreme Court Commissioner's Office to dispatch the JCE in July and September to villages in Bihar that had suffered starvation deaths and were in a state of crisis due to the failure of all right-to-food programmes.

Dr Sajjad Hassan was a Manipur-based IAS officer who was affiliated with the Supreme Court Commissioner's Office and led the JCE team (full disclosure: he was a colleague at the Centre for Equity Studies). The Supreme Court Commissioner's Office considered Jalhi Bongia one of the worst-affected villages in the state, based on media reports and repeated independent investigations. It was the only village that the JCE visited both times. Dr Hassan explained the discrete objectives of each visit. 'The first meeting was intended to be an examination of the conditions of hunger and destitution in the villages, followed by meetings on findings with officials. The second meeting was about institutional set-up—to work off the findings and discussions from the first visit and plan how civil society agencies and government agencies could respond to hunger.'

The July investigation was thorough and non-confrontational. According to the July 2010 JCE report submitted to the Supreme

Court Commissioner's Office, the team held focus group discussions with 'affected communities, mostly Dalits and Maha Dalits [sic]', as well with 'panchayat and block officials' to have a constructive dialogue on how best to fix the broken system. In Jalhi, the team found that of the approximately 'forty-five deaths in the past years' that had occurred, twenty-five 'were due to hunger, and the rest due to people suffering from TB on account of their working in Rajasthan and Delhi at stone-crushing work sites.'

The major socio-economic problem they found was the extensive landlessness of the Bhuiyas ('they had...no agricultural land at all. No land provided to them by government.' And 'no knowledge of land rights'). They also found that each of the right-to-food programmes did not function:

NREGA: 'No one has done any work in the past two–three years. The last year anyone worked was in 2006!'

PDS: 'Only five of the 2005 victims' families had received a ration card'; '25 per cent of families had no BPL [Below Poverty Line] card'; 'those that do have cards, get ration only occasionally'; and 'AAY [Antyodaya Anna Yojana] rice is provided every two–three months for the past year' (it should be provided every month).

Anganwadi centres: 'A pregnant mother says two–three months ago, she received food—0.5 kilogramme rice and dal—and none after that. No evidence of normal provision for infants and young children.'

Mid-day meal schemes: 'School seems to be very irregular. Children say they get rice and dal when it is open.'

After field investigations and discussions with local officials in the July visit, the JCE team shared their findings with district officials in Gaya and state officials in Patna. Officials were open to meeting the team, Dr Hassan said, and accepted the findings as true because, he said, 'you'll find that when people are coming from the Commissioner's Office they can't afford to say no to meetings.' The larger challenge, he said, is ensuring that discussions based on findings result in sustained action.

The team made several recommendations to higher-level officials—the head of the Social Welfare Department, the Food Department and the Health Ministry—including the need to set up block-level committees that would comprise key government officers and civil society representatives to monitor the situation on the ground. The JCE then requested district and state governments to send an official response to the team's findings to the Supreme Court Commissioner's Office, so that the two parties could work together on tackling the severe hunger problem in selected districts.

District and state officials did not respond to the findings. The Supreme Court Commissioner's Office sent the JCE team to Bihar again that September. Dr Sajjad, Father Jose, Rupesh and others met with Gaya's District Magistrate and his staff at the District Circuit House on 19 September 2010 to discuss the July findings and solutions for a way forward. Again, the JCE posed a range of recommendations, particularly regarding the need for the district officials to actively 'work out a plan to provide immediate support to families most vulnerable to hunger', including 'those without land, without earnings, old, infirm and diseased, and those excluded from the BPL list.'

The District Magistrate agreed that the JCE's July findings on defunct social programmes and the conditions of destitution in the village were accurate. He also agreed that hunger and poverty were endemic to the area. But a discussion on the likeliness of people dying from these conditions was more contested. 'The starvation issue itself is contested,' Dr Hassan said. 'The agreement on the findings was less about the cases of starvation deaths and more about the general causes that lead to the breakdowns in the system.' The District Magistrate said that the impending elections made it too busy a time to conceive of and implement a plan immediately.

The lack of political will has meant that the village remains in relatively the same condition as it was when sixteen people died in August 2005. The administrative errors are egregious. Twenty-eight families were mistakenly given above-poverty-line cards. BPL card-holders do get grains from the ration shop each month, but not the full amount due to them. They get 20 kilogrammes (8 kilogrammes of wheat and 12 kilogrammes of rice) instead of 25 kilogrammes.

The 2011 Bihar State Advisor's to the Supreme Court on the Right to Food survey showed that, according to the programme officer's records, 187 people in the village had job cards, but none had been given the application required to assign bank accounts at the post office to deposit their wages. This lapse in the programme is difficult to correct because every member of the Bhuiya community in Jalhi is illiterate and none of the villagers during our time had an understanding of how works are to be sanctioned. The programme is designed to be demand-driven—villagers are to convene at the Gram Sabha and decide collectively on a set of works that are desired and needed in the area. This rarely happens in reality. For one, the Gram Sabha did not take place until 2011. Secondly, officials responsible for the programme do not consult villagers on what works are required or the process.

According to the programme officer's record, card-holders were provided with thirty-two days of work at Rs 114 a day—far less than the guaranteed 100 days of work. But according to surveyors' conversations with the villagers, people had only received twelve days of work, without payment.

On our visit, the programme showed little sign of improvement in that regard too. Thirty-five job cards had been issued. Each of the accounts had been opened. Villagers claimed that they had worked from two to ten days that year, but did not receive pay.

The problem was that the local official responsible for oversight of the programme at the village level, called a rozgar sevak, had the villagers' cards in his possession. Villagers said they were told that they were not allowed to keep the cards with them. This is a violation of the programme. Unfortunately, it is also a common scheme in areas with endemic poverty that lack political power and are beset with very low literacy rates. The cards are supposed to be used to account for the number of days each person worked, to corroborate their wages. The rozgar sevak is responsible for tallying the days worked in the cards, and the wages, based on these figures, are deposited into their accounts. Without the cards, villagers cannot access their own accounts. Amit Kumar filed a report on this incident that appeared in the next day's local edition of *Dainik Jagran* but no action was taken to redress the situation.

***

Back in Delhi, I received a call in February 2013 from one of the local NGO workers that had accompanied us on our visits to Jalhi. I had asked him for updates on who had received BPL cards since we had left. I also asked for a detailed update on Shivdari Manjhi and his family's condition. Our friend called to tell us that Shivdari Manjhi was dead. Forty-six people had died of malnutrition-related causes since we had left. Poverty murdered forty-six souls. I wondered how many of them were the children we saw playing in that circle or going out of the village to fetch firewood to sell in the market to keep their mothers from starving. Such questions have no answers. They are faces inside me that make me burn.

Manjhladhi, Jharkhand

November 2011

Padamchand Hazra (50, Male)

The people of Manjhladhi call Padamchand Hazra's family 'the poorest in the village.' Of the ten villages we visited, Manjhladhi was the smallest, and home to forty scheduled caste families. We went to Jharkhand's Dhanbad district in November 2011 to speak to Paro Devi, the widow of a labourer named Padamchand Hazra who had died the previous year of hunger and poverty.

A group of young people led us through a winding dirt path into the village. We passed stray dogs, small children and a man who was wearing an orange t-shirt with the worn face of Krishna on it, carrying bundles of wood over his shoulder towards the main road that leads to the district town. Paro Devi's home was the first one at the entrance of the small hamlet. It stood on the other side of a crowd of bushes and trees that had no beginning, no end. She was standing outside her home with a group of children, the young adolescents already taller than her. Her house was half-mud, half-brick. The roof had caved in, exposing what looked to be broken bamboo shafts and tufts of hay with holes in them. Dried dung cakes were plastered to a makeshift mud platform just outside the home and a couple of empty baskets and steel pots were placed on a torn piece of tarp just beside the doorway.

She stood calmly with her arms folded, her face half covered under her dupatta. We asked if we could speak to her. She told her children to bring out an extra khattiya for us to sit on. She was forty years old, but looked much older. The bones were sharp against her hollow cheeks, which looked dry and tired, and her lips and forehead were wrinkled and chafed.

Paro Devi was married to Padamchand Hazra when she was a girl and had moved to Manjhladhi as a young woman. Padamchand Hazra had earlier married another woman named Jeera Devi, who still lives in the village. When Paro Devi moved to the village, she and Padamchand Hazra had started a family together in the house she lives in now. Meanwhile, Jeera Devi moved a few doors down, with her young son. Paro Devi said that her husband worked two jobs while they were married. He would find work on construction sites in Dhanbad, where he'd bring in Rs 60 a day. Other days—about once or twice a week—he'd pull a cycle rickshaw in the city and earn about Rs 20 for about seven hours of work. Paro Devi cleaned houses and washed dishes in the village for a half-kilogramme of rice a day.

The family never had enough food to eat. They borrowed money and asked for food from neighbours frequently. Sometimes Padamchand Hazra and Paro Devi would ask Jeera Devi for a small portion of rice too. The couple's oldest son, Akaldev, now twenty-one years old, is blind in one eye with poor vision in the other. He has never been able to work. While Padamchand Hazra and Paro Devi struggled to find enough work and money to feed themselves and attend to Akaldev's special needs, they held hopes that their youngest children, Deepak (15) and Ujala (12) could continue their education and perhaps escape the scourge of poverty. The children got a hot cooked lunch at the village school as part of the national mid-day meal scheme. Meals of rice, dal and sometimes eggs were much-needed respites between many nights they went to bed hungry.

Only fifteen out of forty families in the village had a BPL ration card. Paro Devi's family was one of them. But the local fair price shop, 5 kilometres from their home, was only open one day at a time, in two or three months of the year. When the dealer did open the shop, card-holders never received their due quota. Villagers would cycle to the shop to get 25 kilogrammes of rice. The dealer charged card-holders the state subsidized rate of Rs 1 per kilogramme of rice but they should have been able to buy 35 kilogrammes at that rate. The Jharkhand government had made this a policy during the 2009 assembly elections. In the years before that, consecutive droughts and the struggles poor people faced to either buy cheap grains, or access the public food system at all, resulted in a number of reported hunger deaths in the state.

'When we asked the dealer why he wasn't giving us rations every month,' Paro Devi said, 'He said it was because he was not getting it from the godown.' Yet the dealer would make false entries in the villagers' cards, indicating that people had received more rice than they actually had. In some instances, he'd also write that they had received grains that he wasn't even supplying. Paro Devi's ration card indicated that her family received 19 to 25 kilogrammes of rice and 9 kilogrammes of wheat each month from August 2009 to July 2010. But she and her neighbours told us that the dealer had stopped selling wheat about five years ago. In 2010, the state government had stopped selling subsidized wheat through the PDS altogether.

The NREGA scheme was also not open in the village until 2010. That year, Padamchand Hazra found work through the program, building a road in Manjhladhi with other villagers. The work lasted about fifteen to twenty days—far less than the 100 days guaranteed by law—and ended before the completion of the project: at the time of our visit, most of the road leading into the village was unpaved. As the ration dealer had made false entries in the ledger of the family's ration card, the local official responsible for overseeing the public works programme had also fudged Padamchand Hazra's job card. His job card indicated that he worked forty-eight days under the programme in 2010, but each of the villagers we spoke to in a group discussion say that was not possible. He earned Rs 100 a day, better than wages from other work, but less than the Rs 120 stipulated by law.

That year was also the third consecutive drought year in Jharkhand. In other lean times, Paro Devi had been able to find farm work—sowing paddy a few days a season in exchange for rice. But in 2010 she and Padamchand Hazra could not find any agricultural work.

The years were taking a toll on Padamchand Hazra. He was fifty years old. He had left school at the age of twelve to support his parents and siblings and had spent most of his life overworked and underfed. He had always been thin. But by 2010, villagers said he was starting to become emaciated. Eventually, he was too physically weak to work. The loss of his income was a setback for the family. Paro Devi didn't take him to the doctor because they didn't have any money. She didn't take him to a Public Health Centre (PHC) where treatment is free because she didn't know that such a place existed.

The family coped with the loss of Padamchand Hazra's income by eating less food through the passing days and accepting handouts whenever and wherever they could. But by August 2010, the family was on the brink. That month, they would endure the hardest week of their lives: no work, no food and the ration shop was closed again. They had experienced hunger throughout their lives, but this was the first time they went four straight days without any food at all.

'About six in the evening,' Paro Devi recalled, 'he [Padamchand] asked me to put the khattiya outside. He wanted food. He kept asking for it but there was no food in the house.'

The lack of work, the drought, and the nearly defunct ration shop also created hardship for neighbours too. They could not support the family in their time of need. 'I have two brothers in Purlia,' Paro Devi said, 'but they were unable to help. They had their own families to look after. They're poor too.'

On the night of 17 August 2010 Padamchand Hazra died.

'Had we known that he may die because of hunger,' a villager said in a group discussion, 'we would have tried to arrange some food for him.'

Villagers said that Padamchand's was the first hunger death in Manjhaldhi. Other deaths had occurred in the district in the previous three years. The Jharkhand State Advisor to the Supreme Court Commissioner's Office, Balram, said that problems in the PDS, the drought and the lack of work had been catalysts for starvation deaths in the district during that time. His team conducted an investigation in the summer of 2010, on the socio-economic conditions of the families and the communities, as well as on the functioning of the government schemes in the villages of the deceased.

Five hunger-related deaths occurred in Dhanbad district in August alone. Four in nearby Nirsa block. A man named Shyamlal Manjhi of Chirkunda, died the same day as Padamchand Hazra.

While villagers narrated a story, I saw a hungry and sick man. His face was bloated and his legs were thin. It looked like he was chewing his cheeks. He was balding, but it looked like his hair had been burned off in a fire. He was sitting one knee up, with his elbow draped over it. I asked who he was. The villagers told me it was Padamchand Hazra's brother. I took a picture of him and wondered if Padamchand Hazra looked like him.

Jharkhand experienced three drought years from 2008 to 2010, which correlated to incidences of starvation deaths in several districts. Before, hunger deaths were usually confined to historically impoverished areas of the state with high tribal populations. According to Gurjeet Singh, who oversees the NREGA programme for the State Advisor's Office, hunger deaths had, unfortunately, been common in the northwestern districts with large populations of poor tribal—Latehar, Palamu, Garwha and Chatra—people. Many scheduled tribes in these districts lived in secluded areas. Their poverty and hunger was hastened, in part, by the lack of education and health facilities. Deforestation also struck a blow to tribal livelihood. A few years after Jharkhand achieved statehood in 2000, journalists started to report hunger deaths in other districts. Singh said that the combination of drought, poor performance of government schemes, displacement due to illegal mining activities and the growth of Naxalism led to the rise of destitution in central and eastern districts such as Dhanbad, Hazaribagh, Bokaro, Deoghar and Dumka.

'After repeated drought conditions since 2004,' Singh said, 'we found that hunger deaths were spreading to economically stronger districts like Dhanbad.'

The August 2010 report conducted by the Jharkhand Advisors to the Supreme Court Commissioner's Office on the Right to Food concluded that 'in these areas there is a lack of implementation of the various programmes run by the government. Drought and lack of employment opportunities has created a very alarming starvation and malnutrition situation in these areas. Even food and employment programmes are lacklustre and there is a lack of motivation to implement them.'

The report pointed specifically to flaws in the PDS. Many villagers hadn't received ration cards. Those who did, such as Padamchand Hazra's family, never received grains regularly.

Several local officials and politicians visited the village in the days after Padamchand Hazra's death. Paro Devi and other villagers said that these people not only promised to investigate and fix glaring problems in food and work schemes, but did so with the acknowledgement that Padamchand Hazra died of hunger.

Knowledge of the on-going investigation pushed Govindpur block-level officials to hold a meeting on 19 August 2010. Officials discussed measures to prevent hunger deaths, particularly in times of drought, and decided that each panchayat should hold a quota of grains for emergency situations. Rations would be made available for those in need. Individuals identified as starving would receive 10 kilogrammes of rice. Destitute families would be eligible for either 35 kilogrammes or Rs 400.

But on our visit, fifteen months later, the attention given to Padamchand Hazra's and other hunger deaths by the State Advisors to the Supreme Court Commissioner and by the media had not resulted in long-term changes. Many of the problems that existed at the time of Padamchand Hazra's death persist. People do not receive work from the NREGA Programme.

The anganwadi centre was undersourced at the time of Padamchand Hazra's death, in part because it ran out of a villager's home. She used to provide khichdi for children, but did not have the training or sources to provide the range of intended nutrition, feeding and information services for women. The woman who ran the anganwadi centre had died of a heart ailment the week before Padamchand Hazra died of hunger and the village has yet to replace her.

Paro Devi has also been shut out of other benefits that are recognized as rights under the ambit of the right to food case, such as pension schemes that should be activated upon the death of an earning family member. 'I went to the block official after my husband's death to ask for the widow pension after I hadn't received it and was told that I would get it, but I never have,' she said. The local government has also yet to ensure basic infrastructure in the village like a hand pump for clean drinking water. Manjhladhi's 'poorest family' continues to live on the brink.

'We still don't eat to a full stomach,' Paro Devi said, recalling later, 'I haven't tasted dal in so long I forget what it tastes like.'

***

As in other cases, the media played a vital role in spurring government action by reporting Padamchand Hazra's death within the next day. The earliest reports placed the family's destitute conditions in the context of specific hunger deaths that had occurred in the area and had already been reported on by local newspapers days and weeks before. Villagers said that a *Dainik Jagran* reporter named Anand Pathak was the first journalist to tell Padamchand Hazra's story. He was at a nearby chai stand the morning after Padamchand Hazra died when someone from a neighbouring village told him what happened.

Pathak's article shows that the media had already raised the issue of the deaths of other people in nearby villages who succumbed to similar circumstances during that time. The beginning of his 18 August 2010 article reads: 'While the issue of Rathmani Kisku's hunger death was still fresh, Govindpur block natives Padamchand Hazra of Manjhladhi, Shivlabadi Munda (Chirkunda), and Shyamlal Manjhi also died of hunger on Tuesday.' The article is accompanied by a photo of Paro Devi standing next to Deepak and Ujala on the dirt floor of their kitchen, strewn with empty pots. It highlights the recent events that led to the family having to endure four days without food: Padamchand Hazra's inability to work for two months and the consistently closed ration shop preventing the family from buying grains.

Newspaper reports prompted several local politicians to visit the family four days after the death. They offered money and grains. Phoolchand Mandal, a local MLA, gave the widow 25 kilogrammes of rice and Rs 500. Dhulu Mahto, an MLA from Bagmare district, gave her Rs 1,100. Samresh Singh, an MLA from Bokaro district, gave Rs 6,000. The block supply officer—the official responsible for coordinating the block level food distribution system— ordered the ration dealer to give the family 50 kilogrammes of rice. Journalists also covered the visits and recorded the promises officials and politicians made to authorize pension schemes for which Paro Devi was eligible under the Supreme Court's orders on the right to food. This included a widow's pension and a Rs 10,000 payment known as the National Family Health Benefit Scheme.

In their 19 August 2010 article, the *Dainik Jagran* noted that politicians and officials came to Manjhladhi and provided some immediate financial support to Paro Devi in the form of cash. But they did not address the failure of social welfare programmes in reaching destitute people in the village, or the absence of basic amenities like clean water or shelter. The article also pointed out that a block official, Ashok Kumar, had already ordered ration shops in the area to provide 50 kilogrammes of grain to destitute families in July.

One-time offerings are common in starvation cases that receive media attention, but there is a lack of sustained action that could result in poor people having long-term access to social programmes intended for them. 'Through the media,' Balram, the Jharkhand State Advisor to the Supreme Court Commissioners Office said, 'there is an immediate short-term response. But the problem is that there is no long-term monitoring systems in place, so we don't see long-term changes.' Official orders to ration dealers to provide destitute families grain were not accompanied by discussions and decisions on monitoring procedures to ensure that food reaches the poor.

Journalists and watchdog groups, like the State Advisors to the Supreme Court Commissioner's Office, function as the only local monitoring systems in place, since institutional grievance-redressal mechanisms for the implementation of the court's 2001 orders just don't exist. With this gap, activists are resigned to accepting immediate, short-term responses to case-by-case starvation deaths as small victories, in place of more far-reaching expectations to hold government officials accountable to Constitutional rights, Supreme Court orders, and state and local food policies.

Supreme Court orders direct officials to investigate right-to-food programmes and fix problems in them when hunger deaths occur. But since public officials entrusted with implementing social programmes are often reluctant to admit that starvation deaths happen at all, or when those programmes are rife with corruption and negligence, it may therefore seem futile to trust the local state machinery to fix the problems in the system. If the writ of law does not have much legitimacy on the ground, then it is reason to question how problems in governance, such as negligence that may result in unnecessary and frequent deaths, can be fixed by additional policies alone. The failure to hold officials to task, we observed, is a function of the general acceptance that endemic poverty is a natural part of life in some historically disenfranchized communities in this country. The apathy at the conditions of poverty that Padamchand Hazra suffered is a social crime.

***

Journalists actually informed Dhanbad's District Collector about Padamchand Hazra's death in person. The Collector dispatched Block Development Officer Smriti Kumari to the village. A few days later, other block officials arrived with promises to activate pension schemes and benefit packages. George Kumar, a sub-divisional officer, and Sarojini Annie Tirki, the circle officer, told Paro Devi that she would receive a widow's pension, money for the rural housing programme known as the Indira Awas Yojna (IAY) to build a suitable home, and a payment of Rs 10,000 from the National Family Benefit Scheme. Officials also promised Paro Devi that they would ensure that Deepak and Ujala would be enrolled in a boarding school in Dhanbad. None of the officials probed the issues of the defunct food, nutrition and work programmes and none of them upheld any of the promises made.

Paro Devi did not receive any funds from the Indira Awas Yojana. She and her children still live in a mud hut with dirt floors. The sunken roof of one of the rooms leaks. During the monsoon, water drips into the house. We asked Smriti Kumari over the phone why Paro Devi had not received these benefits.

'It depends,' she said, 'on whether her family's name is on the waitlist of the IAY beneficiaries.'

Khem Narayan Singh, the panchayat mukhiya, confirmed that her name is on that list, but mentioned that no one knows when the funds will be released. What purpose did it serve, we asked, to promise Paro Devi an entitlement that officials did not believe they could honour? Ms Kumari replied that she had not checked if Paro Devi's family was on the waiting list.

We also asked her why Padamchand Hazra's family and others were not receiving grain regularly. Why also was the ration dealer's license not suspended, as Supreme Court orders stipulate?

'I'll only be able to tell the reason,' she said, 'after looking at the report which must have been prepared afterwards.' She could not tell us the official nature of the report, which officials wrote it, or where we could locate it. We asked each of the block officials about this report but no one had any information on it.

Ms Kumari and Ms Tirki both denied that Padamchand died of hunger-related causes. This is not unusual. But in addition to official denials, the high-turnover rate in sub-district offices makes it easier for officials to 'pass the buck', which makes it more unlikely that families of victims will receive benefits. Each of the officials that visited Paro Devi after her husband's death, including Ms Kumari and Ms Tirki, have left their posts.

Some officials are tasked with running numerous posts because vacancies are high. This is a state-wide problem in Jharkhand. According to discussions we had in 2012 with a collector from another district in Jharkhand, the state's recruitment agency for development programmes, the Jharkhand Public Service Commission, had not recruited candidates for needed positions for five years, after allegations of corruption prompted investigations into the organization. In 2012, 75,000 to 80,000 seats in local development programmes remained vacant.

When we asked the current block development officer of Govindpur, Sanjiv Kumar, why Paro's family has yet to receive payments from the Indira Awas Yojana, the National Family Benefit Scheme (NFBS), and her widow's pension, he said that pensions and NFBS are the responsibilities of the circle officer. He also said he was not familiar with the details of Padamchand Hazra's death and did not have an explanation as to why the promises made to Paro were not fulfilled.

It was frustrating to witness how officials were not merely unaware of the range of their duties but indifferent to implementing social programmes and administering benefits. Ms Tirki was the circle officer who promised Padamchand Hazra's family the Rs 10,000 for the National Family Benefit Scheme and was responsible for overseeing the programme at the block level. We asked her why Paro Devi had not received her pension more than a year after her husband's death. She replied that this was the responsibility of the block development official, Ms Kumari. Ms Kumari told *Dainik Jagran* in August 2010 that the form for Paro Devi's pension had been filled and disbursements would begin the following month, in September. That did not happen.

It turned out, moreover, that the circle officer is the official who oversees that program. This was, in fact, your responsibility, we pointed out to Ms Tirki, referring to the mandates we obtained from the block office. She gave no reply.

Smriti Kumari and Sarojini Annie Tirki had attended the 19 August 2010 meeting that took place in the Govindpur block office with local bureaucrats on key measures to avoid hunger deaths in times of drought. Local newspapers documented the meeting. Some panchayat members, such as panchayat sevaks, mukhiyas, members of women self-help groups and other residents, were even selected as committee members. Ms Kumari told us that this meeting was planned before Padamchand Hazra's death and another meeting on the same issue had taken place at the block before his death as well.

***

By the time of our visit, there had been one major improvement since Padamchand's death. BPL card-holders in Manjhladhi were getting their full quota of 35 kilogrammes of rice for Rs 1 per kilogramme each month. Vinay Kumar, the dealer, villagers said, weighs the rice in front of them so they are assured of the amount. Still, Kumar only opened his shop once a month and people that did not have ration cards at the time of Padamchand Hazra's death are yet to receive them. The Supreme Court order of 8 May 2002 directed states to ensure that 'ration shops remain open throughout the months during fixed hours, the details of which shall be placed on the notice board.'

Villagers said that most of the families in Manjhladhi are still at risk of hunger in times of drought and unemployment. In 2010, the Jharkhand state government attempted to address this problem. They conducted a survey that attempted to identify people who were most vulnerable to hunger as a result of economic and weather-related shocks. The idea, Balram told us, was to identify people deserving of BPL status who didn't have it. They identified 12,00,000 people and authorized the release of 20 kilogrammes of rice to each person.

In Manjhladhi, despite relative improvements in the PDS, most families still struggle. 'Officials only do something after someone dies,' Upendra Kumar Hazra, a landless labourer from Manjhaldhi says. 'But many people still do not have a BPL card.' Getting a card is more difficult for people in the village because families have to pay bribes of Rs 100 to a man named Vinod Hazra, the son of a village ward member. Some people have paid bribes but haven't received a card yet, and live, daily, without adequate food.

Large discrepancies also exist between what Vinay Kumar claims is his allocation from the godown and the official numbers on file for the ration shop with Block Supply Officer Satya Manjhi. Kumar, who was in Ranchi during our visit, said on the phone that he receives 24.15 quintals of rice and 960 litres of kerosene each month (1 quintal is 100 kilogrammes). But on the block supply report that Satya Manjhi showed us, Kumar's shop is allotted 105.45

quintals of rice and 1,563 litres of kerosene, because his shop serves multiple villages. None of the officials we spoke to, including the block development officer, had an explanation for this.

By November 2011, none of the villagers had received NREGA work. One problem is that they were unaware that they had the right to demand work. The project is supposed to be demand-driven, and people are supposed to discuss in their local gram sabha meetings what kinds of work would meet the basic and productive needs of the village. But gram sabhas do not take place in Manjhladhi. The people of Manjhladhi are not only ignored in the planning of work in the village but are deliberately deceived. Khem Narayan Singh, the village mukhiya, gave us registries of gram sabhas which supposedly took place on 21 October 2011. We read off the seventeen names listed as present at the gram sabhas to villagers. They had all been fudged: most of the people on the list lived outside the village, one name belonged to a child, and one belonged to a relative of a man named Mahendra Prasad who could not have attended because, according to Prasad, this man is mentally unwell. 'There are many mukhiyas who work hard to improve the lives of the people in their panchayats,' Vishal, a young man from Manjhladhi, says, 'but unfortunately, ours is not one of them.'

Panchayat elections were held in 2010 for the first time in thirty-two years. Khem Narayan Singh was re-elected. He has been the mukhiya since the last election in 1978. Vishal claims that he and others have asked Singh for NREGA work but were told that no work exists.

'It's not true,' Singh said, 'people themselves do not want to work in NREGA because they get better wages in private work.'

Villagers dispute this. People have traveled as far as Orissa for construction work, building petrol stations. Daily wages there are between Rs 130 to Rs 250. But villagers also contend that if they could find work from NREGA at decent wages, they'd stay in the village.

Manan Bhiga, Bihar

September and November 2011.[1]

Kangresh Manjhi (42, Male)

'Meet me at the rest stop off the highway. It's a few kilometres before Manan Bhiga, if you're coming from Bodh Gaya. I live two minutes from there. There's a place for food and chai, and cars and trucks are parked out front.'

'I know that one,' I said.

'Good. I'm looking forward to meeting you.'

'Me too,' I said.

Amit Kumar is a thirty-two-year-old journalist who reports on the district's hunger crisis for the national Hindi daily, *Dainik Jagran*, out of Bihar's Gaya bureau. He was born and lives in a village nestled among others in Barachatti, a block beset with endemic poverty. Kumar's official task for the paper, since he began working there in 2007, is to document the performance of the district's right-to-food programmes. His interest in public service started in childhood.

'My family didn't have money but we had the basic things,' he said, explaining that his father's efforts as a social worker to expand literacy in the area impacted his choice to study political science at Gaya's Magadh University. Kumar's reading there made him believe that 'journalists could change society' and upon graduating in 2003,

1. A version of this chapter first appeared in the *Wall Street Journal*, India Real Time on 13 April 2012.

he began his first job as a reporter for the local *Prabhat Khabar* bureau, covering poverty in the district.

He joined the *Dainik Jagran* in 2007 at a time when the paper decided to report on the performance of social programmes in rural areas as a priority. Since Kumar often writes about people who are denied access to those programmes, he is also a de facto chronicler of hunger deaths.

'We have a team of reporters that are constantly going in and out of the villages,' he told us. 'When there is a case of someone suffering badly due to hunger or sickness...someone from the village will call me.' By reporting on stories that involve multiple dimensions of poverty in Gaya, he has also become a valuable source of local knowledge on cohering problems that plague the area: chronic malnutrition, the high incidence of tuberculosis, the impact that the defunct public works programme has had on people's decision to seek jobs in faraway cities and a dysfunctional local public health system.

We reached out to Kumar after our first visit to the village in September 2011, and asked to meet him upon our return that November, because he had covered the death of a man we were now investigating. In April 2010, Kumar sparked the attention of local officials, politicians and the Bihar State Advisors to the Supreme Court Commissioner's Office, when he reported that the family of Kangresh Manjhi, a middle-aged Bhuiya labourer from Manan Bhiga village who had been diagnosed with tuberculosis, had had no food in the house for four days prior to his death.

On his visit to the village, Manjhi's widow, Kari Devi, and their neighbours told him that the public works and food distribution programme were defunct. An unfortunate incident also precipitated the crisis. A week before her husband's death, a dog bit Kari on her ankle just outside the village. She had to arrange loans for transportation to and treatment at Gaya Medical College, a private hospital about 30 kilometres away from their home. Kangresh

Manjhi was alone with his young daughter when the calamity struck. With no work or access to cheap grains at the local fair price shop, the family ran out of food. Kangresh Manjhi was already ill with tuberculosis. His health plummeted and he died.

We learned this information on our initial visit, through conversations with Kari Devi and neighbours. Numerous public officials came to the village after the deaths to give Kari Devi handouts of grain and cash. But when we presented details of the family's economic condition and the failure of government programmes to local officials, they denied that hunger may have played a role in Manjhi's death.

Officials' denial of a hunger death was not out of step with what we had experienced in other cases. We had discussed the current failings of food and work programmes, based on interviews with villagers, the ration shop dealer and the public works programme officers, with panchayat and block officials. These officials admitted that indeed, some people lived with hunger. But no one died from it. People died of poverty. Malnutrition. Not hunger. Officials gave us their time. They listened to the facts we'd presented. The denial of the extent of hunger in the area—so visible to the outsider—undermined the possibility of an honest conversation on what strategies they had in mind to address the dysfunctional social security system that so many visibly malnourished and dispossessed people depended on to survive.

During further research into media reports on hunger deaths in the area, published in local and national dailies before and after Manjhi's death, we found Amit Kumar's work. Something stood out.

Kumar had actually spent time with Kangresh Manjhi and reported on his struggles with hunger and tuberculosis when he was alive. We had not encountered this before. On 5 October 2009—six months before Manjhi died—Kumar filed a story with a title that translates into English as 'TB-affected Kangresh Dependent on Every Morsel of Grain.' Kumar reported that Kangresh Manjhi had been ill for two years. His declining health, sparse work opportunities and the lack of a ration card required to buy subsidized grains made it increasingly difficult for him and his wife to feed their four children. Manjhi had sought treatment at the public health centre on the National Highway a few kilometres from the village. There, he was diagnosed with tuberculosis. When his health did not improve and he complained to the doctor that the medicines were not working, he was told to seek treatment in Gaya, which he could not afford. He begged for food from neighbours and his wife's family to feed their children. Both of their parents, brothers and sisters lived in another village.

Officials did respond to this report. Block Development Officer S.S. Badhan visited the village and provided the family with 10 kilogrammes of rice and some extra money for food, but the family's inability to access to government programmes was not addressed.

Kumar followed Manjhi's case in the months after his death. His briefs—about 500 words a piece—provided a surprising amount of insight into Manjhi's suffering, and how hunger and malnutrition persist in Barachatti block as a function of broken social programmes, false promises by officials and economic destitution amongst the block's Dalit people. In addition to reporting the short-term calamity that led to Manjhi's death, he chronicled the endemic social and economic problems in the village that played a role in Manjhi's hunger and illness: the lack of clean water, long-term unemployment, starvation wages to low-caste people for sparsely available farm work and the process of decline in Kangresh Manjhi's food security as a result of being shut out of each of the right-to-food programmes over a long period of time. Kumar's reporting was balanced, yet critical. He wrote about how administrators and politicians acknowledged Manjhi's case as symbolic of the area's hunger crisis, and promised to correct failures of government programmes. Block officials ordered all panchayats to distribute rice and wheat immediately to those in the area suffering hunger, while local officials had ordered two ration dealers to provide Kari Devi free grains. He also reported on how officials did not uphold these promises—Kari Devi and others were denied their entitlements a few months after the orders were given.

The controversy over whether Manjhi had actually died of hunger pressured block officials to order an autopsy. Kumar wrote that several officials came to the village days after his death, dug up his body and took it to Gaya Medical College for examination. Officials claimed that the coroner's report concluded that Manjhi had not died of hunger, because a few grains of khichdi were found in his throat. But each of our exhaustive attempts on our first visit to get a copy of the coroner's report to confirm this were unsuccessful.

Three decades ago, Amartya Sen argued that the media plays a vital role in preventing mass hunger deaths in democratic societies. The existence of a free press, he argued, allows for the spread of knowledge on severe poverty and hunger, which incites opposition parties and citizens to move those in power to revise or create new government policies to mitigate egregious social and economic inequalities. 'The government cannot afford to fail to take prompt action when large-scale starvation threatens,' he wrote in an article.[2] 'Newspapers play an important part in this, making the facts known and forcing the challenge to be faced.' The 2001 Right to Food Case was spurred by media reports on starvation deaths in Rajasthan at a time when public storage silos held over 50 million tonnes of grain.

Kumar's reporting was unique. In other cases we studied, media reports only 'forced' governments to act—or take notice—after deaths had actually occurred. In Gaya, journalists and the Bihar

---

2. Sen, Amartya 'Food Battles: Conflicts in the Access to Food' in *Food and Nutrition Journal*, 1984: 10.

State Advisors to the Supreme Court Commissioners were raising public awareness of both starvation deaths and the conditions of endemic hunger and malnutrition simultaneously in 2009. Official discussions on hunger and starvation deaths were actually taking place in Bihar at the time.

In October 2009, several local and national newspapers reported the findings from the State Advisor to the Supreme Court Commissioner's Office's investigation of starvation deaths in select districts, revealing that over a hundred starvation deaths that had occurred in poor districts since 2006. Thirty of them occurred in Gaya district. According to media reports, Bihar's Chief Minister Nitesh Kumar had ordered investigations into two reported starvation deaths in Gaya and Sitamarhi districts on 9 October 2009—four days after *Dainik Jagran* ran Kumar's first story on Kangresh Manjhi. Our attempts to reach the chief minister for comments on the follow-up to these investigations were not successful. According to Rupesh, the State Advisor to the Supreme Court Commissioner's Office, the investigations did not occur and the state administration did not follow up their orders.

***

When I met Amit Kumar at the rest stop off the National Highway in Barachatti block that November, he was wearing a pair of aviator sunglasses and dressed in a white cotton shirt tucked into pressed gray slacks, the strap of a leather satchel draped across his shoulder. We spotted each other in the crowd of men. His attire and youth stood out in the crowd of middle-aged men dressed in dhotis and undershirts and huddled together in groups drinking chai, wiping the sweat from their foreheads and mouths with gamchas under whirring fans. We walked up to each other, extending hands. I went for a shake, he pulled me in for a hug.

'It's nice to meet you,' he said, hands on my shoulders.

'Absolutely,' I said.

'Let's move outside. It's noisy here,' he said. He called out to the young man behind the wooden counter for two cups of chai and we sat on chairs in the gravel area outside the awning. He took out a stash of papers from his bag and placed them atop a stack of upside-down milk crates between us. It was a carefully compiled set of the documents he had used to follow Kangresh Manjhi's case—his own and colleagues' newspaper reports, medical records, local surveys of government programmes and notes of official meetings and public hearings on chronic hunger and malnutrition in the district. 'I never write anything without documentation,' he said, handing the stack over to me.

I told him his work helped us a great deal. It provided us insight into the discrete actions undertaken and gaps between key events: Kangresh Manjhi's demise and death, the context behind initial but then inadequate long-term government responses and the disappointing lack of improvement in Kangresh Manjhi's family's ability to access government programmes.

Why hadn't much changed for Kari Devi's family? She still didn't have a ration card and dealers from two fair price shops had stopped providing grains a few months after they were ordered to do so. One month after Kangresh's death, a public hearing was even held on starvation deaths in Gaya. Those in attendance included the District Magistrate of Gaya and high-level representatives from the National Human Rights Commission and Supreme Court Commissioner's Office on the Right to Food.

He said, 'The problem is the lack of pressure on local officials to carry out their duties and the general acceptance of the people's poverty. No one cares about the poor.'

Continuous coverage of the suffering of the people and rights violations ushers little long-term change. 'After I write a report, there is some improvement,' he said. 'But follow-ups never result into long-term action… I've written on these things so many times,' he said. 'Still, no change.'

During our first visit, the block officer, the village mukhiya, the public health centre physician and the police had all maintained that Kangresh Manjhi's autopsy report concluded that hunger did not play a role in his death. Neighbours said that officials who came to the village had told them the report said that Manjhi could not have died from hunger because a few grains of dry khichdi had been found in his throat. The mukhiya told us to that the report was with the block development office. The block development officer told us the report was kept in the public health centre. The physician at the public health centre told us the report was with the police. The police told us it was with the physician of the public health centre. But each of them claimed that the report clearly stated that, while they could not say the exact cause of death, the coroners had ruled out with certainty that hunger played a role.

'It's there,' he said, pointing to the papers on my lap.

I flipped through the stack of papers and found a file marked 'Postmortem Report.' It was one of the few documents in English. The print was faded, but still legible. The physician, Dr Rajiv Ranjan, did not offer an official cause of Kangresh Manjhi's death. The report says that the cause of death is 'kept reserved' until an additional 'histopathological' exam is conducted.

'Was an additional examination conducted,' I asked.

'No,' he said.

'Was there another official report that stated that he did not die of hunger, or offer any official cause of his death,' I asked.

No, according to his source at the hospital that had helped him obtain this file.

It didn't matter what the official report said. The autopsy story had now become fact amongst the local bureaucracy and the villagers, and officials kept repeating it as a knee-jerk reaction to any question seeking discrete information on the case. Did Kumar ever report this discrepancy?

'I can't,' he said.

'You can't,' I agreed.

'I can't,' he said. He smiled and touched my knee. 'But you people can.'

***

Our September visit to Manan Bhiga got off to a slow start. A young man named Ritwiz, a researcher in Rupesh's Patna office, accompanied us from Patna. He had been to the village before, and knew Kari Devi's situation in some detail. We'd planned to spend that week talking to Kari Devi, neighbours, and local development and public health officials. Our first priority was to spend the first few days with Kari Devi to understand her side of the story in as much detail as she would allow.

We realized, early on, that this was not going to be easy. She was standing in front of her one-room hut when we walked into Manan Bhiga's Bhuiya tola off a stone path that was littered with sticks, mud and animal droppings. Her children, Babita Kumari and Pramod, were tugging at her. Kari Devi was a small woman, less than five feet tall and very thin. She shifted her sari from one side of her face to the other. She had striking eyes—dark and round and alive. She wore a bright yellow sari, a nose ring and plastic bangles on each arm; her hair was tousled and oily. Ritwiz introduced us, explaining why we had come.

There was a long silence. I stood with my hands behind my back, squeezing them. I remember feeling my posture slipping. She smiled, looked away, down at the brick path at our feet. Every now and then she would mumble a few words. She did not want to talk and she said so. She did not see the benefit in discussing what happened. More silences followed. Ritwiz stood between us, looking at her and at us in a way that said: what now? Everything felt slow and wrong. We were standing in this sludge, with bad posture. Ritwiz assured her that we would respect her choice not to talk about her husband but if she was open to sharing her story, we would only ask her to reveal details she felt comfortable discussing.

'Give me some time', she said. Her kids were around. She took both of them by the hand.

We walked around the tola. Do we come back tomorrow? Do we try to politely ask her to speak to us again? Let some time pass, we decided, and see if she is up for it. If not, we'll scrap it.

About an hour later we were sitting with her and her children on the charpai in her hut. We wanted to know what life was like when her husband was alive.

'I was working, but we never had enough to eat. My children's stomachs were half-empty,' she said.

Kangresh Manjhi fell ill with tuberculosis in 2007, making it difficult, then impossible, for him to work. The disease is prevalent amongst Gaya district's Bhuiya community. The people are extremely poor landless labourers who are illiterate and have historically been denied education and employment opportunities. Work options are limited to jobs in stone quarries and brick kilns. When the rains fare well, they find a few days of work a week in the fields of landed farmers. But Gaya is a drought-prone district with poor agricultural production and consistent farm work is hard to find.

All of Manan Bhiga's Bhuiya people live in mud houses. Until 2010, there was no hand pump for clean drinking water. The combination of difficult working conditions with low pay and the generally unclean environment in which they live is one possible explanation—amongst others—for the high incidence of infectious diseases in their community. In 2010, the National Rural Health Mission reported that 360 new cases of tuberculosis are diagnosed each year in Barachatti block alone. In Manan Bhiga, four men amongst seventy Bhuiya households had tuberculosis at the time of our visit. Around ten Bhuiya families take loans specifically for food because, they said, the heads of those households are too ill to work.

Before Kangresh Manjhi's illness, feeding his family was already a struggle. Husband and wife would find about ten days of work a month on construction sites and paddy fields in nearby villages.

They earned wages in grain: four bags of rice per day per person for construction work and three bags per person per day for work in the fields. Whole days were spent side-by-side working together on the paddy fields. Kari sowed crops while Kangresh lifted paddy from one field to plant in another.

'Every month we'd manage about 17 kilogrammes of rice,' she said. 'We'd sell about half the bags of rice for money to the nearby store for about six, seven or eight rupees a bag.' The family would buy vegetables from the market with money earned from rice sales. They'd keep the rest of the bags at home to eat and to store. When Kangresh Manjhi and Kari Devi found steady work they still struggled to feed their four children, because a few months in which resources became scarce were inevitable each year. Two incomes, Kari Devi said, were necessary to scrape by.

***

Kangresh Manjhi and Kari Devi managed to survive for years despite being shut out of each of the food and nutrition programmes in the area. Their economic status entitled them to either a BPL or an AAY ration card to buy subsidized food grains from the local fair price shop. But they didn't receive either, because officials had never added them to the list. On our visit, twenty-five out of the ninety families in the villages faced this problem. Kari Devi's was one of them.

But having a card didn't guarantee benefits. When Kangresh Manjhi was alive, the ration shop was open about two to three months a year. By September 2011, the people said that the situation had improved. The shop opened nine months out of a year—instead of the full twelve—but the ration dealer overcharged card-holders. People had to pay Rs 190 a month for 25 kilogrammes of grain. They should have been paying Rs 154 a month.

The NREGA programme could have eased some of Kangresh Manjhi and Kari Devi's burdens, but it had never functioned properly in the village. At most, people would find twenty to thirty days of work a year since it became law in 2006. By late 2011, none of Manan Bhiga's Bhuiyas had ever worked a full hundred days, as the programme guarantees. Those who do manage to obtain work through the programme are not paid on time. In some cases, several days' pay is withheld. In 2010, for example, one villager told us that he had worked for thirty-five days, while his daughter had worked for two weeks, but both had only received eight days' wages.

This problem is the reason why most families in Manan Bhiga seek work in other districts and states. 'If people don't migrate,' one villager explained, 'our hunger situation worsens, because there is no work, no wages, and therefore no money for food.' People spend about seven to eight months in the factories and brick kilns of Aligarh, Jaipur and Delhi. In some cases, whole families go to these places. They return when work dries up there, or when they fall too ill to continue on the job.

We held discussions with Barachatti's block development officer, Nandlal Choudhary, and Gaya's district magistrate, Bandana Preyashi, on the status of social programmes in the area. Both officials told us that people wouldn't migrate if the district and block received their development funds on time. Mr Choudhary said that development funds had not been released for eight months prior to September 2011. 'We made livelihood opportunities so they could live well, so they wouldn't die of hunger,' he told us. 'But local level corruption has debilitated the efficacy of social programmes. On every level', he said of the NREGA program, 'from preparing of job cards, required photos, disbursing of funds, the process is undercut by middlemen who take advantage of poor peoples' illiteracy, their fear of authority and lack of knowledge of the administrative procedures to extort money from them and take public money with little oversight.' To address this problem, Choudhary said he held instruction camps in the area to inform people on logistics free of charge, such as how to get the required photographs, open bank accounts and how to use pass books.

Ms Preyashi said that the centre did not release funds to the district from February to July 2011. The central government has deemed Gaya a Naxal-affected district. As part of a federal assistance programme known as the Integrated Action Plan, the district is supposed to receive an additional Rs 30,00,00,000 for development programmes. But this designation has not made it easier for the district to collect the development funds the centre says they are entitled to.

Journalists in the area also claimed that the public works programme is beset with corruption problems at the panchayat and gram sabha level. According to a few sources, the NREGA programme officer, panchayat rozgar sewak and the village mukhiya take money from programme funds. Villagers have no check against this kind of corruption because these officers are their only link to the programme. The village mukhiya is responsible for overseeing all of the development programmes in the village. The panchayat rozgar sevak has the task of informing the villagers about the several aspects of the public works programme and its benefits.

***

Kangresh's condition declined after 2007 and the burden of earning enough money and food for the family fell on Kari. 'Before my husband fell ill we had enough to eat. When he fell ill, 3 kilogrammes of rice wasn't enough.'

Life was hard. When she found work on the paddy fields or construction sites, she would worry about her children at home. It hurt her to know that she could not feed them. There was also no one to look after them, since other women in the village went to look for work too.

'We couldn't get help from our neighbours because they were facing similar problems. They said, "You don't have any food in your house, but how can we help you if we don't have any in ours either? Where do you expect us to get it from?"'

One villager in a group discussion said, 'There is no way we could help them because we were in the same situation. We couldn't even get our own roti.'

Amit Kumar's first story highlighted how Kari Devi's family depended on food handouts from relatives because they did not have a ration card. After that story, block officials ordered the local ration dealer to allow Kari Devi's family to buy grains from his shop. But in December 2009, two months after the story ran, the dealer refused to comply with the order and the family was dependant on doles again. Her sister gave her a loan of Rs 700. Twice, her brother-in-law, who lived in a neighbouring village in Mohanpur block, gave Kari Devi a one-kilogramme bag of rice. Even that was a stretch for him. 'He said, "I can give you food a few times, but not daily,"' Kari recalled.

With Kangresh Manjhi ill, Kari was unable to bring in enough money on her own to meet the basic needs of her family. To help the family, her eldest son, Sunil, left Manan Bhiga to work in the factories of Moradabad. He was thirteen years old.

'Right now,' Kari said in September, 'he's in Rajasthan. He works in a plastic-bag-making factory and comes home twice a year after he's saved enough money to give to the family. He came home once between last October and April and gave us Rs 3,000 for rice, flour and other rations.'

But Sunil was not home in early April 2010 when Kangresh fell ill for the last time. Late that March, Kari Devi said, his health took a drastic turn. He was too weak to stand up and remained bedridden for weeks. By this time, the family was starting to lose hope of his recovery.

When Kangresh Manjhi first experienced long bouts of coughing three years earlier, Kari Devi had taken him to the block's primary health centre, about 10 kilometres from the village. He was treated by Dr Dwarka Prasad. Dr Prasad had given him medication for a cough, but his symptoms remained. Kangresh Manjhi sought care at the PHC for six months but his health did not improve. Kari Devi said the last time she had taken him to the centre in 2007, the doctor took an x-ray and told the couple that medication wasn't needed. 'He (the doctor) said it was just a cough and it would go away in time. He said it would get better. But when we came home I said, "Now where will I take him."'

Options were limited. They had to go to a private doctor in Gaya. There, he was diagnosed with tuberculosis. But they could not afford the prescribed medicines and returned home. Over the next three years, Kangresh's health and the family's economic condition would only decline.

In April 2010, with Sunil out of the house, three small children to feed, and her husband bedridden, the family was on the brink. Kari Devi said she struggled alone to keep her family afloat, to keep her husband alive.

Five days after Kangresh Manjhi became bedridden, a dog bit Kari Devi on the foot. Infected, her foot swelled and she was unable to work. Getting treatment meant more money for care, as well as travel to Gaya. Kari would have to make one of the most painful decisions of her life. If she stayed at home to care for her husband and children, who would work for daily wages of grain to ensure that the already scarce food they cooked and ate would be earned? And if the infection spread and debilitated her, who would care for her, Kangresh and her children? Yet, if she left home to seek treatment while her husband was sick, who would care for her husband and children?[3]

As her own condition worsened, Kari decided to treat her infected foot and return home to her family as soon as possible. Her sister borrowed Rs 600 from a moneylender, which paid for her commute and treatment at Gaya Medical College. As she feared,

3. Parulkar, Ashwin, 'Starving in India: A Scribe Tries To Save A Life,' *Wall Street Journal* 'India Real Time', 13 April 2012

the condition at home took a drastic turn for the worse. The little stock of grain in the house was soon depleted. For four to five days, there was no food was in the house. To keep Kangresh alive, Babita, Kari's youngest daughter, would bring a single meal of khichdi from the supplemental nutrition centre home for her father. But it wasn't enough to keep him alive, and on 13 April 2010, Kangresh died.[4]

***

Along with Amit Kumar's reporting in *Dainik Jagran*, several media outlets covered Kangresh's death. Rupesh's 2009 report on hunger deaths in Bihar provided some context for journalists to raise questions about why poor people in the area were being shut out of government programmes and dying brutal and unnecessary deaths. Widespread newspaper coverage pressured government officials to visit the village. Kari Devi said she'd received more visitors after her husband died than she had in her lifetime put together: local and state politicians and bureaucrats, journalists and members of human rights organizations. Kshamta Devi, a Vidhan Sabha MLA of Barachatti block, Chhottu Khan, the panchayat adhyaksh of Janata Dal United, and the village mukhiya, Tafiq Ali Khan, all came with cash handouts and promises to rectify the problems in social programmes.

Tafiq Ali Khan gave Kari Devi Rs 1,500 under the Kabeer Antyoshti Yojana. But officials did not ensure that the family received a ration card. The block development officer gave Kari Devi Rs 5,000 and the zilla parishad gave her Rs 1,000. Her widow's pension was also sanctioned, though the post office takes a Rs 10 cut from her before they release it each month. Officials also installed a hand pump in front of her house, though it had stopped working by the time we visited. Soon after Kangresh's death, Gaya's District Magistrate ordered the local ration shop dealer to provide Kari

4. Parulkar, Ashwin, 'Starving in India: A Scribe Tries To Save A Life,' *Wall Street Journal* 'India Real Time', 13 April 2012

Devi 10 kilogrammes of wheat and rice each, free of cost. She only received these rations for the first three to four months.

Media reports and pressure from activists also resulted in a public hearing in Gaya on the starvation deaths that took place in May 2010. After Father Jose read about the case in the *Dainik Jagran*, he sent staff members to the village to inquire into the government's response and Kari Devi's status. Father Jose and Rupesh's team then went with officials from the district administration and asked the District Deputy Commissioner to provide Kari Devi's family the Rs 10,000 she was entitled to under the National Family Health Benefit Scheme. In the village, the activists initiated discussions with district officials in front of the people about opening up the public works programme to help those under perpetual financial duress.

The organizers of the May 2010 public hearing selected a few cases to present to the panel of national officials and representatives. Father Jose said that they asked Kari Devi to come. He sent a jeep with a staff member to pick her up. The staff member arrived at the public hearing without her and told Father Jose that the block development officer and Tafiq Ali Khan had prevented her from coming to the event. Kari Devi told us that she made the decision to remain in the village, because she didn't want to leave her children.

A year after we had left Gaya, we were frustrated to find that Kari Devi had still not received her ration card. Block official Nandlal Choudhary acknowledged in a November 2012 conversation that Mr Manjhi's family's name had been mistakenly left off the list of families that should receive ration cards. He said a public servant from the state agriculture department had been suspended for the error as long ago as 2010. Mr Choudhary said that he had submitted a request in April 2011 to get the family their card.

Ancillary acts of mercy by officials in the form of cash handouts at the time of hunger deaths are no substitute for the implementation of programmes meant to provide poor people long-term access to the social protection system. Such visits simply don't address the structural problems that prevent poor people in rural areas like Barachatti block from accessing their right-to-food programmes and healthcare. These include corruption, the lack of communication and knowledge of processes necessary for accessing and assuring benefits on a consistent basis, and the deep-rooted forms of segregation and exclusion that keep people in the same village physically isolated from each other, yet dependent on one another through unequal and exploitative economic relationships. Short-term government action to poverty-inducing death is only a reaction. Not a response.

We realized in our conversations with local officials that it may not be wise to expect them to uphold their duties to protect, respect and enforce the rights of the poor to such programmes when they deny that hunger is a chronic problem afflicting the people whom they are accountable to. That denial is, at least in part, a result of notions held by local officials about low-caste people, who suffer most from hunger and malnutrition, as undeserving of equal status and treatment, let alone, in many cases, special treatment to redress inequality and prevent death. It is well known that a high number of people of vulnerable groups, such as Dalits and economically backward castes, experience chronic malnutrition and persistent economic distress. For Kangresh Manjhi, a dimension of this kind of destitution was the failure of government programmes intended for people like him.

After our field days were done, I would go through my notes. It seemed as though the distance between the Bhuiya tola to the office of a bureaucrat or the home of an elected official was farther than from New York to New Delhi. There is no personal interaction between those in power and those who live in impoverished hamlets.

We met the village mukhiya, Tafiq Ali Khan, a man in his late sixties, at his house, located about a kilometre from the Bhuiya tola, along a series of dirt roads that lead to acres of farm land. We sat on plastic chairs under an awning that protected us from the rain, sipping tea. A white Ambassador car was parked in a concrete square plot. 'He (Kangresh Manjhi) did not die of starvation, he died of TB,' he repeated more than once. He maintained that the family had had food in the house at the time of the deaths and that Kari Devi was currently receiving 15 to 20 kilogrammes of grain from the fair price shop, following local government orders.

We presented the findings from our recent visit to the Bhuiya tola. Kari Devi still does not have a ration card, we said, and according to her and her neighbours, she is still unable to buy subsidized grains from the fair price shop. 'Many people in the village say they are not getting their rations even after the death,' we countered.

'Look,' he said, 'these people look at you and know you're from the outside. There's this thinking that "the people from Delhi" will give us things.'

Local officials are the closest contact the poor have to the state. In the absence of accountability measures to check corruption and malaise, the way these officials think determines the extent to which the poor can exercise their rights. Researchers and journalists, when working in poverty-stricken areas of India, routinely hear the poor say that social laws and policies appear 'only on paper.' Social policies are not machines. And while implementation may depend on the integrity of those in power to do their jobs, it also depends on redressal mechanisms that can protect the rights of the poor when they are violated. For people in extreme poverty in India, the apathy and negligence amongst officials in the absence of functioning redressal systems marks the line between life and death.

Officials only acknowledge failed government programmes when death or some other calamity is too outrageous to go unnoticed. This puts them on the defensive and forces them to act, but the window for change is still limited to the span of time during which newspapers will pay attention to select cases. Officials don't actually follow up on promises to fix the problems that have been identified. The people affected most, the hungry and dying, are not mobilized or informed. Their silence is exploited.

Government responses to hunger deaths in Barachatti block were viewed by local officials as separate from addressing the misery of those living with hunger. Officials we spoke to in Manan Bhiga village view the conditions of people who die from hunger as different from those who live with it. Some officials acknowledged that many people whom they know and see live in a state of destitution. But when asked how the kinds of illnesses and hunger associated with that kind of destitution may serve as a pretext for death, straight answers were hard to come by.

This was apparent when we spoke to Dr M.E. Haque, the physician who treated Kangresh Manjhi at the public health centre in the last months of his life. Dr Haque had replaced Dr Prasad as the centre's physician in 2008. He said he was encouraged to treat Kangresh Manjhi when Amit Kumar reported his first story in October 2009 detailing the poor state of Manjhi's health and treatment.

'When he was very sick and many people knew about his case I was informed,' Dr Haque said. 'I did what was possible for him.'

We asked Dr Haque if Kangresh Manjhi's inability to get enough nutritious food on a regular basis may have hastened his decline and death.

Dr Haque did not agree that Kangresh's death was due to hunger. 'Everyone in every house has something to eat,' he said. Outside the window of his office an elderly, poor woman was standing alone by a tree. 'See, there is a beggar outside and if she is starving, then someone from the hospital will give her at least something to eat.'

'With any disease, if there is malnutrition, the patient's immunity will suffer,' Dr Haque said. 'It's possible that Kangresh didn't take his medicines regularly. There are multiple causes,' he continued. 'But it's impossible to say that the exact cause (of death) is hunger or starvation.'

Corruption, apathy, inefficiencies in running government programmes and empty promises by officials make it impossible for poor people to access to food and work in Manan Bhiga. The numbers of young people who leave home to support their families tell a story of how people find ways to survive against impossible odds. The visible suffering endured by those who cannot leave the village raised questions in my mind of how such odds can ever be overcome.

One of the reasons that inefficiencies in poverty reduction programmes in Gaya persist may be due to the fact that while local officials acknowledge, in a limited sense, that problems of hunger, malnutrition and poverty are interrelated, they fail to see how solutions to these problems also demand an integrated approach. We asked Dr Haque how the government programmes aimed at reducing illness, malnutrition and hunger should coordinate outreach between different departments to target the numerous deprivations afflicting a large number of poor people in matters of health, nutrition and food security.

'As far as our duty is concerned, it is only treatment. We have no facilities or resources of providing diet or nutrition. The block development officer and marketing officers are the people responsible for nutrition,' he said.

***

'So many people have come,' Kari Devi said in our last conversation inside her home in November 2011, 'but nothing changes.'

In March 2013, I saw her, unexpectedly. She was sitting in a circle of women near the stage at a dharna in Jantar Mantar in New Delhi. The Right to Food Campaign had organized a rally, protesting the Standing Committee's recommendations for the impending National Food Security Bill. They were discussing the proposal for reducing grain entitlements to 5 kilogrammes per person and the lack of legal entitlements to nutrition services for women and children under the anganwadi centres. Badri Pasman, a local NGO worker who had come with us into the villages on each of our visits, was standing by the water tank. A group of villagers were washing their hands and faces under the tap. 'Kari Devi is here,' he said, pointing her out to me in the crowd. 'You should talk to her.'

She was sitting with a group of women next to the stage. I had spoken to Nandlal Choudhary on the phone a few months before, while the socio-economic caste survey was being conducted in those villages, and he had said he would ensure she received her ration card and would check to see if she was getting her grains on time. I asked her if she had received her ration card yet. She hadn't. Her son was still going to Rajasthan to work.

I don't know how, but the person on the stage speaking on the microphone knew of Kari Devi's situation. She saw us and told us to come up on stage to tell the crowd what had happened to her. I didn't feel right about it. I asked her what she wanted to do. She said it was okay. We stood up and walked to the front and I tried to narrate her story. I was looking out at these faces and looking at Kari Devi. She was just standing there with her arms folded. I told the people the basic events that I've narrated in this chapter. But I told them badly, I was filled with fear.

I thought of that line, *I'll know my song well before I start singing.* This was not my song, it was hers, and I felt like maybe, if someone could tell it right, maybe, if there was some other language to express this insanity, maybe, if she could at least get her damn ration card, that could count for a bit of justice in this God-forsaken world.

Malgusa, Madhya Pradesh

October 2011

Ramkali Mawasi (30, Female)

The story of Ramkali Mawasi's life and death would be told to us by her sister Munni in a small room of the office of the Adivasi Adhikar Manch in the district town of Satna. We had taken for granted the relative ease with which people spoke to us before. There had been difficulties, but we were usually able to make our way through them in the first few hours. For the first few days in Malgusa, Ankita and I were forced to ask each other who Ramkali Mawasi had been, how did she live, how did she really die. Her family members and neighbours were afraid to talk.

Ankita and I didn't talk much between deaths—I mean, en route from one district to the next. In the villages we had the hours to calculate to keep us busy: between demise and death, death and denial, denial and action, being born and being acknowledged. I guess we got to know each other via getting to know the dead. We'd met once two months before the work began, and in earnest, about a week before we headed to Bihar from Delhi. Digging through newspaper reports, constructing timelines and formulating questions was team work. But when sitting together on beds where these people had died, seeing their brothers and sisters sick and hungry, or ostensibly alive yet vacant, thoughts of how the dead had lived circulated privately. The imagination *is* real.

In autos, on buses or motor bikes in Madhya Pradesh, from one village to the next on the National Highway in Gaya or on dirt roads up to desolate hamlets in Jharkhand, the mind wanders, especially before sunset: they must have walked this road on the way back from collecting wood from the forest to sell in the market, and that woman with a bundle may be dead next week, next month, or else she's already dead.

By nightfall, you only see headlights, you only hear horns, and we were always told to be out of the villages by dark. We didn't talk about how the people who died of hunger must have lived—we asked how much they earned, how many children they had. But not who they were. We did the math. Death was a legitimate concern, since facts had been disputed. No one contested how these people lived. It seemed so easy for officials to reveal that these lives didn't count. No one can corrupt what doesn't exist. You would have to be insane not to see that people who lived like this were on the brink. And neighbours we had yet to meet were slipping away in front of the world. The lives of the dead were impossible not to visualize. 'The past is never dead', Faulkner wrote, 'it isn't even past.' I remember the president back home quoting that line in a speech, but in America you never live the past; you only feel it in documentaries and music.

In other villagers, if you thought you couldn't tell if the person laying on a charpai, or the kids against the walls, were slipping away, you had to just wait, and one question would lead a villager to tell you about a family member too close to the edge or else they would bring you to them. These were India's discarded worlds of the continuous present.

Every time stories were repeated, or deepened, we would stare at each other, start scribbling again, excavating the ghosts of death. And if I were to have submitted wholly to my conscience, I would have done something more than write about those villages, but here I am, speaking to you....

When we didn't talk death, meaning work, we talked about her father, the demands of the father of a girl I left back home for a respectable life, Charlie Chaplin's autobiography, which she had lent me that Diwali, Orwell's *1984*, and, as the weeks unfolded, the fall of Gaddafi which we read about in the *Frontline* reports we bought at train stations. On trains between districts we'd read or sleep or listen to the music on my phone, one earphone each—the songs on Illmatic and this Woody Guthrie compilation had sounded true back in the States, but in Madhya Pradesh there was something more urgent in them to be heard than truth.

Usually, there was a twenty-four-hour window between work ending in one district and work starting in another—travel between districts, meeting the State Advisors to identify starvation cases, logistics for contacts and travel into the villages.

But we had to retrieve information on Ramkali Mawasi of Malgusa from Prashant Dubey, a Bhopal-based journalist working with the Madhya Pradesh State Advisor's Office on the Right to Food. He was in Reeva district and his office identified Ramkali's case as a starvation death, based on media reports and investigations done by their Satna-based partner, Adavasi Adhikar Manch. We stayed in Reeva for two days and tagged along with Prashant into Reeva's villages, where he was conducting surveys on child deaths, severely acute malnutrition among children and the status of anganwadi centres and National Resource Centres. The resource centres were residential spaces for malnourished mothers and children to gain immediate medical care for up to fourteen days. The state established them to reach the large number of women and children left untreated by the anganwandi centres, since there was a shortage of those centres, health workers and funds.

Prashant had a way with the people in those villages. He talked to the women holding their babies with respect, warmth and humour. He and two interns weighed the small babies in scales provided by

UNICEF. He told them about the centres and the provisions and breastfeeding practices, while writing away in his notebook. Those people really liked him. They knew he was sincere. There was a lot of sadness in those villages, but there were things to feel good about too. In one village, women talked about this kind doctor that came there and how he was looking after the kids. By the time we left Prashant for Malgusa, I had this feeling that I had learned something. That there was a way to speak to people without letting the mind get in the way too much.

But in Malgusa we were outsiders asking direction questions of death. I realized it then. We had no weighing scales, we were not coming back. This would be the only time we would speak to these people. We were strangers asking about death.

And so these are the basic details that the men and women of Malgusa who knew Ramkali Mawasi shared with us on our visit to their village in Satna district in October 2011. She was a thirty-year-old mother of five children who worked in the fields owned by members of the landed Yadav castes to support her family. Three of her children died before their second birthdays and in the spring of 2005, her husband, Pyare Lal, a labourer who worked in brick kilns and small plots of farm land for Rs 40 a day, died of tuberculosis.

After his death, Ramkali worked twelve to fourteen hour days for about Rs 40 a day and the burden of child care took a toll on her health. First, she experienced chronic back pain. She coped for months, but the pain didn't go away. In early 2006, she caught fever. She went to work each morning, but her symptoms got worse. She worked through the back pain and fever to feed her children and by April, almost a year after her husband's death, she was bedridden. She died that month.

According to the Advasi Adhikar Manch, local TV and newspaper outlets covered Ramkali Mawasi's story in the days after her death and told of her family's struggles with food, money and health, that undermined Ramkali's brief life. The local ration shop and public works programme functioned erratically in the village; she hadn't received pension schemes after her husband died; she was unable to get healthcare when she was ill; and although the state government had granted land rights to her husband and other Mawasi families in the mid-1990s, no one actually obtained possession of their land.

Her brother and sister, Munni and Ramkesh, disputed these facts. They both said that her sister's family never experienced a shortage of food or work.

Malgusa is located in Majhgava block, where malnutrition is alarming. Surveys by the Adivasi Adhikari Manch, a local tribal advocacy group that works on the implementation of food and nutrition programmes in the area, found that 200 children died in twenty villages in the block between 2008 and 2011. Satna is one of the worst hunger and malnutrition-affected districts in the country. In 2008, Prime Minister Manmohan Singh—lampooned often for his reticence—cited 145 starvation deaths in Satna in the previous three years. Investigations by the Right to Food campaign also revealed that sixty-four children in Satna died of malnutrition-related deaths between May and September 2008 alone.

Media coverage of the district's malnutrition crisis, especially amongst Mawasi children, led to repeated investigations in the area by the Asian Human Rights Commission (AHRC). Their 2010 survey uncovered numerous problems. Food and nutrition programmes were not reaching the poor and officials were underreporting malnutrition figures. 'The administration lacks an independent first-hand investigation methodology and strong willingness to eradicate malnutrition and hunger,' the report said.

Ramkali Mawasi's brother, Ramkesh, and sister, Munni Devi, corroborated each of the facts mentioned above, but said that their sister was neither hungry nor poor. The proximate events preceding her death mirrored other cases we studied in Bihar, Jharkhand and

Madhya Pradesh—shut out of food and work programmes, the inability to obtain rightful control over land, the loss of children to malnutrition (an indication of the mother's nutritional status), overworked, poorly paid, stressed about providing for children without adequate means and not receiving medical attention in time to ward off death. Based on these patterns, which we'd encountered frequently in the field, it was very difficult to believe that Ramkali Mawasi did not experience a kind of poverty intimately linked with economic struggle, dispossession and hunger.

In the village, local officials and people who belonged to landed castes ensured that Ramkali Mawasi's sister and brother could not speak to us alone. Yadav men stood by Ramkesh's window, looking into his hut as we spoke to him. Initially, three men came inside and stood against the wall. Two sat on either side of Ramkesh on his khattiya. More men eventually walked into the hut. A legitimate conversation was impossible.

When we spoke to Munni at the NREGA worksite, Yadav men, some of them village officials like the secretary, spoke over her. They would either interrupt us or her when we asked questions about Ramkali's family's access to food and nutrition programmes before her death.

Munni spoke to us alone once, but the persistent sense of fear in her eyes made us aware that our inquiries may be intrusive. Her voice was quiet and low, her head always down. After all, she had her own struggles. She had the right to not want to speak about the death of her sister, whose kids she was now raising with little means.

Fear of retribution from the higher castes that wield power is one reason family members won't discuss the deaths of loved ones who succumbed to some form of hunger and malnutrition. It is odd to see visibly malnourished children, emaciated, with watery eyes and yellow hair, and hear, simultaneously, that hunger and poverty are not a problem. It is even sadder to know that the people who are telling you this perhaps suffer the most from those conditions, under a system of power that is extractive and requires, for its continuance, for people to live in a kind of fear as paralyzing to the mind as hunger and malnutrition—so obvious to the eyes—is to the body.

Madhya Pradesh ranks lowest on the State Hunger Index and has the highest under-five mortality rate in the country (9.4 per 100 live births). According to UNICEF, the state's maternal mortality rate (700 per 1,000) is far above the national average of 407. In Malgusa alone, villagers say between twenty to twenty-five people have died in the last few years of tuberculosis.

The poor and public officials are inured to malnutrition deaths. 'Hunger' is politicized, because media reports put the spotlight on 'starvation' deaths. But, as each of our stories show, people don't die *only* because of lack of food intake. They die due to a combination of factors caused, in part, by social exclusion—malnutrition, lack of access to basic amenities like sanitation, water and healthcare *and* the lack of adequate nutritious food, hastened, in part, by failed public food and works programmes. As other cases have shown, drawing clear lines between chronic malnutrition, hunger and starvation is difficult. India's destitute often suffer a combination of poor health and long periods without adequate intake of nutritious food.

People who live in these conditions are prone to premature death for three reasons: lack of access to safe drinking water, inadequate sanitation and a compromised immune system due to chronic malnutrition. Dr John Butterly, professor of Dartmouth University's Medical School, told us 'The first two issues expose the malnourished population to a contaminated water supply and constant viral and bacterial infections. The compromised immune system causes severe and eventually fatal illness, frequently caused by organisms that a normally fed human would barely notice.'

'Hunger' is a word that is a part of daily life in rural India, but with so little focus on the role malnutrition plays in mortality, public officials have reason to label such deaths as ones by 'illness' or even 'poverty'. As Dan Banik, author of *Starvation and India's Democracy*, a study of starvation deaths in Orissa and West Bengal, has argued, 'those in authority do not expect to be held accountable for persistently high levels of under-nutrition and are confident that such issues are accepted by society as a natural feature of a poor country with a large population.'

***

We first met Munni Devi a kilometre from the village, on the NREGA work site where twenty-five men and women were digging trenches for the construction of a road, while children were standing in the trenches. The sun was out and it was a hot afternoon. Munni was working in a group of women, transporting a pile of bricks from one trench to the other.

We stood at the bank and she stood on a small mound looking at us, with the edge of her hand shading her forehead.

'Can we talk to you about your sister?'

She draped her shawl across her head, put the bricks down, and walked over to us in the shade. A group of men, women and children stood around us, as we sat on a dirt mound just off the work site. Later, a group of men came, accompanied by the sarpanch. The sarpanch laid on his side on the crest of the small hill, picking at rocks and weeds.

A few days later, Ramkali agreed to meet us in the office where we were staying, in the district town of Satna.

She told us that before Ramkali's husband, Pyare Lal, died of tuberculosis in 2005, husband and wife worked the fields owned by Yadavs under the adhiya-bataee system: the landowner provided the seeds and necessary inputs for labourers to grow crops, with the agreement that the landowner recoups a share of the seeds and inputs above the original quantity, along with 50 per cent of the harvest. The other half of the harvest is divided equally among the tillers. When possible, the family also sold minor forest produce (MFP) such as wood, honey, amla, mahua flowers, tendu leaves for making beedis and a local fruit, called bahera, in local markets. They earned about Rs 5,000–6,000 a year (a bundle of hundred beedis sold for 40 paise) and were able to bring home daan, jowar and kodo harvests. A farm labourer like Pyare Lal could expect to bring home 50 kilogrammes to 4 quintals a year under the adhiya-bateeya system, to feed the family.

Around 10 million tribal people in India depend on forest produce sales to survive. But they've struggled since India nationalized MFP trade under the 1952 national forest policy. The idea was to place control of forest use under the jurisdiction of individual states, to promote MFP sales to local industries for economic growth. A 2010 *Down to Earth* report showed that the eight Indian states with the highest concentration of MFP—with 92.5 per cent of tendu production and 99 per cent of sal seed production—are also the country's poorest. Each state also has the highest concentration of tribal people.

In the 1970s, Madhya Pradesh was the only state to recognize community rights over MFP, but since then state monopolies have continued to expand. These policies undermined the survival of tribal people. Most tribals today are sharecroppers under agricultural production systems where land holdings and wage rates are dictated by caste. The central government intended to address these inequalities by passing the 2006 Forest Rights Act, a law that ensures tribal people community-based land rights to areas they have historically tilled. In some cases, it also entitles them to ownership over the production and sale of MFPs.

In the mid-1990s, the local government issued Pyare Lal a legal deed to 1.25 acres of land. By the early 2000s, twelve other adavisis in Malgusa also obtained legal deeds to the same amount of land.

The problem was that none of them were able to wrest control of it. Munni told us that landed Yadavs threatened him and other Mawasis with death if they sought ownership over their own plots. 'He didn't get the land,' she told us privately, 'because Yadavs said, "If you keep asking for it we'll kill you."'

Of the 200 households in Malgusa, fifty are advisasis, 100 are Yadavs, and the other fifty belong to the general category, Each general category family owns land, while only thirty Yadavs and twenty adivasi households do. The concentration of land reflects the balance of power in the village. Landed Yadavs occupy key political and bureaucratic positions at the village and block level and have a stake in village labour markets. Yadav tekhadars—labour contractors—offer the promise of manual labour in other cities for a daily wage of about Rs 120. Ramkali's eighteen-year-old son, Rajesh, had left a month before our visit with two other young men who had been contracted by a local Yadav tekhadar for manual labour in Chennai. Rajesh had gone to Chennai once before under the tekhadar, but had not been paid the Rs 11,000 due to him. It is not uncommon for young men to continue to leave the village for work, despite unsafe, insecure conditions, including not getting paid, as they have no other options.

The dominance of the Yadav caste over adivasis in Malgusa is one reason that tribal people have been denied their rights to land. Still, local administrations and the state government do not enforce the Forest Rights Act.

A 2010 Union Ministry of Tribal Affairs report cited by *Down to Earth* recorded 2.9 million claims under the Act. Just 1.6 percent (46,156) of applicants received community rights. Most of these did not include rights over MFP. According to the Campaign for Survival and Dignity, an advocacy group for tribal and forest dwellers in ten states, forest departments continue to violate the Act by encroaching on tribal areas. A report on the Campaign's website claims that in

Satna district, in 2009, 'the SDM (Satna) and officials of two-three blocks agreed to come and see the forest department's encroachment themselves and accepted that this was illegal. They promised to distribute 1,200 claim forms for community rights by 25th October and to support their claims for CFR rights.' But the administration did not uphold that promise.

The AHRC's investigations confirm that this problem persists in Satna district. In August 2010, they found that twenty-six Mawasi families in one village were denied land rights because village committees did not submit land applications to authorities. The Adavasi Adhikar Manch has tried to address the problem by holding monthly meetings with villagers to discuss ongoing conflicts over land, provide information on their rights through the Forest Act and file applications for land on their behalf.

Still, a larger problem is that the Act, which protects tribal land rights, is at odds with the older nationalization policy, which vests control of production with the state. The Forest Rights Act was intended to reduce inequalities that arose from the old nationalization policies, but the state still upholds the nationalization of lucrative MFP items, such as mahua, sal seeds and flowers, tendu leaves and certain gums.

Eventually, Pyare Lal stopped asking for control over his own land and continued to work as a sharecropper for low wages. He worked long hours with little to no clean water or adequate food. When he fell ill with tuberculosis he traveled 60 kilometres outside the village to seek care in a town called Chitrakoot. His sister lived in a nearby village and cared for him. The family couldn't afford private care. They took a Rs 7,000–8,000 loan at 3 per cent interest a month from a local Yadav.

'He was sick one year before he died,' Munni told us. 'He stayed in the hospital for ten to fifteen days and then came back home and started working again. But he kept falling sick.' In the spring of 2005, Pyare Lal's sister came to Malgusa and took him back to her village. He stayed with her for one month and died at her home.

Ramkali should have received Rs 10,000 under the National Family Health Benefit Scheme within four weeks of her husband's death, but local officials told her that she wasn't eligible for that benefit because her husband died of tuberculosis. The cause of death of the head of household has no bearing on a BPL card-holder's rights to the benefit. The Supreme Court Orders simply state, 'BPL families are to be paid Rs 10,000 within four weeks through the local Sarpanch when the breadwinner dies.' Ramkali didn't complain to anyone to get the money. She did not know she had a right to it. Munni didn't either. 'The family did not receive any help because he died of illness,' she said.

After Pyare Lal's death, the burden of feeding five children fell on Ramkali. She continued to work on Yadav fields where she earned about 2 quintals of grain that year. Leela started to work with her mother to meet the burden. Both earned about Rs 300–400 a month. Ramkali's health started to decline. She had developed a back problem two years before her husband's death. The pain got worse after she became a widow, compromising her ability to work. She pulled through it as much as she could, but she would soon be debilitated with bouts of chronic fever.

Munni said that Ramkali and her children did not experience hunger at all during this period. According to her, the family received about 15 kilogrammes of rice and 5 kilogrammes of wheat each month from the ration shop. When there was a food shortage, Munni or her brother would help their sister by feeding the children.

Journalist and researcher Pravin Patik works for an organization called the Madhya Pradesh Jan Adhikar Manch. He visited the village after the deaths. His report, based on events narrated by Ramkali's brother, Ramkesh, told a different story. Ramkesh told Patik that Ramkali's family was having a difficult time making ends meet, so they asked the secretary to change their ration card status from BPL to Antyodaya after Pyare Lal's death. The

Antyodaya card is reserved for destitute families and would have enabled Ramkali to buy even cheaper grains from the ration shop. Their status was temporarily changed, but switched back to BPL status for reasons we were not able to confirm. When officials re-categorized the family to BPL status, the ration dealer, a man named Ramdev Yadav, refused to sell grains to the family. Other families in Malgusa were also unable to help them as their situation deteriorated.

Ramkali worked through illness and pain to keep her children from starving. Work opportunities at this time started to dry up. There was no other option to bring in money. The family went to the ration dealer to ask for mercy, but he said there was no grain available.

As mentioned earlier, when we spoke to Ramkesh at his home, we weren't alone. Several Yadavs stood outside the small window. A few came in and stood with their arms folded, leaning up against his dry mud wall. Some would begin to answer questions directed to Ramkesh, particularly those having to do with the last days of his sister's life. After some time, we knew it may be futile to ask Ramkesh what happened that night but we thought we would take our chances. He had already mentioned that he could not give us too much time because his days were spent going into the forest to collect and sell wood.

'When you went to the PDS dealer to ask for grain,' we said, 'what did he say?' There was a long silence. A few of the men standing against the wall started to speak. One sat down on the bed next to Ramkesh. There was little room separating our faces in the tight space.

'Ramkali didn't die of hunger,' Ramkesh said. 'Ramkali died of sickness.'

The Sahara TV channel aired a story days after Ramkali's death. They reported that the family went days at a time without any food in the house. In an interview, Leela said that the family would eat about once every two to three days. Leela died about a year after Ramkali. None of the family members were willing to say how.

Eventually, Ramkali was bedridden. One day, Manish Rastogi, the District Collector of Satna, came to Malgusa to see an ongoing watershed project. People told him of Ramkali's condition. Mr Rastogi ordered the Sub-District Magistrate of Majhgava to arrange for Ramkali's immediate treatment. The Sub-Divisional Magistrate delegated these responsibilities to the block development officer, who arranged a jeep to take Ramkali from the village to the nearest public health centre. Ramkesh accompanied her. In Mr Patik's account, Ramkesh states that no one was at the health centre when they arrived.

'I pleaded with the driver, "Sahib, can you please take my sister to any hospital in Chitrakoot or Satna because if not, she'll die,"' Patik's report reads. 'He didn't listen to anything I said. He yelled at us and dropped us off at the doctor's office in Majhgava, and drove off.' Later in this account, Ramkesh tells of how he wandered the streets looking for help, since the doctor's office was also closed. He asked a nearby person where the nurse lived. In desperation, he walked to her house and asked if she could help. 'I asked the nurse if she could give my sister medicine, but she said she couldn't. I couldn't do anything.' Ramkesh then rented a jeep to take his sister back to the village. She died that night.

Ramkesh denied that he made these statements. He told us that it was his fault that Ramkali could not find medical treatment in the hours before her death. 'I went with my sister to the hospital and, because I yelled at the driver on the way, he dropped us off at the edge of the road,' he told us in his cramped hut full of men. 'Ramkali fainted then, and when she fainted I brought her back home. I rented a car for Rs 500 and brought her back at twelve at night. She died here at home.'

Ramkesh then said something that surprised us. The block official called him the morning after Ramkali died and asked him to come to the block office. There, the official told him to give a statement that Ramkali died of illness.

The deaths of both parents were disastrous for the children. The dealer would not sell them grains under their mother's ration card. Munni had even requested the ration dealer to give her rations on Ramkali's card so that she could feed her late sister's children. She and her husband were their guardians now. They were all under eighteen at the time. She raised them with five of her own children—three daughters and two sons. The panchayat secretary ordered the ration dealer to give Munni's family 50 kilogrammes of free grain a month. This helped them, but a short time after the order was given, the dealer stopped complying. Munni went to the panchayat secretary and told him that she needed those grains to feed her children and nieces and nephews. He replied that the stock was depleted and there was nothing he could do.

At the time of our visit, the people in Malgusa were receiving grains each month. But the shop is only open three days a month. Villagers are also unable to buy rations in installments, and sometimes the quality of grains is poor or they find insects in their rations.

Today, Munni and her husband are raising eight children. As mentioned earlier, Leela died about two or three years after her mother. Munni and her husband had arranged Leela's marriage shortly after her mother's death, but the young woman passed away six months after her wedding.

Life is hard for the family. They are landless wage labourers and depend on work provided by the NREGA programme to meet income needs. But the programme has its problems. Works are only opened one to two months a year, far below the 100 days stipulated by the act. Payments are always delayed. When we visited the workers in October 2011, villagers said they had yet to be paid for work completed in September. The year before, villagers said, payments were made three to four months late. They only received Rs 100 a day, Rs 20 less than the entitled wage payment by law.

Munni told us that her family never struggles for food. She buys about 50 kilogrammes of wheat each month from the market and 25 kilogrammes of rice from the ration dealer. But the family can only afford to eat dal or vegetables once every eight to ten days and her youngest daughter has been identified by the anganwadi workers as severe acutely malnourished. At the time of Ramkali's death, Munni's struggle to buy enough nutritious food to feed eight children was intensified by the fact that the anganwadi centre was not up and running. That has now changed. According to the school teacher, Bans Bahadur Yadav, and Anand, head of the Adivasi Adhikar Manch, the anganwadi has improved since the time of Ramkali's death because of pressure by local activists and NGO workers.

'Until 2008, anganwadi workers in Majhgava block didn't perform their responsibilities as much as they do now,' Anand said. The Adivasi Adhikar Manch has raised the issue of the poor quality of anganwadi centres through rallies, advocacy campaigns, surveys and partnerships with journalists and research organizations. The organization's efforts put pressure on the local administration to open centres and implement the programmes outlined by the Supreme Court. In September and October 2011, a Special Malnutrition Programme was launched for three weeks to identify malnourished children throughout the block. National guidelines require anganwadi centres to test for malnutrition by weighing children, measuring their mid-upper arm circumference and testing for signs of edema. Based on these indicators, six children in Malgusa, including Munni's daughter, were identified as severe acute malnourished. Five are adivasi children.

Today, children receive rice, roti, dal, vegetables and khichdi, as well as a nutritional supplement packet consisting of wheat flour, sugar, soy flower, chana dal and milk powder. But Bans Bahadur Yadav also claims that, due to corruption and lack of timely funding, the anganwadi is only able to give children half the required amount.

'Adavasi children are weak and malnourished because of the lack of rations,' the anganwadi sevak told us. She said that the centre never gets the full quota of rations. She and other workers have complained about this.

Limited income and the underperformance of the Integrated Child Development Services (ICDS) are reasons, in part, why Munni struggles to feed all eight of her children enough nutritious food. When another daughter was identified as malnourished a few years ago, she had to send her to a National Rehabilitation Centre (NRC) in Satna. In Madhya Pradesh, these centres were set up as an extension of the supplementary health programmes provided by the national nutrition centres. The national nutrition centres were intended to be in each village in the country, but the programme was stricken with performance, funding and corruption problems.

According to the Supreme Court Commissioner's Eighth report, of the 1,32,000 centres required in the state, only about 60 per cent (79,238) are functioning, which could help explain why 60 per cent of Madhya Pradesh's children under the age of six are malnourished and 12 per cent are severely acutely malnourished. According to a *Frontline* report, the state only spends 0.86 per cent of its budget through the ICDS on children under six.

A few years ago, there was no NRC in Majhgava block. Media reports of the area's child malnutrition problem, as well as health campaigns conducted by NGOs put pressure on the local administration to build an NRC in the block in 2010. Per guidelines, NRCs provide adequate nutrition to admitted children for a fifteen-day period. Mothers are recommended to bring their children to the NRC once every fifteen days after they're discharged, to track their progress. The problem is that NRCs are still understaffed and undersourced. When we visited the Majhgava NRC, twenty-two children were admitted, but the facility only has ten beds. District guidelines state that each facility should have twenty beds. According to the *Frontline* report, of 121 NRCs in Madhya Pradesh in 2008, only ninety-five were fully functional, and forty-nine have no trained staff.

Munni and the people of her community continue to work in a labour environment dictated by caste. Through groups like the Adivasi Adhikar Manch, poor people in Satna district are more aware of laws, such as the Forest Rights Act, which entitle them to land rights, and of the range of social protection programmes and health services that are intended for them, but the feudal dynamics that control land use and employment have trumped the political will to ensure those rights.

Back in Delhi, pooling information from notebook paper and Munni's voice on recordings, I could hear the fear in her voice; I could see the fear in Ramkesh's face. Did I have the right to brush that aside and plough through to the facts? My frustration was a violation of their privacy.

A friend told me that some of the stories of people living with hunger in India sounded to her like war. I had no idea about that. But there was another kind of war too. In *Jesus and the Disinherited*, Howard Thurman called the state of fear faced by destitute people who live with a constant threat of organized violence, 'a war of nerves.' The death threats that Pyare Lal faced over land that was lawfully his. The silence in Ramkesh's room among men who told him with their eyes what to say, what not to say. These were impending realities. The kind to make, as Thurman wrote, 'their bodies commit to memory ways of behaving that will tend to reduce their exposure to violence.' My friend was talking about physical war and she gave me a copy of *Dispatches*, by Michael Herr, a former war correspondent who was embedded in Vietnam in the late 1960s. 'If dead ground could come back and haunt you the way dead people do,' Herr wrote, 'they'd have been able to mark my map current and burn the ones they'd been using since '64, but count on it, nothing like that was going to happen...even the most detailed maps didn't reveal much anymore; reading them was like trying to read the faces of the Vietnamese, and that was like trying to read the wind.'

All the facts from media reports, NGO workers, villagers, Munni Devi, Ramkesh and village officials were maps that could only lead you to facts: no land, no access to social programmes, menial wages, illnesses, low food intake—but it was the fear in people who had to live that way that has to be understood. I don't know if that is possible.

Heta, Jharkhand

November 2011

Kalacharan Lohra (55, Male),
Sanjay Lohra (24, Male)

Heta was the first village we visited in ten weeks where people were busy living. There was a tailor stitching clothes outside his shop and a few boys across the road laughing, playing carom on the lid of a rusted oil barrel. Yellow and green lilies shimmered in a large pond at the entrance, while a girl was sitting on the brick wall looking out at the fields. The houses were blue with smooth walls, and we were walking down the path leading to the village's hamlets to speak to Basanti Devi about her husband and son, who had died within hours of each other in August 2007 because the family could not feed itself.

Kalacharan Lohra was a former rickshaw puller who hadn't worked in years. He had contracted a rare illness as a young man and his health had deteriorated steadily until that summer when there was no food in the house for days. One night, he complained to his wife of chest and body pain.

'We massaged his hands and feet,' his daughter-in-law, Munni Devi, told us. 'But his head slowly went cold and he died.' He was fifty-five years old.

The stories of Kangresh Manjhi and Ramkali Mawasi had revealed to us the role malnutrition-related illness and hunger play in the death of the poor when they work under exploitative conditions and cannot access social programmes and healthcare. Our time with Kalacharan Loha's family showed that medical attention for other physical maladies is essential for poor families who struggle to find work and food. In this case, Kalacharan Lohra's family had no knowledge that free medical care was available in nearby public health centres, which made him and his son vulnerable to death when work became scarce during the monsoons and food was not available from the public distribution system.

Ranchi district has the most public health centres and sub-centres of all districts in Jharkhand. Villagers told us they were aware that health centres exist, but said that they don't avail those free services because treatment is poor. They also don't usually consult the private doctor who makes visits to the village because they don't have enough money to pay for treatment.

On average, there is one doctor for every six health centres in the area. Block officials told us that the caseload deters physicians from making frequent visits to each one. In Heta, people claimed that the doctor doesn't show up consistently to the nearest centre, which is walking distance from the village. Patients with serious illnesses like tuberculosis and malaria say they get turned away.

According to the World Health Organization, there are six physicians for every 10,000 people in India, compared with fourteen in China, the only other country with a larger population. In 2012, public debate on India's poor health expenditure was cause for policymakers to promise to increase the current outlay of 1 per cent of its gross domestic product on public health to 2.5 per cent of GDP in five years. The main criticism of the 2015-2016 budget focused on the centre's scaling back of social expenditure overall, placing the burden on states to fund social programmes out of their own budgets.

That afternoon in November, we found Basanti Devi hanging clothes on the line at the family's small but newly painted cement home, built recently with funds they had received from the Indira Awas Yojana.

'I have brought up my children with great difficulty,' she said. She was forty-seven years old but looked much older. She had deep set wrinkles on her forehead and held a perpetual squint with her eyes when she spoke. Eventually, we sat down on a blue rug in the yard and talked. She was the head of this household, looking after her two sons and one daughter, as well as three grandchildren. Her daughter-in-law, Munni Devi, had given birth to a boy, Kanhaiya, eight days before our visit. She was twenty-two years old, very kind, in the way she smiled at us and told us to sit on the mat outside the house. She and Basanti Devi would take turns holding him while we spoke.

Basanti Devi had been the main income earner in the house since her marriage to Kalacharan Lohra. She used to clean houses in Ranchi for Rs 300 a month when she was young, but when she started to have children she began doing manual labour at construction sites in the capital for Rs 60 a day, a few days a week.

Thirty years ago, Mr Lohra contracted filiariasis, a parasitic disease that can lead to elephantiasis, a thickening of skin and underlying tissues. Basanti Devi recalled that her husband's leg started swelling in the days just before their marriage. About two to three years before his death, the swelling overtook his entire leg, leaving him unable to walk. They never saw a doctor, she said, because the family couldn't afford medical care.

The couple had three sons: Sanjay, Ajay and Krishna. Sanjay was twenty-four years old when his father become unable to work, but he couldn't help the family's economic situation because he'd been disabled since childhood. The family said he contracted jaundice when he was ten years old, which later developed into a physical disability that affected both legs and left him unfit for manual labour. Since childhood he had been very weak and walked with a limp, Basanti Devi said, and the family didn't have enough money to pay medical expenses for two sick people. She never visited any of the district's public health centres because she didn't know any existed.

'Today we know about such things because of the television,' she told us. The television was on inside the house and her grandchildren were watching a cartoon.

By the time her boys had grown up, there were three income earners in the house. Basanti Devi's younger sons, Ajay and Krishna, also worked on construction sites but the family's earnings weren't enough to feed six people. They were only able to hold ground because Ajay and Krishna found a little extra work on neighbouring farms for about Rs 20 a day. In 2006, Ajay and Munni Devi were married and the couple moved to Ranchi where Ajay worked on construction sites and Munni cleaned houses.

Basanti Devi recalled that the family's struggle became more intense after the household lost an income earner. It's not that Ajay and Munni Devi didn't help. But bouts of chronic fever in Ranchi rendered Ajay unable to work for days at a time. Ajay and Munni decided to return to Heta to live with the family, but in the summer of 2007, construction and farm work were scarce. For a short period, Basanti Devi was the only member of the family earning somewhat regularly.

Most families in Heta owned small plots of land. When work and food were scarce, the little amount of rice they could produce from it made the difference between living with hunger and succumbing to it. 'Almost everyone else in the village has land,' the anganwadi worker told us, 'so even though their food situation is only a little better than Basanti Devi's, they can rely on farming for six to eight months a year.'

Land was the key asset in Heta that determined if family a family was poor or destitute. Stephan Devereux attempted to define the condition of destitution as separate from poverty, based on his field work in rural Ethiopia. He said those in rural areas of developing countries who are destitute are 'people who have failed in the struggle to preserve themselves and their dependents from physical want' while those who are poor who 'struggle continuously to preserve themselves and their dependents from physical want.'[5]

In Dhanbad and Manan Bhiga, neighbours could not come to the aid of Padamchand Hazra and Kangresh Manjhi because they faced shortages of food as well. In Heta, everyone may have been struggling, but Basanti Devi's family was set back in two ways: the disabilities of her husband and son, and no recurring source of food from the land.

Before she married Kalacharan, he had mortgaged his land holdings to another family in an arrangement known as bandik: a landed family sells its plot for a specified amount of time, with an agreement to reacquire the land at an agreed-upon date in the future. Basanti Devi said the family never got their land back and that she didn't know the details of the arrangement or when it was first made.

In 2007, several factors led to the tragedy. First, the local ration shop was closed most days and when it was open, the dealer claimed he didn't have grains on hand. At most, Basanti Devi's family could buy grains once every two to three months. When they did, they never got their full quota of 10 kilogrammes of wheat, 15 kilogrammes of rice and 3.5 litres of kerosene. In 2006, the family only received rations twice, according to her ration card records.

Between January and September 2007, the family only received a single food ration from the government. That year, Basanti Devi would leave home for work in Ranchi at 8 a.m., and return by 7 p.m. On days she couldn't find work, she'd return empty-handed.

That year, Ajay's wife, Munni Devi, had given birth to a boy, Kishan. Ajay had fallen ill with a chronic fever and was also not able to work as much as the family needed him to. According to Munni

---

5. Devereux, Stephan. *Conceptualising Destitution*. Institute of Development Studies: Brighton, UK. December 2003.

Devi, the family would eat rice acquired with the money Basanti Devi and Krishna could bring in. Some days they'd eat maadh bhaat (rice with starch water). They stored the rice in two 200-gramme tin jars and when they ran out of food they'd ask for help from neighbours. Most neighbours were relatively better off, but no one, villagers told us in a group discussion, was secure enough to offer food consistently.

Other social programmes were also defunct. The NREGA programme had not been opened in the village. The ICDS programme, which guarantees all children in India under the age of six, adolescent girls, and pregnant and lactating mothers free supplementary meals of adequate protein and nutrients based on international standards to target malnutrition, never received funds on time from the state, so women and children didn't get the nutritional supplements they are entitled to. The only programme that fared well in the village was one that gave school children mid-day meals, another initiative the Supreme Court has said must be available nation-wide.

In 2007, panchayat elections had not yet taken place in Heta, so the family had no local politicians to approach to air their grievances and no local system to depend on to implement social programmes. Lack of clean drinking water and inadequate shelter made matters worse. There was no hand pump in the village and their home, at the time, was made of mud and was collapsing in the rains. The absence of social programmes, insufficient income from Basanti Devi being the only earning member, and the required care of two ill family members resulted that summer in days without food. Basanti rejected the idea of taking loans at the time because she knew the family wouldn't be able to pay the money back.

On the night of 7 August 2007, Kalicharan Lohra complained of body pain and a headache.

That night, Basanti Devi fed her husband two spoonfuls of rice and gave him his nightly massage. He died a few moments later.

Later that night, her son, Sanjay, also complained of a headache and was in too much pain to eat the bit of rice offered to him. He died five hours later.

As in other cases, the local media reported the deaths, detailing the state of chronic food shortages, prolonged illnesses and the absence of public programmes in the village. The block development officer, responsible for overseeing developing programmes in the region, and the medical officer conducted a joint investigation and concluded that the cause of Kalicharan Lohra's death was filiariasis and that Sanjay Lohra died of chronic fever.

Four years after the deaths in Heta, villagers were still being denied most of their rights to food. Despite media reports, investigations by activists and visits by high-level officials, including the chief minister of Jharkhand, Arjun Munda, poor governance, high turnover rates in the local bureaucracy and insufficient funding of the food distribution programme continued to plague access and delivery

Panchayat elections did take place in the years after the deaths. The rural job guarantee programme was implemented in the first half of 2011, but as of our visit, workers were yet to get wages for those months because, the panchayat leader says, he isn't getting consistent funding. That's why, to avoid hunger many villagers, like Basanti Devi's son Krishna, were leaving the village as contracted labour for other states like Karnataka.

According to Kamal Kishor Sen, Ranchi's district collector, the source of the problem was the central government. In the year of our visit, the district had not received funds from the centre for five months, despite the submission of repeated reports to central government officials.

The ICDS was also not receiving monthly payments from the state. This included the anganwadi worker's salary, which she hadn't received in the four months before our visit. She was unable to provide women and children their full entitlements (for women: 80 grammes of rice, 10 grammes of lentils, 10 grammes of soya beans and 15 grammes of sugar, six days a week; for children: 60 grammes of rice, lentils and soya beans, six days a week). She was still trying to keep the programme running, despite a peculiar system, which she and local officials explained to us.

Under this system, the anganwadi worker does not receive monthly advances from the block office to buy rations. Instead, she has to buy rations on credit from the shopkeeper in the local market and submits her credit bills to the child development programme officer (CDPO), a state-appointed official responsible for all the ICDS centres in the block. This official collects the bills of all 192 centres in the block and sends them to the district. The district then releases funds to pay for the credit slips through the same channels in which the bills were sent. It's a three to four-month-long process. That's why the anganwadi worker buys less food than she would if the state was able to provide her an advance equal to the amount needed to meet nutrition requirements. And these funds are separate from cheques she receives for salary and other expenses, such as toys and charts used to weigh children and inform parents of their malnutrition status. In fact, there is still no facility for the ICDS centre. The anganwadi worker runs the programme for thirty of Heta's children out of her home.

Market traders take advantage of this. Since she doesn't have cash on hand and payment will eventually come from public accounts, they inflate prices. Worse, she told us, she had to give 10 per cent of the ration money she gets to the CDPO, the highest-level local official in charge of the implementation of programmes in anganwadi centres.

Sen acknowledged that this is a problem throughout his district, but told us he is powerless to check the corruption because the CDPO is a state-appointed official, and hence out of his jurisdiction. That's why he's petitioned the state government to provide each anganwadi worker a two-month advance for purchasing rations. 'If I'm an anganwadi and I have to purchase rations in the month of April, then the money should be made available in February,' he says. 'The shopkeeper is not a social worker. He has to have an incentive to provide rations on credit. Which is why he inflates prices.'

When officials visited Heta after the deaths, they didn't call for investigations into failed government schemes, as the Supreme Court has mandated should be done after suspected starvation deaths.

Targeting breakdowns in these programmes is difficult without a unified grievance redressal mechanism. In the absence of that, even well-meaning officials, like Sen, cannot check the extent of corruption that takes place. He acknowledged the problems of corruption and incompetence that prevent social programmes from working, but said that he can't hold officials accountable if they don't have enough funds to run their programmes.

***

We received updates from the village a few months later. The public distribution programme was functioning. In September 2011, people took action for not having received their monthly grains and decided that Heta's all-woman Self-Help Group should take charge of the management and distribution of grains in the village. Kamal Kishore Sen arranged for all ration-shop owners to certify the amount of monthly grains they distribute with the panchayats. And, at the urging of activists, Sen also pushed for changes in the system by which grains are transported from the Food Corporation of India (FCI) warehouses and distributed to local dealers.

After the deaths, villagers were still only accessing grains from the PDS once every two or four months, with the problem lasting until 2011. Villagers were denied access to the shop from February through May and once, in August. In addition to problems with

NREGA employment, the lack of food added to the villagers' struggle and hunger. 'The situation didn't improve after the deaths,' one villager said in a group discussion. 'The problem continued until recently. We didn't know why we were not getting grains. The dealer would say he doesn't have the rice.'

So villagers took action. The Self-Help Group, led by Sushma Oraon, a local villager, petitioned to transfer the charge of the ration shop from the private dealer to their authority. This meant that Ms Oraon would run the shop out of her home in the village. The ration shop was previously in Bajpur, a village about 7 kilometres away. The Self-Help Group also assured accountability, since Ms Oraon was from the village and knew all of the families well. Ms Oraon described the work as public service. She didn't earn commission on the rice or kerosene and paid for the transportation costs of the kerosene herself. To weigh the rice, she made her own scales from stones and operated the shop in the small room where she lived. The grain truck from the state godown comes once a month and villagers do get grains monthly. But Ms Oraon still does not get the full quota from the godown. She is supposed to get 26 quintals. She gets only 23. She complained to the block supply officer about this but was disappointed in his reply. 'He told me to just give a little less to the villagers,' she says.

Since Jharkhand became a state in 2000, low off-take of grains from public stock houses has been a problem. Until 2010, Jharkhand didn't have its own State Food Corporation (SFC) and had to rely on the Bihar SFC to procure grains through FCI for Jharkhand's public distribution shops. Today, the state's own SFC still lifts fewer grains than their allotted quota, which makes it difficult to assure beneficiaries their full entitlements. In the year of our visit, according to FCI allocation and off-take data, Jharkhand and Gujarat had the third worst off-take percentages in the country, at just over 78 per cent. For 2011, through September, Jharkhand's off-take was just under 77 per cent.

But another reason for low off-take ratios was that grains were lifted from the FCI and distributed to shops on an ad-hoc basis. 'Earlier what was happening was that there was no match between lifting and distribution of grains. The amount of grains needed for April would actually be lifted in the month of July or August,' Sen said. Called a 'chain system,' as detailed in a 2011 *Frontline* report, one month's quota would actually be lifted in the following month. These mismatches were the result of a lack of fixed distribution dates and systems that required adequate record keeping. In June 2011, the state ordered reforms to this system, insisting that grains have to be lifted and distributed in the same month. If dealers don't distribute their quotas in the same month they've lifted them, they're penalized and have to request an extension. It's good to note there have been improvements in the system. But problems still persist in getting the full quotas from the FCI.

In the case of Heta, Mr Sen suggests that villagers didn't receive grains from February through June because of the mismatches and erratic distribution before policy changes took place. And in August, the villagers didn't get their grains because the district had only distributed 20 per cent of the quota that month. For August, he explained, 'We had to get an extension, but we didn't get it, so we didn't have the authority to distribute.' He added: 'If this is the situation in the capital, it's very pathetic.'

Basanti Devi told us before we left that her family's food situation was better than it was four years ago. More family members are able to work and they earn higher wages than in the years earlier, she explained.

I hope that in the future her life, and those of others who have struggled as she had, improve because they are able to access their democratic rights. I hope they demand them, as the people of Heta eventually did that September in 2011. But officials have to demand more from their state too. Sen called us a few months after we had left the village to tell us that he'd instituted a local plan for anganwadi workers to procure food for their centres from local farmers. 'There is a truth to whatever the villagers are telling you,' he says. 'There is no issue about that. And we have to admit it. If we want to correct the system, we have to admit it.'

Hindiyankalan, Jharkhand[6]

November 2011

Hindiyankalan, in Jharkhand's tribal district of Chatra, is a village that is arguably one of the poorest in the country and home to fifty Birhor tribal families who experience hunger and illness as a daily reality. In 1952, the Indian government identified the Birhor community as one of the country's seventy-five Particularly Vulnerable Tribal Groups (PVTGs)—nine of which are highly concentrated in Chatra—on the basis of low literacy rates, threats to their population through stagnation or decline and vulnerabilities associated with livelihoods that depend on pre-agricultural technology.

Tribal communities in India suffer higher rates of malnutrition and have less access to health care than even the abysmal national averages. According to the National Family Health Survey, 54 per cent of their children under five are underweight compared with 43 per cent nationally and the percentages of tribal children who are both born in hospitals and fully immunized are far lower than national averages.

The Birhors, like other PVTGs, live in isolated hamlets with little to no access to basic services and routinely suffer malnutrition-related diseases and deaths because they live in the poorest regions of the country. Chatra district was ranked the second-least-developed

---

6. A version of this chapter appeared in the *Wall Street Journal*, India Real Time on 11 April 2012.

district in Jharkhand. It was ranked 583 of the 593 districts in the country in 2006 by the International Institute for Population Sciences (IIPS), on the basis of the under-five mortality rate, access to safe drinking water, immunization of children and female literacy.

The work of local journalists and a few prominent academics brought the Birhors' hunger crisis—in Hindiyankalan and other villages in Jharkhand—to the attention of the state government and national right-to-food monitoring agencies. They continued to publicize the failure of government promises and mandates to reach the people.

The village is located in the desolate hills of Jharkhand, isolated from needed health and social services. There is no electricity and it is about 10 kilometres away from the nearest paved road. We stopped for a night in the block town, Prattapur, on our way from Ranchi and traveled the next morning on two motorcycles up the hills with Balram and a local journalist, Nandkishor Yadav. The road was treacherous—large rocks and ditches, surrounded by forest on both sides. No one on the road for miles. Then we passed a man, woman and their daughter on a bicycle. The man was riding the bicycle and the mother and daughter were sharing the half-seat behind him, facing opposite directions. The daughter was sick, in pain, holding her stomach. Her father said he was taking her to the health centre in Prattapur. 'There are no resources for her in the village,' he said, 'so I have to take her to Prattapur.'

We passed a group of children, one little girl holding her baby brother or sister in her arms. They had these scared little looks on their faces, and when we stopped to talk to them, they didn't say anything. It took us an hour and half to get into Hindiyankalan. Ten Birhors were crouched in a circle next to slabs of rock at the entrance to the village. They knew Balram and Nandkishor. Balram had conducted an investigation three days after eight people were reported to have died of hunger and Nandkishor had filed several stories on the deaths in Hindiyankalan and nearby villages for *Dainik Jagran*. 'We were going there frequently, every day, making sure the reports reached officials, people in the administration, the Chief Minister,' he said.

The starvation deaths of eight Birhors in Hindiyankalan between 1 and 2 October, 2008—two other people were reported to have died from complications in the days after— received more local and state-level attention than other starvation death cases we covered in our three months in the field. Nandkishor took us to a library in Prattapur one day, an office building where troves of newspapers were kept in file cabinets. A worker there spent half a day with us, sifting through reports on the incident. It was remarkable how much ground they covered in such a short amount of time. It was remarkable that none of it seemed to have mattered. I remember the first headline he pulled out of the cabinet: 'Birhors Can't Remember the Last Time They Ate Rice.'

Continual media coverage and official investigations of the conditions of the village were put in the context of the hunger and malnutrition crises afflicting other vulnerable groups and regions in the state, leading then-Chief Minister Shibu Soren to initiate a state-wide programme called the Mukhiya Mantri Khadyan Suraksha Yojana (The Chief Minister's Food Security Plan) which assured all PVTG groups 35 kilogrammes of free rice from local ration shops. The state government also ordered each panchayat to reserve 5 quintals of grain in one ration shop as buffer stock to prevent future starvation deaths. Yet by the time we visited, it was clear in conversations with local health and development officials that there was no legitimate pressure to follow through on those and other promises.

We sat with family members and discussed the current state of social programmes in the village. The village school was only open four to five days a month, which meant that children could only receive a hot cooked meal under the mid-day meal programme that many times each month. Parents were previously sending their children to the nearest school a few kilometres away in Narayanpur village, but stopped after they got word that the teacher refused them meals, claiming that Birhor children would pollute the utensils. Work under NREGA opened only after the 2008 tragedy, but only twice, for short spans, and workers never received their wages.

The people in the circle seemed to be the only people in the village. With no work and food, many villagers migrate to other states like Chhattisgarh where, we were told, they earn about Rs 5,000 a month as contract labour. But about twelve Birhors left to find work in other states in the last few years and their families have lost contact with them entirely.

Saharia Devi, a sixty-five-year-old widow, was one of the people who sat next to us in that circle. She was alert, but quiet, and wore a nose ring and a blue sari. Deep wrinkles lined her forehead. After the two-and-a-half-hour-long meeting, we met her outside her home at the end of a narrow dirt path lined with bushes, where she was carving a stick of bamboo with a shearing knife, making a soop—a basket used to separate the husk from rice. The Birhors, whose total population is around 10,000, were previously farmers and hunters and traders of forest produce, but today the community survives largely by collecting and selling honey and wood from the forest and selling soops for Rs 15 each.

Saharia Devi lived in a brick house constructed through a rural housing programme called the Birsa Awas Yojana, which Chatra's district administration had opened in 2008, after the deaths. The intention was to build brick houses for Chatra's nearly 1,600 Birhors who lived predominantly in mud huts that would collapse during the rainy season. Saharia Devi's house was complete, but most of Hindiyankalan's Birhor families were still living in halfway-built brick homes or mud huts.

We asked her if we could speak to her about what happened in October 2008.

She and other villagers had not been receiving food from the local ration shop since 1998. Most of the villagers didn't even have a ration card. Only four families during those ten years had cards, a problem that Balram had tried to address in an investigation shortly after the deaths. He found that the local ration shop dealer held the villager's ration cards, made fake entries of the cards in his possession and sold the grain on the open market.

'My family was starving,' she said. In 2008, Saharia Devi's family's only source of came from selling soops. The rate then was seven rupees. She, her three sons—Lalhan, Anil and Sunil—and two daughters-in-law made two to three a day. The Rs 40–60 a day they brought in was never enough to feed the household's eight people, including her grandsons, Kuldeep and Korhiya, who were two and four years old at the time. Sometimes, the family would trade soops for one kilogramme of rice.

Each of the Birhors were legally entitled to an Antyodaya Anna Yojaana ration card, which would have enabled each family to buy 35 kilogrammes of grain at highly discounted prices. In 2003, the Supreme Court ordered that all PVTGs would qualify for this benefit, but none of the court-mandated programmes were functioning.

Birhor families survived on a once-daily portion of rice, which they would eat with chakora, a local variant of spinach, and a wild root known as gethi that grows in the forest. They would boil the spinach and root in hot water, but since gethi is poisonous, they would need to drain the toxins by steeping the root in water for one or two days before eating.

On the night of 1 October 2008, villagers were so hungry they could not wait to detoxify the gethi. Twenty to twenty-five people ate the raw root and fell ill immediately with vomiting and diarrhea. The nearest hospital was 13 kilometres away in Prattapur. None of the Birhors in Hindiyankalan own a car or motorcycle, so villagers have to rely on a charpai to take anyone who is ill to the hospital. Beside the challenge of navigating unpaved roads with deep ditches and sharp rocks at night with no light, carrying someone on a charpai requires at least four able-bodied men for each sick person.

Eight people died in the village that night, including Saharia's two grandchildren and her daughter-in-law, Jethi Devi, who was Lalhan's wife.

That October, *Naya Duniya, Dainak Jagran, Hindustan Times* and *Prabhat Khabar* reported the deaths in over thirty stories. They documented the defunct food and nutrition programmes, lack of health and transportation infrastructure, the physical isolation and neglect of tribal communities in the area and the people from tribal and other vulnerable groups in the region who had either died or were in a precarious state due to hunger and tuberculosis—including the additional twenty to twenty-five Birhors of Hindiyankalan who hadn't died that night, but were seriously ill.

'The deaths of Birhors within 24 hours has raised serious concern for the government,' one report said. 'The deaths of people belonging to primitive tribal groups has [sic] been occurring while deaths of members of Scheduled Castes are now also being reported.' The report lists death tolls in neighbouring blocks: five Birhors had died in Sehada village that year, five Baigra tribals had died in Malgu village twenty days before, and about a dozen tuberculosis deaths of the Scheduled Caste Bhuiyas were reported in Pindarkala village. Reports we gathered calculated thirty-five starvation deaths of Particularly Vulnerable Tribal Groups that October alone. As with the Jalia Bongia deaths, the reports drew attention to the extreme deprivation the community must have faced to have decided to eat toxic food.

Twelve days after the deaths, the public health centre in Prattapur sent a physician, Dr Shivshankar Pandey, and a team of doctors to treat the Birhors who had fallen sick from the toxin. The doctor and his team took blood samples from fifty people to test for malaria, gave out mosquito nets and administered saline solution for fifteen villagers suffering dehydration. But they didn't refer those in critical condition back to block or district hospitals for further treatment. This proved fatal for one woman who was taken to the block hospital from Hindiyankalan the next day by villagers, and who died there awaiting transport to another hospital for treatment the day after that.

According to one news report, this was the first time a physician had ever visited the village. State officials and politicians visited the village days before and gave orders for investigation and the issuance of all required social protection programmes. New Antyodaya ration cards were distributed to all villagers immediately in line with Supreme Court orders, and according to news reports, Jharkhand's health minister Bhanu Pratap Sahi met with the families of victims and acknowledged that the shoddy implementation of the government's food and work programmes was denying Birhors state benefits. Yet, coverage at the time also told of how Mr Sahi and other officials, including Prattapur block medical officer Dr Shivshanker Pandey, and Chatra's Deputy Commissioner Abu Bakr Siddique, concluded after visits that October that the cause of the deaths was food poisoning.

The chief minister's free grain scheme did ensure that villagers do have access to the local ration shop on a monthly basis, but they say they are still only getting about 24 to 25 kilogrammes of their food benefit. The lack of paved roads is part of the problem—grains are distributed 13 kilometres away at the block office in Prattapur and villagers have to rent a tractor to make the difficult journey, which costs each family Rs 70.

Unlike previous official visits, the four-member investigation committee comprising the Secretary of Welfare, Food and Civil

Supplies Secretary, Rural Development Secretary and Health Secretary, didn't go to the village to witness the lack of basic infrastructure, the absence of right to food programmes or the state of destitution in which the people lived. Citing the threat of Naxals, which are active in the area, they called Birhors to the block office and held a nominal meeting. The report they submitted to Jharkhand's chief secretary on 31 October 2008 did raise questions on the government's poor delivery of schemes. But like other officials, they concluded the cause of death was food poisoning. No autopsies were conducted on the bodies.

We observed three major problems affecting the implementation of nutrition, food and health programmes: vacancies among several administrative posts in charge of the implementation of programmes at the block level, the lack of coordination between these programmes, and the lack of will from the few officials left in charge of individual programmes. Since 2000, there have been eighteen district collectors of Chatra district—six were in office for less than a month. At the block level, one officer was doing the duties of five official positions. And the supervisor of the ICDS programme was in charge of all ICDS centres in two blocks. There are 144 alone in Prattapur block. She could not answer simple questions about the percentage of malnourished children in the area.

The lack of coordination undermines the implementation of development programmes in any of the interrelated areas of nutrition, food security and health. The lack of needed infrastructure impacts the health and well-being of Scheduled Tribe communities drastically. In a survey conducted by the Ministry of Tribal Affairs, 44 per cent of Scheduled Tribes reported that the distance to a facility posed the greatest problem in accessing healthcare. Only 17.7 per cent of births to women from Scheduled Tribes are delivered in health facilities, compared to 51.0 per cent of all others.

The central government established the National Rural Health Mission in 2005 to attend to the needs of the rural poor, with a focus on eighteen states, through building rural health infrastructure and providing adequate specialized human resources for people in these areas. Since nearly 90 per cent of tribal people live in rural areas, the health of the overall community is largely dependent on the extent to which this programme can deliver. The mission should have in place one sub-centre for every 5,000 residents and, in tribal-dominated areas, a sub-centre for every 3,000 people.

Aside from the lack of infrastructure in Prattapur, officials responsible for nutrition and health programmes still don't acknowledge that chronic hunger and malnutrition afflict the people of Hindiyankalan. The official responsible for the implementation of the anganwadi centres in the Prattapur block insisted that all 144 centres were fully functional, including Hindiyankalan, and that child malnutrition is not a problem in the area. But their primary concerns are to meet the mandates of their respective departments.

Other officials do acknowledge the severity of the problem, but insisted that the obligations to address health and hunger are divided amongst various departments. 'There is a lot of malnutrition here,' said Dr Ravinder Lal, the block physician at the Public Health Centre said. 'But we're from the medical side. We can only treat health problems. They're from their side [referring to the block office responsible for ICDS] and we're from our side.'

Dr Lal was part of the team of physicians that visited Hindiyankalan after the deaths to examine the rest of the villagers. Balram, the State Advisor on the Right to Food, was with us while we spoke to Dr Lal. He mentioned to the doctor that in his investigation a few days after the deaths he assessed a severe problem of malnutrition. He was speaking of children, specifically, who were all underweight in the village. An official block level report shows that 46 per cent of children in Prattapur are underweight. It is likely that actual numbers are higher, since these figures do not account for children in villages like Hindiyankalan that have no proper ICDS centre for weighing facilities. Officials are also likely to under-report.

Dr Lal told us that food poisoning was the cause of death. We mentioned that before people had decided to eat the poisonous roots, they were living with hunger, since they had not accessed the public food grains for ten years and that facilities that could have prevented outright starvation, such as a school for the mid-day meal or an ICDS, were not in the village. We wanted to know if this was taken into consideration during the team's investigation to assess the people's medical condition.

'Do you agree that the people weren't receiving food grains at the time of the deaths?'

'Perhaps,' he said. 'I am not willing to say. That is their problem.'

Banwara, Bihar

***September and November 2011*[7]**

Gita Devi (42, Female), Phoolkumari Devi (24, Female), Unnamed (newborn, female), Sunita Devi (24, Female)

I was seeing a woman then, who was back home in the States, and in Bihar I would see her name everywhere. On buses, storefronts, doorways and I would hear her name in the streets; in the villages, girls and boys would say her name. I saw her name a million times. I heard her name a million times. That November I was on the bus solo to Banwara village between Domuhan and Dobhi blocks, sitting between a boy who was holding a rucksack looking out the window and a blind man who was staring at my fingers. Other old men were singing a song on the bus and there was life on the road between the villages: trees, fields, marshes, cars, trucks, crops that had come that year, crops that had almost come that year.

This was the road that Buddha had walked and, as we were driving down that road, people from all over the world were huddled around the fourth iteration of his enlightenment tree, under which he had sat ten kilometres away, in Bodh Gaya, over two thousand years ago, and where monks had set themselves on fire a few months or days ago. That day, it seemed that no one who had ever been born outside of these villages was walking this road

---

7. A version of this chapter appeared in the *Wall Street Journal*, India Real Time on 10 April 2012

that Buddha had walked. It was just dirt and fields and trees in his day, too. What had he seen then, and was that the spot where a little girl had given him rice and milk on this road, and were any of these old ladies, and little boys walking alone on this road, her progeny? Perhaps there were fewer poor people then, since this was before money as we know it now, but people must have still been killed and tortured for something.

I was always writing back home to her between two walls that were about to smash together. That day, I would see a woman who had just been knifed on the arm by an angry husband and children working their makeshift wells for drinking water and water for the fields. One child said, 'This is why we can't go to school; if we don't do this, what will we drink?' and a man, maybe his father, said 'How will the crops grow?'

Time is a fix, I wrote to her later that day, what do you do with it? Equality takes time, shady governments take time. I have met little girls with your name, I wrote to her, I have seen fathers invoke you. Buddha had no problem with your name, but the way rulers invoke it told him something was off. And that day I had met a man whose wife had had her name. Five months ago, the gas tank had exploded on his wife's face when she was cooking and she died. We got on like old friends and I didn't tell him I had a woman back home who shares his wife's name, but I fell in love with this man's heart. I wrote to her: when he said your name and spoke of what a good woman his wife was and that was just before getting to Banwara where, unlike Heta, there was no life at the entrance of the village, but a dead dog lay in a ditch on that dirt road into the Mahadalit tolas of the village. It was slashed and nicked about the ribs and genitals, its snout in the dirt and flies or mosquitoes fed off his belly and worked their way about the teeth, inside the flaps of his black lips.

I just stood over it and heard: 'Ha ha ha ha ha!'

These boys and girls were laughing, standing on one of the small hills that lined the dirt road where the trees end. We recognized each other since we had met on the dirt patch on our way out of Banwara two months before that. It was hot then and just before dark on our way out, Badri called for an auto to help us get around the drop-offs that you would otherwise fall into, in the dark. They were all over the place, with cement slabs and rod irons of half-constructed beam bridges jutting out in different directions. Now, early November, the sun was out and we were wearing sweaters and the kids were playing some game with sticks, rocks and two ripped chappals.

Two little girls remembered us. I had pictures of them on my phone. I showed them. They laughed. The rest of them pointed at us or covered their mouths, ran around each other or stood with their hands on their heads. I got a big kick out of that. In most other villages we visited, the children stood up against the wall with their hands behind their backs. They were scared to look at you.

'This way or that way to Banwara,' I asked. One dirt path went straight and the other curved to the right along the hills and dried-out streams. We'd made the wrong turn last time and Badri himself was unsure.

They pointed in unison, like that photo of Jesse Jackson and the rest pointing to the warehouse after Dr Martin Luther King Jr. was shot.

We reached Banwara twenty-five minutes later. A crowd was forming in front of the first row of kachcha houses where the first hamlet begins. The thirty-eight Bhuiya families of Banwara live in an L-shaped tola that is essentially two little hamlets. One hamlet begins at the entrance of the village, along a small brick pathway, about a hundred yards long. The row of kachcha huts with charpais out front is lined up on the right side of the path. The other hamlet begins at the end of the left bend, huts lined up on the right side of the path, tightly wedged together. The brick pathway breaks off into the dirt and begins again as stones, leading into the thickets of fields that spread far ahead.

Fifteen to twenty people packed in a circle, shouting, cursing, putting their hands on each other. Off to the side, a group of young men sat on a khattiya, dividing up a stack of flyers and talking amongst themselves.

A woman's head poked out of the circle. She could have been forty, she could have been sixty. Tears were just part of the rest of her wrenched expression, obscuring all of her features. I still can't know for sure what she actually looked like. She was crying, screaming and the tears and sweat were smudging her face. Some black substance oozed down her eyes and cheeks and into her mouth, while the sun illuminated miniscule droplets of spit and dust and the crowd spread out. The desperation in her voice made them back down. The men on the khattiya stopped talking, stood quiet with their arms folded. They weren't exactly listening. They were waiting.

Her voice was all nerves and gut, pointing us to her left arm, which was bleeding. She had been knifed somewhere on her forearm. I couldn't see the gash exactly. The blood was rushing. It was on her sari and on her feet. The dirt below her looked like lava. Tiny streams of spit flew out of her mouth. She was shaking, holding her bleeding arm out with her right hand. 'Look! Look!'

'What happened,' I asked Badriji, who translated from the local dialect to Hindi.

'Just wait,' he said. 'Just be quiet for a moment,' he said. He went to scope it out and disappeared in the circle.

'Look at what he did to me!' the woman screamed.

Another woman stepped out of the circle. She was about thirty and was wearing a blue sari. She was holding herself, one hand on each opposite shoulder. She had a warm smile. We had spoken to her about the government programmes on our last visit. 'Right, you did say you were coming back,' she said.

The men, who had become silent, started to shout back again, while two other women got hold of the distraught woman. I thought they meant harm, but they patted the screaming woman on the back, not flinching one bit while she swung chaotic punches indiscriminately, and walked her off to an empty khattiya. 'Sit down!' they said. 'Sit down!' She sat, beating her palms against her wrinkled forehead.

'You said you would come back', the woman in the blue sari said. 'But that was a long time ago.'

It had been six weeks. Six weeks can be an unforeseeable future. I watched these two women simultaneously: one, holding herself smiling at us, the other apparently losing—having already lost—something dear to her…

'We have to talk to Vilas Manjhi again. And also Tulsi Manjhi,' I said to Badri. 'What happened,' I said, nodding towards the crowd. 'Who did that to her?'

Some people were laughing now. The men on the khattiya were busy again, dividing up the flyers, talking amongst themselves.

Badri said the woman's husband had knifed her in an argument. He had been drunk. Things had turned violent when the husband had declared that he had asked his mistress to move in with them. The woman had said she would not accept that. So her husband had knifed her arm and threatened to kill her if she did not leave. The woman had tried to fight back. And the husband had fled that morning.

'What should we do,' I asked Badri.

He mumbled something, looking at the group of men stacking flyers on the khattiya. One of them got up, holding a stack in each hand. He was wearing a white shirt tucked into gray slacks.

'Who are they?' the man asked the woman in the blue sari, looking at me. His name was Ramlakand Prasad. He was a CPI-ML member and was trying organize about forty villagers to wrest land rights back from the government.

'They were here when Sunita Devi was ill,' she said.

'You're some kind of officer?' he asked.

I told him we were not from the government.

'What are you here for?'

The bleeding woman zipped through the crowd. She wasn't crying anymore. She was just talking to herself, stomping down the road we had come, holding her arm.

She was getting smaller.

Badri said, 'It happens.'

'What happens,' I asked.

'What are you here for?' Ramlakand Prasad said.

'Anything, everything,' Badri said to me while the woman's lower half disappeared and the rest of her was swivels of heat.

~

The Bihar State Supreme Court Commissioner's Office identified the death of Gita Devi as a starvation death. She was a forty-two-year-old mother of seven from Banwara's Bhuiya community and we had met her eldest son, Vilas Manjhi, in late September. He was twenty-eight years old when we met and had quit school after the fourth grade to bring in money and food for his family. Vilas's face was the face of the man Harper Lee was talking about when she wrote about courage. *He had been licked too many times before it all began, but he started out anyway and kept going, no matter what.* He had a small build, clenched jaw, a strong forehead, but these vacant eyes. He had thick and full black hair and smooth skin but was an aged young man.

He told his mother's story on the khattiya outside a neighbour's hut. Young men formed a circle. He spoke slowly and quietly. Fatigued. Resigned. But he was a survivor. He had been coaxed unwillingly to recount the worst days of his life to journalists more times than he could bear. In subjecting himself to the pain of reliving those days time and again, he'd managed remarkable grace and courage. I crouched in the dirt with my notebook on my thigh and would lose balance now and then as he spoke, having sometimes to clasp his knee to regain it. He would grab my hand, squeeze it, hold his over mine and continue on with his story.

For four days prior to Gita Devi's death, he said, there had been no food in the house. This was the longest the family had ever gone without *any* food, but the struggle to avoid hunger was one they faced every day of their lives. The family had never owned a ration card. Officials had not counted their family on the list in the original poverty-line survey in 2002. They could not buy cheap grains from the local fair price shop, which according to villagers, was never open more than three to four days a month during that time. Several other families in the village did not have a ration card either. The village also lacked an anganwadi centre. Village children, old people and the infirm could not count on a meal that way either.

In 2006, Bihar was hit with drought. The family did not own land and what little work was available could not sustain their needs. At most, Vilas and his father, Tulsi Manjhi, would find ten to twelve days of farm work a year during the paddy harvest. Both men earned a daily wage of 3 kilogrammes of rice. They would sell a share of their grain at the local market to buy other items. The family could not afford dal or roti so they would eat a small ration of rice and salt twice daily. 'The last time we could afford to buy dal,' Tulsi recalled, 'was two years before my wife's death.'

They would take loans from the panchayat mukhiya of either Rs 1,000 at 10 per cent interest, or 10 kilogrammes of rice which they'd trade for money, and work the interest off by sending more of the children off to work. Aside from farm labour, Tulsi could find about ten days of house-building work in neighbouring villages in June and July, during the rains. That brought in about Rs 70–80 a day.

In late September 2006, Gita delivered another baby, Muniya. There were now eight people to feed. But the family could not bring in enough food to avoid hunger, because work had dried up in the last month. Sometimes the family would supplement the rice and salt with wild local flora. They would boil a green fruit called mungha—which some villagers also call sajna—into a sabzi. They would also make sabzis out of jinghi (the leaves from a tree), and a vegetable the villagers call ninua. Each of these plants grew in their village and in areas close to villages nearby.

By early October 2006, Vilas and Tulsi said, Gita Devi fell ill and was too weak to walk or talk. She had complained to her husband and son of chest pain days before and was now losing weight rapidly. Some family members would tear a bit of jinghi from a tree to feed her. They would also try to nurse her with water. But the quality of that water was questionable. There was no hand pump in the village at the time, so people constructed a well, called a latha, on their own for drinking water. The well by Tulsi Manjhi's house, we saw, was full of frogs and flies.

Neighbours said they couldn't provide financial support or food since their economic situation was dire too. Tulsi also said all of their family members from neighbouring villages could not help for the same reason. Gita's worsening condition, after having had just given birth to Muniya days before without help, put economic and emotional strain on the family. 'I would just lie next to her at night,' Tulsi said, 'Feeling bad that I could not do anything.' He tried once to feed her a handful of jinghi leaves.

According to Dr Vandana Prasad, a paediatrician and founding secretary and National Convener of the Public Health Resource Network in New Delhi, a woman in Gita Devi's condition is more vulnerable to death compared to both malnourished women who are not pregnant, and malnourished men, of a similar age. Gita Devi, Dr Prasad said, likely suffered from anaemia, which afflicts 72 per cent of Scheduled Caste women in Bihar, according to the last National Family Health Survey. She was thus more at risk for 'dying from primary postpartum haemorrhaging,' which is a loss of blood from the genital tract within twenty-four hours of delivery. According to Dr Prasad, breastfeeding women in Gita Devi's condition are more at risk because the mother expends 'calories and essential nutrients, which can lead to osteoporosis, vitamin deficiencies of all kinds and an increased susceptibility to sepsis which is also fatal post-partum.'

These possible complications were likely more difficult for Gita Devi's body to bear because she had suffered a life of prolonged hunger and malnutrition. 'Basically,' Dr Prasad said of a death of a person struggling with hunger and malnutrition, 'the intestinal mucosa gets flattened, which leads to poorer absorption of nutrients. Since all vital organs require energy to function, the inability to absorb required nutrients leads to the failure of the kidneys and liver to expend toxic elements that accumulate in the body. But the main point to remember is that before any of this would happen, the person would get an infection and die of illness.'

Vilas then told us a part of the story that we were unprepared to hear. 'My own wife had also given birth to a girl at that time,' he told us.

'While your mother was dying?' we asked.

'My mother died in the morning after drinking water,' he said. 'The same night, my daughter passed away. The next morning, my wife also died of starvation,' he added. He was straight-faced.

Phool Kumari was Vilas's wife. According to Vilas and other villagers, she had eaten no food for days until the moment she gave birth. Vilas or Tulsi could not find work for over a month prior to the demise of Gita Devi, Phool Kumari and the unnamed baby. This is despite the fact that Gaya was one of the first hundred districts selected for the beginning of NREGA work in 2005. Villagers say that the programme did not begin in the village until 2010, when many did about fifteen days of brick-laying work that year. Vilas's wife lost large amounts of blood during childbirth. Since she had eaten no food, she was unable to feed her day-old daughter, who died the day she was born.

Young men stood around us. There was no emotion on their faces. Had they witnessed these events? Had they heard these details retold before? I scribbled my disbelief in my notebook and held it in check on my thigh with my elbow, looking at the questions I had written in all caps, afraid to look at Vilas and the blank faces. It would take a while to comprehend the fact that these events had actually taken place. I wrote: *Three people of different generations in the same family had died of conditions related to destitution within twenty-four hours.*

We sat there for a few seconds. I looked up at Vilas and the young men. Some of them had their arms around each other.

Cornell West had said the condition of truth is to let suffering speak. There was silence.

'Now, my second wife is ill,' Vilas said, after much silence. 'And we don't have enough food to give her.'

'Where is she?' I asked.

'Home,' he said.

'Can we see her?' I said.

***

Sunita Devi lay on a khattiya outside their mud house. She was covered by a woollen blanket from the waist down, and wore a red sari. Flies buzzed about her dark face. Her eyes were liquid. The pupils darted back and forth. Her tears did not drop. They pooled about the rims. Her mouth stayed open so that her teeth showed. She moaned. Her belly and cheeks were swollen, but the flesh on her arms had withered to a tight, dry, wrinkled sheet of skin, outlining the bones. She would rest the back of her hand on her forehead every few seconds and make a sound, like a gag. She was trying to breathe. She was twenty-four years old but her swollen face and the look in her eyes that she did not know what was happening to her made her appear like a child, confused and sad.

My God, I thought.

The family could not say when exactly Sunita Devi first fell ill. But by August 2011 her condition worsened. Tulsi Manjhi said his family took a Rs 15,000 loan from the local labour contractor, Sanjay Singh, to pay for transportation and medical expenses to Magadh Medical College, a private hospital in Gaya. Sunita Devi's records indicate that she was given a range of free oral medications, including antibiotics and vitamins, a standard treatment for a liver abscess, doctors in New Delhi told us.

Tulsi Manjhi said that he and his sons—Vilas, Umesh (21), Arjun (19) and Sarjun (13)—worked in the brick kilns in the nearby town of Chanda to pay back the loans while Sunita Devi's parents stayed with her in the hospital as she underwent treatment.

Villagers say that Sanjay Singh has been taking migrant workers from Banwara and other neighbouring villages to districts in Uttar Pradesh—Khanpur, Allahabad and Rampur—to work in the brick kilns since 2007 or 2008. Leaving the village is the only way to avoid hunger, they said. Work is scarce. The NREGA programme has never provided the full 100 days of work. The programme was defunct until 2010.

Singh provides an initial cash handout of Rs 5,000 to individual male workers and Rs 6,000–8,000 to heads of households who move with whole families. Peak seasons are between October to June, after and before the monsoons. In our last visit to Banwara, Vilas was not present because he and twelve other men from the village had left for Kanpur that October, where they earned about Rs 300 for every 1,000 bricks made. Two men, his father said, can make about 600 to 700 bricks a day. The days are long and brutal. Young men and whole families work from 4 a.m. until 7 p.m. and live in cramped rooms near the work site.

'How long has she been like this?' we asked.

Vilas told us that the doctor had discharged her about a week ago. 'But we don't have any money to take her to another doctor,' he said.

'Bhaiya (brother),' he said, 'We don't know what to do.'

According to hospital records, Dr Rahul Kumar indicated that the family requested Sunita's discharge before she was healthy enough to leave. But Tulsi Manjhi denied this. 'No, no. Why would we ask her to be discharged,' he said. He claimed the doctor told the family that the hospital did not have the necessary medicines and suggested they seek treatment elsewhere. Dr Kumar refused to comment after repeated requests.

We stood silent for ten minutes. Her eyes kept wobbling back and forth, her mouth open in pain. Something inside me died. I kept looking at her hands, her fingers, reaching out.

'Is it okay to talk to her?' I asked.

Vilas nodded.

More villagers filed in, a group of young men formed a circle behind us.

I got on my knees, dropped my notebook in the dirt, and took her hand in mine. It was cold and dry. Her fingers were searching my palm, my wrist.

Vilas stood just above my head, one hand on his hip, looking down.

'What do you feed her?' I asked him.

'We can only give her this much rice, once in the morning,' he said, cupping his empty hand. 'We don't have enough food in the house.'

She started to cry. She was saying something but I couldn't make out what. An empty feeling in me started to widen. I put my free hand on her shoulder, then atop her head.

'Are you in pain,' I said to her.

She nodded. The water that had pooled around her eyes started to fall in large tears.

'I'm hungry,' she said. 'Please give me something to eat.'

I looked up at Vilas, standing over me. He was a broken man. Lost.

'When we come back tomorrow,' I said, 'we'll bring food.'

***

The Supreme Court has issued hundreds of interim orders on starvation as part of the 2001 Right to Food Case. An October 2002 interim order states that starvation deaths 'would be taken as evidence of the status of the implementation of orders relevant to the Right to Food Case.' These orders refer to all food, nutrition and employment related schemes: the Public Distribution System, Integrated Child Development Services (referred to locally as anganwandi centres), the mid-day meal scheme, the National Rural Employment Guarantee Scheme, and pension programmes for widows and the elderly.

The right to food at the time was currently upheld by the court's conversion of food, nutrition, work and pension programmes into legal rights. Local officials therefore have duties to enforce the right to food through each of those programmes. When starvation deaths occur, local officials have to investigate the status of each of the 'right to food' programmes meant to enable poor people to access sufficient amounts of nutritious food. They also have duties to correct problems in the implementation of the programmes immediately. The goal is not only to prevent future cases of starvation deaths, but to uphold the Constitutional right to life, and ensure that the destitute, who live with chronic huger and malnutrition and have endured the deaths of their loved ones to those conditions, can access the social safety-net system. The interim order of 29 October 2002 says that when governments are aware of starvation conditions, 'The Central and State Governments are directed to ensure that Antyodaya Anna Yojana is extended to the destitute population.'

Officials admitted that Gita Devi's family and neighbours could not access basic schemes at the time of her death. Yet, the panchayat mukhiya, Ashok Singh, and the block development officer, denied that this means that Gita Devi, her daughter-in-law, and the newborn who was not able to feed, died of conditions of hunger. Instead, they claimed that Phool Kumari died due to complications in childbirth and that Gita Devi died from tuberculosis.

No medical official had ever diagnosed Gita Devi with tuberculosis while she was alive and no post mortem was conducted after her death. Tuberculosis is rampant in the village. Twelve people from Banwara were afflicted with the disease during our visit. It is possible that officials are more at ease acknowledging deaths by illness, since there are no binding duties on the state to ensure affordable and sufficient healthcare through public health centres.

The *Dainik Jagran* covered Gita Devi's story over several pieces in the days after her death. The stories didn't just draw from immediate calamities the family faced in the four days without food. They detailed the lack of access to subsidized grains, a defunct anganwadi centre, no hand pump for drinking water, no work from the public works programme, and the general conditions of destitution in which Banwara's Mahadalit community live. A local reporter, whose name we won't disclose, confirmed after one of our interviews with local officials that, on the basis of the information highlighting these failings, 'several officials admitted off-the-record that the cause of death was due to hunger. '

News reports put pressure on government officials to visit the family, but this did not lead to official investigations into programmes to ascertain why families were denied their rights of access. The block development officer at the time, Ravi Bhushan, gave Tulsi Manjhi 15 kilogrammes of rice and a cheque of Rs 10, 000 under the National Family Benefit Scheme. Jitan Ram Manjhi, the Janata Dal United (JDU) MLA of Barachatti, visited the family and stated publicly that the deaths were due to administrative negligence.

Ashok Kumar Singh, the panchayat mukhiya since 2001, visited the family two days after the deaths and offered them Rs 1,000, 10 kilogrammes of flour and 20 kilogrammes of rice. According to the *Dainik Jagran*, the grains, money, and promises to provide needed infrastructure for the village were only given on the condition that Tulsi Manjhi, who is illiterate, gave his thumb impression on a document proclaiming that Gita Devi had died of tuberculosis. We later called Singh to confirm this allegation, but he hung up on us.

'At the time I thought, "If she died of illness, where is the doctor to verify this?" She wasn't ill before she died. She died of hunger,' Tulsi Manjhi said.

No post mortem was conducted on the body since the family had buried her by the time Singh arrived. Doctors did arrive ten days after the deaths. A team of officials, including a civil surgeon, Bhola Prasad Sinha, the block medical officer (BMO) Dr Halda, Block Development Officer Ravi Bhushan, Circle Officer Durgesh Nandan, IAS intern Devesh Sehra and Shaldeep Prasad Singh, the district upsamaharta came to Banwara and told villagers that they were there to inquire about the cause of the deaths. But villagers later told the *Dainik Jagarn* that, despite their telling the team about the family's conditions of hunger, the officials insisted that the two women died of illness and told them to comply with this decision.

In the days after the deaths, several aam sabhas were held in the village to discuss the issue. Block and district level politicians, Jitan Ram Manjhi (JDU MLA, Barachatti) and Rajesh Manjhi (Rashtriya Janta Dal), visited and stated publicly that the failures of the social safety-net had contributed to the deaths. Rajesh Manjhi went as far as to say that the state government should be held accountable. But villagers—most importantly, Gita Devi's family members—were not able to speak at the meeting to give their own accounts of those failures. Tulsi Manjhi and neighbours sat quietly while officials made promises they would not fulfill.

'Why did you not share your own experiences at the sabha?' we asked.

'Poor people aren't allowed to speak. Only the leaders are allowed to speak,' he said.

~

In their 2009 investigation of statewide starvation deaths, the Bihar Advisors to the Supreme Court Commissioner's Office flagged the issue of accountability. As mentioned in a previous chapter,

Rupesh, the State Advisor on the Right to Food, led the investigation and compiled a list of nearly 100 cases which he sent to the chief minister's office that August. Rupesh used the report as the basis for a public interest litigation his organization filed in the Bihar High Court that December. The High Court did not hear the case.

'There has been no actual result of the PIL,' Rupesh says. 'The High Court pushed the issue to the (Bihar) Human Rights Commission for further investigation, but nothing has come about in the last two years. ' This situation continues as of this writing.

In Banwara, despite immediate media attention, official investigations and local politicians calling for state accountability, there has been little progress on fixing defunct programmes.

A September 2010 Dobhi Block Office report we obtained entitled, 'An Investigation of Death by Hunger', signed by the child development programme officer, is a two-page document with factual errors about Gita Devi's family's socio-economic situation. Officials write in the report that the family had received benefits from government programmes, including the Indira Awas Yojna (the rural housing scheme), Swastya Bhima Yojna (the rural health scheme) and the Aam Aadmi Yojna. It does state that the anganwadi centre, which had not been functional until that year, was run in a private home instead of a government centre. In the year since the report was signed no attempts had been made to build the required centre, needed to provide services to eighty children in the village.

In 2007, officials distributed BPL ration cards to villagers. All of the Bhuiya families of Banwara, including Tulsi Manjhi's, should have received Antyodaya cards in line with Supreme Court Orders which list Scheduled Caste groups identified as Mahadalits as destitute. Only two of the thirty-eight Mahadalit families have such cards.

Meanwhile, BPL card-holding families are only able to buy grains from the ration shop six to eight months a year. They are being overcharged and not getting their full quotas. They have to pay Rs 180 for 23 kilogrammes of grains. At most, they should be paying no more than Rs 152 for 25 kilogrammes. In 2010, a group of ten villagers tried to address this problem. They walked to the block office and told the block official about their situation and the impact it was having on their lives. The official told them that it would be fixed, but nothing happened. They revisited the office a few times, before giving up hope that their problems would be resolved.

Job cards for the public works programme were distributed just after the deaths. As mentioned earlier, villagers are provided about fifteen days of work a year.

But the problems in the functioning of this programme reveal some constraints that are out of the hands of local officials. Gaya district does not receive timely and adequate funds from the centre. Each year, district officials compile data from each panchayat on how much of the allotted money for the programme was officially used for wages and capital expenses. The central government uses these figures to determine the allocation to each district for the coming year. Districts receive that amount twice a year: in April and October, the beginning and mid-point of each fiscal year.

But the process has never gone according to plan. Officials in Gaya told us that the funds for the programme are always delayed.

'Last year's second allotment didn't come until this February,' Vandana Priyasi, Gaya's District Magistrate said, 'And this year's first installment didn't come until July.' Long delays in payments for the public work programme are a major barrier to alleviating poverty in districts like Gaya, where the poorest people starve and die.

Funding problems make it difficult for local officials to run the programme effectively. I'll illustrate this problem with an example from the panchayat budget. According to official records, there were 566 job card-holders at the time of our visit in the panchayat where Banwara is located. If the programme ran according to plan—assuring a hundred days of work to each card-holder, the panchayat would have to spend Rs 64,52,000 (566 workers x 100 days x Rs 114/ workday) for wages alone. That figure does not include expenses for infrastructure and materials, which are 40 per cent of each budget. We know the programme has never come close to providing the full hundred days of work, in part, because, as officials say, the district never receives payments on time. It is not clear how much money, exactly the panchayat asked for—which is important to know since the programme is supposed to be demand-driven—but we do know that they only received Rs 3,18,000 in total for both wages and materials. That paltry amount makes it impossible to assure workers the legally guaranteed 100 days of work.

Do officials spend what funds are on hand efficiently? Records show that the panchayat used Rs 79,340 of the budget on wages through September-end, or just under 21 per cent. We asked the panchayat mukhiya, Ashok Singh, how much the panchayat spent on wages that year. He said Rs 15,000, a gap of over Rs 64,000. It is not possible to conclude why, exactly, there are gaps between the official reports and what one of the lead officials of the programme tells us. What is possible to say is that funding constraints do restrict the efficacy of the programme, while the lack of local-level accountability compounds the disadvantage against the poor. They have no reason to believe—no proof has ever been given to them—that officials entrusted with a public good will carry out their duties in line with the law.

'The buck stops here,' the District Magistrate said, when we asked what accountability measures are in place to make sure that funds reach the panchayat and are spent without graft. But she was unable to elaborate how she holds officials in her district to task for administering the public work programme and if, or how, the lack of accountability in the overall social safety-net system impacts the lives of people who depend on such programmes to survive.

Is the disparity between required and allotted funding a problem of centre to district allocations or is it that that budget demands are not truly demand-driven? Or, perhaps, both? Under NREGA guidelines, budget demands are to be decided upon in the gram sabhas, through discussions amongst villagers about what works are needed. The panchayat mukhiya is then required to report these demands to the NREGA programme officer at the block office, who is charged with vetting the demands and deciding the budget requests to send to the district. In reality, this process does not occur. There are no regular gram sabhas, according to Gita Devi's family members and several interviews with other villagers, and no consultation with villagers about what works are to be included. In the absence of this, and the fact there is no real accountability, there is absolutely no pressure on local officials to assure the proper functioning of a programme so vital to addressing the daily hardships of poverty.

***

The NREGA programme officer, Shiv Prakash claims plantation and farm work won't open in Banwara due to a land dispute. 'The land problem,' CPI-ML member Ramlakand Prasad, says on the other hand, 'is the reason the government won't implement *any* of the programmes properly.'

In the late 1980s Banwara's Mahadalit community, historically landless, obtained land rights from the government after they'd seized 40 acres of land from Balram Singh. Singh, the local landlord, controlled all of the farmland in Banwara, claiming ancestral ownership, despite the fact the land was deemed state-owned in 1985.

Due to land-ceiling laws, however, the legal limit of ownership of non-irrigated land in Bihar was set between 12 and 18 acres. In the late '80s, several landless Mahadalits, with the help of CPI-ML members, seized the land from Singh. He moved to nearby Sargohtti, while his two sons remain in the large house that sits in the middle of Banwara at the midpoint between two Mahadalit hamlets. CPI-ML members distributed the 40 acres amongst the thirty-eight

Mahadalit families, who tilled small patches of land where they grew tomatoes, wheat, potatoes and corn, until 2002.

That year, Singh filed a case against the villagers in the Gaya Circuit Court under Articles 379 (theft), 143 (unlawful assembly), and 146 (violent force by unlawful assembly). This resulted in the cancellation of the villagers' land rights. Despite not having legal authority, they continued to till the land and in 2005, says Anjani Prasad, the attorney representing the Bhuiyas. Gaya's sub-district judicial magistrate ordered the arrest of twenty-three villagers, who were apprehended and jailed. Tulsi Manjhi spent three months in jail. During that time, his sons worked in the brick kilns to bring in money.

'Government officials came and arrested us all at once,' Jathand Mandal, a villager who spent four months in jail, said. 'Some of us spent two to three months in jail. While we were in jail, our families had to struggle for work.'

Singh filed an FIR in 2007 and the case was still pending in 2011.

~

'The Mahadalits of Banwara are extremely poor,' the mukhiya, Ashok Singh, said. But they were not hungry.

About ten men sat around him on khattiyas. They were silent, watching our conversation. Singh was wearing shorts and a tight undershirt. We sat outside his house, a two-storey fully furnished bungalow, with a new white paint finish and a large tractor in the yard.

'Gita Devi,' he said between a gulp of tea and a bite of biscuit, 'died of tuberculosis.'

'These people are poor,' he explained. 'They drink. So they have health problems.' They get sick. And die.

We presented what we knew—there was no food in Gita Devi's house for four days, no access to subsidized food grains, no work, no road to travel for help. No doctor had diagnosed her with the tuberculosis prior to death. No post mortem was conducted.

We wanted to know how local officials assessed the socio-economic conditions responsible for the deaths of three people who could not access their legal entitlements to food. He stood up, retrieved a sheet of paper from inside his house, walked back, and placed it our hands.

'See', he said.

'What's this?' we asked before looking.

These people are poor, he said. They get sick. And die.

'Sunita Devi', he said.

'Sunita Devi', we said. 'We just saw her last night.'

'She died this morning', he said, 'just before you came here.'

In our hands was a death notice.

***

She was under the woolen blanket now. They were going to bury her soon. We placed the bags of grain and dal we had bought in the middle of the ring of people. Vilas walked up to us slowly and stood with one hand on his hip, facing down. We stood there looking at each other, at him, at her, the people.

We were silent.

I am in a lot of pain, he said.

Pain.

I thought, What if my soul was born in his body? An image came into mind: I lunge for him, hugging him as hard as I could, I pull the pain out of him, I hold it.

But I just stood there, watching him condemned.

~

I had bad dreams back in Delhi. I would wake up breathing like I had smoked a pack of cigarettes. I couldn't remember much about most of them when I came to. There was one, though. It was Badri and I coming up over that hill into the village, and that circle of people in the dirt patch are screaming and shouting. The woman steps out of the circle bleeding at the arm, darkening her red sari yelling 'Look! Look!'

'What happened,' I ask Badri.

'Just wait,' he says, and disappears into the crowd.

'Look at what he did to me!' she screams.

The young woman in the blue sari steps out: 'Right, you did say you were coming back.'

'We have to talk to Vilas Manjhi again. And also Tulsi Manjhi,' I say.

'What happened,' I say. 'Who did that to her?'

People are laughing.

'What should we do,' I ask Badri.

He's beside me again. Ramlakand Prasad walks up, white shirt, gray slacks.

'Who are they?' he says.

'They were here when Sunita Devi was ill,' the woman in the blue sari says.

'What are you here for,' he says.

Sunita Devi zips through the crowd, holding both arms. Still bleeding. Same eyes, same mouth. I watch her get smaller down the hill.

Badri says, 'It happens.'

'What happens,' I say.

'What are you here for…' Ramlakand Prasad says.

***

'Do you feel as though you have sinned,' the doctor asked in the first session.

I told her yes.

'Do you still have the dreams,' the doctor asked in the last session.

'Sometimes,' I said.

'How does that make you feel?'

'Bad,' I said.

'Can you be more specific?'

'I don't know how to say it.'

'Try,' she said. 'The first thing that comes to your mind.'

'Grief.'

'You are mourning her.'

'Yeah.'

'You are mourning for her. But you are also mourning for who you once were. You're not the person you were before her, are you.'

'No.'

'You look like the same person, but you will never be that person again because it is not possible, is that right.'

'I don't know.'

'You are reborn. It is painful.'

I heard 'possible'. But she said 'painful'. Rebirth. Is it so? And how many human brothers and sisters are born busy dying.

PART II

ENGAGING WITH UNEQUAL INDIA

This Land Is Their Land

Ashwin Parulkar

This story is based on fieldwork conducted with Kanchan Gandhi in Jaipur, Rajasthan during the months of March, April, July and August in 2012 for a study on destitution.

New life. A baby was born at 11 o'clock on the morning of 27 July 2012 in Jaipur's Monohorapur kachchi basti. We heard the news when we got to Shukuran's house. It was noon, Friday.

'My daughter-in-law just delivered a girl,' she said, standing in the hallway. She was smiling. The parakeets were chirping in their cage and the goat was chewing thorns from the stems of the channa plants stashed at the doorway, next to its stake. 'Come inside,' she said, 'we have to celebrate.' Kanchan and I walked through the beaded curtains and sat on a single bed wedged next to a stack of pots and pans. Pinky was in the corner holding her baby. Pinky is Shukuran's seventeen-year-old grand-daughter. I like her nice large eyes looking at everyone, her always carrying her baby. She had always been thin. But between our March and July visits she'd really lost weight. She'd stopped eating since her husband left her and the baby. No windows in the room. The bedsheets were damp. Shukuran walked in, holding a tray with half-filled plastic cups of Fanta.

'Drink,' Shukuran said. All around us were voices of women.

'Where is she?' Kanchan asked.

'In the room across the hallway.'

Our room was low lit, dusty, and very hot. We were dripping. It reminded me of a subway stop in Brooklyn in the late summer nights, when trains run local. But the baby's room had a window that faced the main vein of the basti—the dirt road between the mosque and the trash mound where the Valmiki neighbourhood begins.

That road is alive. The kids bounce red rubber balls back and forth and torture stray cats ('There is life in these animals too!' Kanchan had told them). The women peel channa in a circle in front of the storekeeper's stoop for Rs 30 a day. Some men laugh horrendous drunken laughter while drinking warm beers. They sit you down to talk of the original landscape of the basti when it was jungle and don't recognize you one day to the next. The pigs get chased off, flinging mud, the chickens stabbed in their cages with sticks.

Mid-day, the road is chaos. The sun in July will blind you and ferment the beer and meat and vegetables in the alleyways. It's the burning hay and morning breath you smell in your sleep. By dark, the lanes go black and silent, except the lights of beedis and the goats and drunken cackles. Now, I imagined in the half-dark of the room on a Friday afternoon, the sun shining on the baby through the metal bars in the room across the hallway.

We could hear Rajiya's voice in there. She's the midwife who lives across the street and delivers babies in the basti for Rs 500 a birth. She was not well. A blood pressure condition for the last five years, always holding her stomach and waist. Her husband lives in a village in West Bengal. Deliveries fund her medical expenses: Rs 450 for five days of medicine. So her sons and her daughter-in-law, Saveena, look after her. Saveena gives Rajiya hope. She was in her final year of college with plans to open a school in the future. In March, money had been tight because her oldest son, Buddal, needed care for liver and kidney failures. She moaned back in March while she talked about Buddal, with all the ladies around her sitting on her floor. He was dead by the time we returned in July.

There were the birds and the laughter and the talking ladies outside, but she had preserved that room across the hallway in peace. God bless that baby's first hour on earth.

'What will you name her?' I asked.

The baby was Shukuran's fifth grandchild. Four generations of women worked about the house—cleaning, peeling channa, scolding children. But Shukuran's daughter-in-law—Pinky's mother—wasn't home. Her name is Rabiya and she was forty years old at the time. She had gone to Garg Gate to beg again. That's in the Old City in Jaipur. It was Friday. Usually Rabiya, Shukuran and two other women—Momina and Sahara—took the Number 6 bus together to the Old City on Thursdays. They're all widows. They all beg. Shukuran and Rabiya are ill with respiratory problems.

Momina is sick of being alone in the world. She's less than four-and-a-half feet tall and when her face is hidden under dupatta you'd think she was a little girl. And when she yells at you, you'd think she was a little girl. She is one of the oldest residents of the basti, one of the originals who walked from Old City to this spot of jungle in the 1980s with her little girl. Her daughter lives in the basti but they don't get along. People say her daughter is crazy. People say Momina is crazy.

'She doesn't know anything. She doesn't even know how to speak,' Zyada said. Zyada is the leader of the channa circle.

But Momina can speak. 'My daughter is the crazy one,' she said.

And her daughter: 'My mother is crazy.'

Either way, she doesn't have a home, and her friends don't call her by name. Buddhi (old woman), they say. Sometimes she sleeps on the street. Sometimes she sleeps outside the mosque. Sometimes she sleeps in the homes of different widows, week to week. Shukuran takes her in, feeds her. Sahara takes her in, lets her watch TV and drink Fanta with her grandchildren. Afroza takes her in, lets her scream at her children. Afroza is a newcomer. Thirty-five years old, she rents a small room, tortured by her inability to stop her ten-year-old son from getting high.

Thursdays, the four women start at five in the morning sharp. First, they go to the exit gate of the graveyard, where some people give them one or two rupees. But most of the money comes in on their rounds in the city. They break up for the afternoon to knock on the doors of houses in neighbourhoods laid out in squares. The last leg is through numerous galis in the markets.

The shopkeepers expect them. Some of the people that give them a few rupees a week have known the women from the old days when groups of migrants from West Bengal and Assam came to Jaipur in the 1960s, '70s, and '80s and lived on the footpaths of Janta Market near Govinda Mandir in the Old City.

Each week, they split the pot. An average Thursday brings in about Rs 50 to 90 each, subtracting expenses—the bus fare, an afternoon samosa, maybe a bathroom break. Better than the Rs 30 to 40 a day when they go alone.

But today is Friday. Rabiya went to the Old City alone that morning again to test her luck, Shukuran said. Since Pinky gave birth months before, Rabiya has had to bring in money seven days a week. The family already had enough trouble getting food. But things got worse when Pinky stopped eating because she started to fall ill. Rabiya thought she understood heartbreak. Her husband Sayavelli—Shukuran's eldest—was an alcoholic throughout their marriage and died of jaundice in 2003 when her son and daughter were very young. Soon after, her son died. He was three-and-a-half years old. Malnourished. She didn't understand why Pinky was torturing herself. Not eating when every day was survival? Pinky's mother and grandmother tried to get her to eat while they struggled for food. But she was broken. Why did he leave? They were his only family. He came from a broken home.

When he left, the mother and grandmother worried. When daughter/grandaughter fell sick, they had permanent anxiety. Between our visits in March and July Rabiya took a Rs 5,000 loan to get her daughter a glucose drip and iron supplements. She was working it off as fast as she could. 'People are more generous to the beggars during Ramadan, so…' Shukuran said.

Tafiq Ali Khan appeared through the doorway blinds. Old age may have slowed him down but there is a grace about him. Maybe that's because he's always smiling. He felt for the empty chair in front of us with his left hand and kept his balance with the wooden cane in his right. Pinky's baby started crying.

'I remember you,' he said to us, now comfortably seated.

Pinky put the baby on Tafiq Ali Khan's lap. He patted the boy a few times before Pinky scooped him up again.

'How are you,' I said.

He nodded and smiled. Tafiq Ali looks like Fyodor Dostoevsky: bearded, about seventy years old, with thick, young man's hair. He's blind and sits in one position for long periods: hunched over, rocking back and forth, elbow on knee half-exposed through dhoti, palm on chin. He doesn't bother anyone. He lives with his daughter and son-in-law across from Shukuran's house in one he built thirty years ago. It's not on the main road. It's on the other side, in an alley with other closely cramped homes that make up the Bengali Basti. Most Bengalis in the basti, including Shukuran and her late husband, built their own houses when the community moved to what was vacant land in the 1980s. Tafiq Ali Khan's son-in-law, Ismael, paints houses.

When work dries up, Tafiq begs to bring in money. But always alone, his daughter told us. He likes the women. They watch over him while they work and talk and laugh. The way they move about him, it seems they love him very much. They smile at him. He feels it. He smiles back, at the ground. His eyes dart back and forth when he does that. He hardly talks. Never answers questions. The women do that for him.

'What will you name her?' I asked again. Shukuran went down the list: generations of women in the house, how they got their names.

'When she was born,' she said, nodding to a voice in the hallway, 'about ten people came to the house. We had a meal. Drinks and meat. Maybe fish. And after the meal it was decided—Sonia. We liked that name. So we kept the name Sonia.' Sonia was in the hallway talking to one of the older babies. All through the small blue house, voices of women and babies.

'And when she was born,' she said nodding to another voice in the hallway, 'we had some people come to the house again, and just the same, we had a meal, but no one could decide on a name. Well, there was an old lady who sat outside the mosque back then. I went to see her. I asked her what she thought. She said, "Why not Amina. It's in the Koran." It *was* in the Koran so we kept the name Amina.'

'And Pinky,' Shukuran said, 'Pinky's real name is M____,' I couldn't make out what she said. 'But one of our relatives said, "You can't call her that." I told her, "It's a good Muslim name." "It's a good Muslim name," she said, "but she'll get fat if you call her that. You have to give her a thin girl's name. Call her Pinky and she'll always stay thin." So that's why we call her Pinky.' Pinky was standing in front of us, turning her son upside down, back and forth, patting the back of his fluorescent-green basketball shirt. He was reaching for the picture of a little girl on the poster taped to the wall.

'Allah gave me some things,' Shukuran said a bit later. 'Look, He gave me a house. He gave me a family. The only problem is food.'

***

The story of Bengali Muslim life in Monohorapur basti has its roots in the history of Bengali migration into Jaipur. According to the People's Union of Civil Liberties (PUCL), skilled workers from West Bengal started coming to the city after Independence. Religious leaders and educated elites found government jobs as administrators, city planners and teachers. But labourers from a community known as the Cooch Beharis also came to the city from a few West Bengal districts such as Maldad, Nadiad, Hooghly and Howrah. The men found construction work. The women worked as maids in middle-class homes.

Things started to change in the early 1970s, with war on the eastern border and Bangladesh's Independence from Pakistan. The government banned Bangladeshi immigration after the conflict, but people facing violence from the Pakistani Army were eager to make their way into India for a better life. Human traffickers skirted India's immigration policy. Dalals (middlemen) smuggled refugees into Rajasthan through informal labour networks.

The older Bengali Muslims of Monohorapur basti were part of a parallel wave of working-class migrants from West Bengal and Assam who began moving to Jaipur in the early 1970s as a result of communal violence, the loss of land, floods and poverty. The trend continued through the 1980s. Some were orphans who hopped on the train from Calcutta alone. Kids who never knew their parents. But some were boys with physical disabilities, like Illyas, who dreamed of the outside world as a place of potential opportunities and affections that eluded him in rural West Bengal.

'When I was a child,' Illyas said, 'I had that feeling of going somewhere new. I had that feeling on my own.' He left home at nine for the streets of Calcutta. A few months later, he got word that people were making their way west. He's been in Jaipur ever since. His right leg is deformed and he walks with a limp. Beggar families on the streets looked after him when he got to the city. Fifteen years on the streets. At twenty-four, surrogate mothers and fathers got him married to an orphan girl who begged in the galis of Janta Market. The couple has four daughters together.

As for opportunity? He has begged for alms since the day he got off that train in Jaipur Railway Station. Resting his hand on top of his cane while leaning on Shukuran's doorway, he said there are small perks—the nearby hospital, Sawai Man Singh, is kind to disabled people, which is good for him, because he is often ill with respiratory infections. These, including tuberculosis, are perhaps the most common illnesses in the basti. And most people in the basti can't afford treatment—the public health centres turn them away.

Some were born migrants, like Hamida, a woman in her fifties, who actually lived on the streets of Jaipur in the 1960s when she was a little girl. Her father was a cow-herder in West Bengal. Her family lived in West Bengal, Rajasthan and Bihar. Her father died when she was a teenager and she went back to Calcutta alone. She got married there and came back with her husband as a young woman to Jaipur, where she raised three sons and a daughter on the streets and in the basti.

Some people were young joint families—siblings whose parents died when they were young. When one got married on the streets of Calcutta, s/he brought the others along and arranged their marriages too. Security in numbers. That's how Hanupa and Khadija, two sisters from West Bengal's Barishar district, made their way to Jaipur. Hanupa married Mozit Syed Ali in Calcutta in the 1970s. He needed family as much as the sisters did. According to Hanupa, Mozit Syed Ali's parents died in a Hindu-Muslim riot in a West Bengal jute mill after a mob burned it down. The boy grew up with the girls in the same village and when they made it to Calcutta, they all begged together. A few months later, the three of them came to the footpaths of Janta Market in Jaipur. Early on, Mozit Syed Ali and Hanupa arranged Khadija's marriage to a Rajasthani man named Rashid. Hanupa had two children—a boy and a girl. Khadija had five. They all died of smallpox on the streets or in the basti.

Now the sisters live together a few minutes away from Shukuran, in a wood shack with a makeshift outdoor toilet and using black tarp and canvas over four wooden planks as a roof that doesn't hold water during the monsoons. It's still a joint family, but the husbands are dead. It's Hanupa, Khadija, Hanupa's son and his three daughters. People say they are the poorest family in the basti—Hanupa doesn't bathe or change out of her long green kurta. It's been years since people have seen her any other way. Food comes from Khadija's begging.

Looking at her picture on the copy of an old identity card from the 1990s, Kanchan said of Khadija, 'She was so pretty.'

'That's the way it was, didi,' Khadija said. Today she walks around the basti mumbling to herself or cursing at people while rubbing prayer beads. People say that Hanupa's son has gone mad since his wife left him with the kids for another man. Since then, mother and son haven't been the same. Hanupa's three granddaughters, aged between eight and thirteen years old, are blooming. Pretty and polite, they go to school every day, and when they smile you sense a force. 'They've had to get used to living on an empty stomach,' Hanupa said. 'But I worry about them. Thankfully, because of God, they haven't fallen sick, but if they get sick…'

Shukuran's story was a bit of everything. Orphaned. Potentially disabled (her son Avaliya said she's had a long history of mental illness, sometimes madness). Married for protection. 'I had no one,' she said of her childhood. Shukuran left her village as a young girl after her parents died and tried to survive on the streets of Calcutta. She begged. That's where she met her husband. She was nineteen years old. He was, by her account, about thirty-five years older. A widower. A beedi-roller. 'He had nobody and I had nobody to call my own,' she said. First, they were friends. He protected her and taught her to roll beedis so she could earn some money. They weren't going to make it on their own, so they decided to get married. Her husband died in 2011. Shukuran claims that he was a hundred years old. She showed us a picture. Old indeed. But a century on the streets and slums of India. Was it possible? The couple lived on the streets and slums of Jaipur together for about forty years. They made their way on a train from Calcutta to Jaipur in the early 1970s.

Shukuran, Hanupa, Khadija, Rajiya, Momina, Tafiq Ali Khan, Illyas. They weren't alone when they got to the city. Several other Bengali Muslims—many from a district called North 24 Parganas—lived on the streets of Janta Market in the Old City. They did whatever work they could find: domestic work to rag picking. They found family, enemies, squalor, hunger.

Older Bengali Muslims had lived on the streets of the Old City for fifteen years. In the mid-1980s, a member of the Communist Party of India created a 'basti federation' which led the state government to sanction ten plots of land in Jaipur to house the city's homeless. People called the man Comrade Baqaar. Monohorapur basti got carved out of the forest land near the train tracks of Jaipur's Malviya Nagar section. People recalled Comrade Baqaar sending trucks to the Old City. Tafiq Ali Khan, Shukuran, Hanupa and others hopped on and built new lives for themselves in the vacant land in Malviya Nagar, now home to 10,000 people—some 2,200 families. Momina walked, roaming the basti and the city ever since.

Legend grew in the basti that Prime Minister Indira Gandhi asked Comrade Baqaar to reserve that land for the homeless, but we still don't know if that's true. The Bengali Muslims were one of a handful of communities that settled there. Religious or occupational castes built homes, carved out their own neighbourhoods. No barriers between the hamlets, except the ones in peoples' minds. They've lived in segregated enclaves since. Valimikis. Tamils. Regars. Kal Belias (snake charmers). And in the last few years, the Katputlis, puppet-makers known for performing traditional Rajasthani marionette and dance acts in festivals.

There's no animosity between communities, people said. Only tension over resources. Rag picking and manual scavenging are the mainstays of livelihood, so money is tight for anyone. Access to healthcare, subsidized food grains and clean water are prized. Besides poverty, every community in the basti knows sickness: chronic fever, tuberculosis, respiratory infections, liver problems. The Regars have a water line and decent drainage systems. The rest wait for the water truck to come. They haul out empty bins and buckets to fill up for the day's needs. In all other bastis, there is open sewage. Men scoop waste out of the drains with their hands in the Valmiki basti. It overflows into the dirt pathways that line houses and khattiyas where sick people sleep.

There may be little tension between communities. There is also little mixing. Some people said that when the Bengalis first moved to the basti, their women were harrased by men of the Meena community.

1989. It was jungle then. Not like today, with samosa, chai and sweet vendors, Chinese food stalls, butcher shops, movie rentals, fruit vendors lined up on the main road that borders the basti. No hourly jitneys or regular buses either, for people coming in from other parts of the city. No electricity. Rajiya and a group of women said men would drag women into the jungle at night and rape them. So Rajiya formed a self-help group. The problem went on for nine years. No nearby police stations back then. Then, one day in 1998, a group in the Bengali basti beat a man who'd abused one of the girls to within an inch of his death. Rapes stopped. Rajiya's group took on other problems.

The people needed identification, deeds to their houses, employment, ration cards for food grains. She spent days trying to work with ward administrators to provide basic services to her people. Frustration. Nothing was getting done. Then a man named Hanuman Meena got elected. 'After Hanuman Meena came, a lot was accomplished,' she said. 'He got the ration cards issued for us.' The cards authorized them to buy subsidized food grains from the local fair price shop, which helped. Some people even got deeds to their houses. That gave them security. Things weren't exactly great, but little improvements in people's access to basic services earned Rajiya some esteem. Life was a little better for the people than it had been on the streets, when they struggled for everything, all the time. Maybe not good, but better. But all of that would change.

***

13 May 2008. Terrorists plant bombs in the walls of the Old City. By nightfall, there are sixty-eight dead. They come from five states. Fifty-two Hindus, sixteen Muslims. Over 200 injured.

Newspapers praised the responsiveness of hospitals and the immediate cooperation between Hindus and Muslims in extending help for relief work to the injured in the wake of the attack. The surprise at the relative peace which followed in the city was justified: Jaipur had witnessed three communal riots in the last two decades, in 1989, 1990 and 1992.

Violence was contained. But while state and national officials were trying to ascertain the veracity of emails sent by members of the Indian Mujhadeen claiming responsibility for the act, the media served as a platform for BJP leaders to voice the need for tougher anti-terrorism laws to protect against threats from insurgency groups based in Bangladesh. L.K. Advani and then-chief minister Vasundhara Raje called specifically for the reinstatement of the Prevention of Terrorism Act.

The Act had been hastily issued after the 2001 Parliament bombing. Parliament had repealed the Act in 2003, after evidence had come forth that states had abused the special powers granted to enforcement bodies to hold suspects in custody for six months without warrants for arrest. The lack of monitoring and review bodies and of binding accountability measures on states had resulted in politically motivated crackdowns.

The notion of bringing back the Act was shot down by Left parties, but the rhetoric of hunting down terrorists had already built momentum within the state administration and other BJP leaders. This momentum was quickly directed towards what became framed within the administration as the Bangladeshi threat.

According to a report filed by the People's Union of Civil Liberties, Rajasthan State BJP President Omprakash Mathu stated in the press days after the blast that 'we support all the actions of the administration, as they have substantial evidence to link Bangladeshis with the terror attack. Lots of calls been [sic] made from Bangladesh and administration [sic] has all the evidence.' The evidence was not presented to the press. The PUCL report also stated that Chief Minister Raje claimed on NDTV and in *The Indian Express* that Bangladeshis are known to induldge in a 'lot of illegal activities.' But these assertions did not remain rhetoric.

Two days after the blasts, all District Collectors and police departments in Rajasthan were issued orders to identify Bangladeshi immigrants by checking voter ID and ration cards. On 19 May, four days after the attack, an Australian national daily reported that 'senior members of the Rajasthan Government announced last night that the estimated 50,000 Bangladeshi migrants living illegally in the state would be questioned and, if they could not provide acceptable explanations about what they were doing, deported.'

The orders had an immediate impact on the lives of Bengali Muslims in the slums of Jaipur. In the first week after the blasts, 116 Muslims in the ten slums of the 'basti federation' were arrested without warrants under Section 109 of the Criminal Procedure Code (aiding and abetting a crime). Twelve men were from Monohorapur basti. In all, the police would arrest twenty-six people, including a pregnant woman, from the basti. Ilyas, Hanupa's son, and Sahara's son, Mintu, and seven male members of Hamida's family, among others. The police asked for proof of identification. Each complied. But they were arrested and taken to prison. Questioned. Beaten.

According to Kavita Srivastav, Secretary of PUCL, when the Central Bureau of Investigation ordered the investigation into the citizenship status of suspected Bangladeshis—and not of people suspected of links to terrorist organizations based in Bangladesh—the responsibility for carrying out the surveys fell on the Station House Officer (SHO) of each police station.

The Malviya Nagar Police Department SHO did not carry out the investigation in an honest way. Door to door, he asked for identification. Each person complied. All had in their possession Government-of-India-issued Below Poverty Line ration cards and identification cards. All were born in India. Most families had lived in Monohorapur basti for two generations. The young men were born there, some through Rajiya's hands, whose son was arrested that month. All who were arrested were held in prison for days to weeks. Those who were not arrested were fearful of what was happening to their friends and family. And since many of the men who were picked up were income earners, many families felt the brunt of not having at least the possibility of a daily wage.

The SHO reported to the District Collector that each of the Below Poverty Line and identification cards presented to him by the Bengali Muslims in Monohorapur basti were fake and recommended the cancellation of those cards. The District Collector obliged. The immediate impact, of course, was that the community no longer had rights of access to the social protection programmes granted to BPL card holders, such as pension schemes and subsidized food grains. The larger implication was that the SHO's recommendation rendered the community without rights of citizenship. Each of the cards that were returned to them were marked 'red' to indicate that they were no longer valid. Many did not receive their cards back at all.

Prem Kishan, a High Court lawyer associated with the People's Union of Civil Liberties, took the Bengali Muslims' case to the Jaipur High Court on the grounds that their BPL cards were cancelled unjustly and should be reinstated immediately. If they could not be instituted, he urged, allow them the right to reapply. He had asked an independent team from an NGO called MASUM, based in Calcutta, to go to a number of villages, to verify the residence status, and even birth, of the men who were arrested that May. The team reported that their investigation 'proves conclusively that they have links in the State of West Bengal; the confusion, if any, is due to the fact that these people left the State in the early seventies and have never gone back to live.'

Mr Kishan sent this report to the police station and filed it in the courts in 2009. But the deck was stacked against him. The evidence the court cited to prove that the people were 'Bangladeshis' was the documentation submitted by the SHO to the District Collector. In another Catch-22, the court also cited that the fact that some Bengalis in the basti went back to West Bengal after the arrests and in the run-up the case, to retrieve evidence of their previous residence, was also a ground for suspicion.

Illyas was one of those men. He sold the goats he was rearing for his daughter's future marriage to pay the train fare. 'The police said the documents I brought back from Calcutta were fake. But how can they be fake? I've spent my entire life here.' He said that he retrieved documents for his family members, including his sister and his father. The only victory was a stay order on their deportation. But this puts them in a bind all the same. They are stateless people within their own country.

The only recourse now for the community is to move the case to the civil courts to fight a case against the state for their citizenship. But this is not likely to happen. No one in the community has the money to pay for the lengthy procedure. And although the PUCL had taken their case after the attacks, Mr Kishan told us that a team of new laywers would have to be assembled to get a lengthy set of documents for each person in the basti—birth certificates, parents' birth certificates, duration of stay in India, proof of work and proof that they have never travelled abroad.

The people are poor and they want their BPL cards badly to allow them to access basic services needed for survival. But even before that, they want respect. 'What we want is for the government to recognize that we live here, that we're from here. We are not Bangladeshi.'

Pilgrims and Patients

Shikha Sethia

This piece is based on a series of interviews conducted with persons living with locomotor disabilities, caregivers and staff members at the two Bhagwan Mahaveer Viklang Sahayata Samiti (BMVSS) centres in Jaipur, during the summer of 2013. It draws extensively on notes and fieldwork reports prepared by my co-researcher, Vikrant Dadawala, a student at TISS, Mumbai, and various students from national law colleges who were interning with the People's Union of Civil Liberties, Jaipur, at the time of the study. The names of the patients have been changed to protect their identities. The title has been taken from the first chapter of Emile Zola's novel, Lourdes.

As we climbed out of the auto-rickshaw on Guru Nanak Path in Malviya Nagar, Jaipur, we were greeted by the sight of a stream of people slowly and deliberately progressing through the main gate of a large building complex. This was a community of people barely visible in everyday life, and to see them in such numbers was a rarity. Some were sliding across the floor with the aid of their hands, some were leaning on crutches and others had their arms around a friend or a relative for support. We took in the scene, which appeared to be in almost caricaturish contrast to the busy road outside where both vehicles and pedestrians moved briskly and effortlessly towards their destinations. The people moving through the gate and an unobtrusive signboard announcing the Bhagwan Mahaveer Viklang

Sahayata Samiti were the only signs of what lay on the other side of these walls: the headquarters of BMVSS, a charitable organization that offers prosthetic and orthotic devices, and other forms of aid, to people with disabilities, free of charge.

BMVSS's growing reputation brought people here from all over India, and as far away as Bangladesh and Nepal, to seek treatment. They were generally extremely poor and had scant hope of receiving such treatment elsewhere. Mohammed Salim, for instance, had come all the way from Mymensingh in Bangladesh, a fact that he attempted to initially conceal, presumably fearing that he would not receive treatment or be asked to return to his country. Once a rapport had been established between him and one of our researchers, Vikrant (who spoke fluent Bengali), he became more candid and recounted stories of his travels through Allahabad, Mumbai, Nagpur and Agra.

'I won't lie to you since you are my friend now', said Salim. 'I had told you I'm from West Bengal, like you are. That's not really true. I'm actually from Bangladesh, Mymensingh district. I wander about like this a lot.' Salim had been on his way to the dargah at Ajmer Sharif when he saw a disabled man running to a water cooler and back with an artificial foot. He showed Vikrant a scrap of paper that said *Sawai Man Singh Hospital, Malviya Nagar, Jaipur*. 'He wrote this address down for me in English', Salim said. 'That's how I came to be here. As soon as I get a foot replacement, I'll take a train and go back home. Crossing the border isn't difficult at all, but your BSF [Border Security Force] is much crueller than our Bangladesh Rifles.'

Even in the unrelenting heat of a Jaipur summer, anywhere between fifty and seventy people would visit the Malviya Nagar campus every day, hoping for a similar transformation. They congregated in and around the medical centre, one of the busiest buildings in the complex, which also housed a library, a temple, a physiotherapy centre and a tricycle workshop. Inside the medical centre, separate rooms dealt with the measuring, fitting and manufacturing process for the artificial limbs and callipers. Clouds of plaster of Paris-dust enveloped some of the staff, hard at work in the room where the casts were made. The miracles performed here were intensely mechanical. Behind the manufacturing unit, on the path leading up to the physiotherapy centre, a small hill of discarded prosthetic legs was awaiting disposal and recycling. While we were a little disconcerted at the sight, staff members would nonchalantly fill their bottles of water at the cooler next to the heap and walk back inside.

Once they had registered themselves at the medical centre, the patients began their two to three-day-long wait before they could undergo the procedure and return home. Even the seemingly simple task of sitting on a chair required significant manoeuvring and patience for many of them, leading most to reject the stuffy, chair-lined waiting room in the medical centre in favour of the cool shade of the trees in the front courtyard, where they could spread their durries out on the ground and sit comfortably. An air of fatigue and melancholy shrouded them, and to see any two of them speaking to each other was a rare sight. The journey here had been dangerous and uncomfortable—buses were crowded and difficult for them to climb into and out of, especially for the ones that were travelling alone, while railway coaches reserved for them were frequently occupied by the able-bodied. Rohit Gupta, a young man of about thirty who was an amputee, was threatened with being pushed off the train when he protested. Whatever optimism they had started with had long since dissipated. Even those who were leaving the centre did not look particularly jubilant—merely relieved.

The guard at the medical centre, known to the staff as 'Panditji', came out intermittently to bark orders at the patients, ordering them to move from where they had settled down to rest or to call one of them inside. The patients nervously gathered themselves up and shuffled to find another spot in the shade. I turned to look at Jai Singh and his wife, next to whom I was squatting. They were glaring at the retreating figure of the guard. '*Ye sabko bhadka raha hai.*'

(He is provoking us.) Jai Singh had lost both his legs and I could only see stubs where his knees had been. His crutches were lying next to him, one crossed over the other. Another patient remarked, '*Ye log battameezi se baat nahin kartein hain par dhang se bhi nahin bolte.*' (They are not rude but they are not respectful, either.) Two of our researchers, Prapti and Ankita, spoke to the guard later, who attributed his brash manner to a career in the army. He only shouted at the patients to get their attention, he told them, somewhat unconvincingly.

When we approached the patients, we were treated with a mix of curiosity and suspicion. 'Why are you doing this?' one of our researchers was asked. 'To learn about what your experience has been with your family, community and the government,' was the stock answer. 'What will you do with this?' asked the patient. 'This research will help us make recommendations to the government on your behalf.' So far, so good, I thought, but the patient looked sceptical. 'Can you help me get a tricycle?' he asked after a pause. This wasn't part of the script. The researcher was starting to look nervous. 'No, we can't do that.' The tricycles produced at BMVSS for people with significant impairments in both legs were in high demand. Word was that they were of much better quality than the ones given by the government. 'These are young students,' I offered, unsure as I was of my own position in this process. Realizing that the patients themselves would derive little benefit from this study, I continued, 'This will help them learn about a life very different from their own.' This at last seemed to satisfy him. '*Theek hai. Poochho kya poochhna hai.*' (Okay, go ahead and ask what you want to.)

Ours wasn't the only group of students on the campus. The library was right next to the medical centre and a popular place to study, which ensured that there were always hundreds of local students present. Scanning the area, I realized, however, that our researchers were very easy to identify—conspicuously clutching identical survey forms, talking to the patients or staff and taking furious notes at every opportunity. The students on their way to the library, however, barely seemed to register the silent, brooding groups of patients sitting in the courtyard.

At this library, Pranav, another researcher, met Reyazul Hassan. Reyazul was a twenty-one-year-old man working for BMVSS, little older than the researchers themselves. He was from the village of Noorpur in Bihar. The youngest of three brothers in a family of nine, Reyazul was born with a deformity in his legs. The family's savings were meagre and what little they had accumulated, about two to three lakh rupees, was spent on Reyazul's treatment. As luck would have it, all the operations he underwent were unsuccessful. The family said, '*Ab sab allah ki marzi,*' (It is now up to God.)

Despite this setback, the ingenuity with which Reyazul had carried himself through life was astounding. As a child, though Reyazul could not walk properly, he was the captain of his village cricket team. When it was his turn to bat, he would use a runner to run on his behalf. The same resourcefulness was also evident later in his life. When his brothers were old enough to earn, they all went to work, but Reyazul himself was unable to find a job in his village. He recounts: '*Main to dharti par bojh hun. Sabhi bhai apna kamate the aur apne kamre mein chale jaate the; mujhey koi nahin poochhta tha. Kabhi kabhi mujhe sirf ek bar khaana milta tha.*' (I am a burden. All my brothers would earn during the day and then go into their rooms, when they returned. No one cared about me. Sometimes, I would only get one meal a day.) Reyazul started to draw sketches and it was quickly evident that he was extremely talented. He said to Pranav, '*Allah kuch leta hai to kuch deta bhi hai. Usne mujhse mera pair le liya par ye kala muje di, jiske sahare me aaj is sthithi me hun*'. (When God takes something away, he also gives you something in return. He took my leg but gave me this talent, as a result of which I am here now.) He drew a sketch of the collector of his district and asked to be provided with some form of employment. Pleased with the drawing, the collector assigned him a subsidized shop for distributing rations. Reyazul took loans from the bank and some relatives to get the shop going, but soon had to close it down when he was unable to raise more money. After another failed attempt to establish himself in Gujarat, he made for Delhi with only Rs 150 in his pocket.

In Delhi, he managed to arrive at the office of a politician, Bhupendra Singh, who was reputedly an art enthusiast, and presented him with a painting. Bhupendra Singh paid him Rs 1000 for the work. It was in Delhi that he heard of BMVSS and the work that they are doing in Jaipur. Reyazul travelled to Jaipur and waited for a few days at the hospital for an audience with Mr Mehta, who runs the trust. He used his usual methods and drew a sketch of Mehtaji, asking for employment and was instantly given a post at the campus library. Reyazul had arrived in Jaipur with little hope of achieving anything other than an operation or a tricycle. He now resides there and manages to even send some money home to his mother. He still wishes, though, that he had someone to take care of him and hopes to have a family of his own some day. Pranav related all of this to us with some awe, showing us some of the paintings that Reyazul had with him there.

Reyazul was not the only person who had come here for treatment and had succeeded in making a permanent place of their own at BMVSS. We often stopped for tea at the parantha shop next to the main gate of the campus. Seema Sharma, a fiercely independent forty-year-old lady ran the shop. Fifteen years ago, while she was pregnant, she had lost one of her legs in a train accident. Soon after, her husband deserted her and their two children to marry another woman. After a year of living alone, without the use of her legs, she underwent the leg replacement procedure at BMVSS and was able to walk again. Since then, her life had turned around completely and she had been successfully running the parantha shop by herself. She told two of our researchers, Kunal and Sonal, that she had also since found herself another husband and had some land in her name.

Many of the patients we spoke to said that they had been sent to the Malviya Nagar campus from the SMS Hospital on Sawai Man Singh Road. The centre there had been running since 1975, preceding the one in Malviya Nagar by many years and was the first stop for most people traveling to Jaipur for treatment. Mr Mehta said that even the rickshaw drivers at the railway station no longer needed to be told—if they saw someone with a disability and in need of assistance, they automatically brought them there. It took us a while to locate it, though. Used to the sprawling, well-maintained campus in Malviya Nagar, we took two rounds of an imposing-looking building in the hospital complex and were unceremoniously ejected from the rehabilitation centre (the security guards thought we were journalists) before we found the small shed-like construction tucked away in one corner. As most patients still only knew of the centre at the SMS Hospital, BMVSS thought it best to maintain a presence within the hospital premises and construct some dormitories in the little space available to them there.

The change in context made the desperate circumstances of the patients that much more apparent. Many wore tattered clothes and looked completely worn out. Several of them had been here for the last two to three weeks, waiting for the tricycles to be restocked or to be given tea-kits or sewing machines, as a form of livelihood support. This shortage was not a normal feature, the staff informed us. The existing stock of tricycles had been sent to the mobile camps that BMVSS was organizing with the government across Rajasthan. The dormitories were full as a result, and some patients had even chosen to sleep outside on the lawns of the hospital. The long wait had also made them restless.

Everyone we met held tiny pieces of paper torn off a notepad, with words like 'tricycle' or 'tea kit' scrawled on them and a signature. This was the receipt, I realized, that allowed them to claim whatever

Mr Mehta had authorized them to receive: the golden ticket. In a tiny office, manual records are kept of all forms of assistance BMVSS has given each visitor over the last few years. This is supposed to prevent them from selling the free tricycles and kits, since they would be unable to claim fresh ones from the centre. The paperwork does not dissuade everyone, however: Mr Mehta estimates that nearly 20 per cent of them still sell the kits that are given to them.

While at SMS, I befriended Suresh, a young man of thirty from Khairthal, Rajasthan. Suresh is nearly bent over double as a result of a condition that affected his spine and hips when he was fifteen years old. He said that the pain was getting worse now. His mother does household chores and earns about Rs 500-700 a month. His father is a barber, but Suresh says that he only earns Rs 10-20 in a day, as people are afraid that his eyesight is failing and he might hurt them while shaving. Suresh, too, was offered training and a job at the Malviya Nagar campus, but declined. He said he needed to be near his parents, who are getting on in years and have no one else to support them. Suresh was earlier employed at a local factory as a weaver. The seth was good to him, he said. However, when Suresh went to have an operation done at a hospital in Alwar six months ago, he was replaced. He had been unemployed since then. He wanted some livelihood assistance from BMVSS—'*loan chahiye*' (I want a loan), he said—so he could start a chai-churi ki dukaan (tea and snack shop) in his village. When Suresh and I met, he had been waiting for a fortnight to collect a tea-kit and tricycle from the centre. He said his parents were getting worried about him.

While we waited together for his name to be called, I asked Suresh what the happiest moment in his life had been. He said that when he was eight years old, he won a race at school, in front of five hundred children.

'And since then?' I asked.

'Nothing', he replied.

I quickly changed the subject. 'Can you get an operation done to correct this problem?' I asked. They would need to heat his bones to correct it now. There was a small risk that it would fail and he would not be able to move again, so he decided against it. I left my number with him and asked him to call, when he had set the tea stall up.

A few weeks later, Suresh called. He said, 'I remember now. My second happiest moment was ten years ago, when we managed to build our own house.' He said his tea stall was up and running.

His mother then took the phone from him and complained, 'Can't you get him a nice job somewhere? I don't like the idea of him selling tea.' Suresh called again in a month—this time to tell me that he had sold the tea kit as the seth at the cloth-weaving company had taken him back. His mother was very happy, he said.

'And the tricycle?' I asked.

'I gave that to my friend. I can ride a bicycle but he needs it to travel to his workplace.' This made sense to me, as the tricycle was now with someone who clearly needed it more but had not made it to Jaipur, like Rajesh. One saw Mr Mehta's point, though.

Not every story that wound its way through BMVSS ended as happily. The promise of transformation eluded Salman Sheikh, a man of forty from Bulsar, Gujarat. Salman was waiting at the SMS hospital for a pair of crutches, when Vikrant approached him. Salman used to work as a casual labourer until an accident at his workplace in 2001 left him badly injured and he had to have his leg amputated. Since then, he has had no permanent address and wanders from place to place, begging to survive. 'I don't like to beg in the same basti day after day. I've been all around Gujarat, Rajasthan, Allahabad…' Salman's brother and sister-in-law live in a basti in Mumbai, where they grew up, but he doesn't stay with them. '*Wahan jamta nahin tha*,' [It didn't work for me] was all that he would say about it.

And foot replacement—had he tried it? 'I've come to Jaipur before. I have got a foot made here three times. *Magar shareer mein takat nahi hai.* [But I have no strength left in my body]. I could not walk properly even with the foot.'

When the conversation drifted to his present condition, Salman would fall silent. '*Baaki sab garibi hi garibi hai.* We were very poor even in our childhood. I can't read or write.' He paused and said, '*aur baat nahi karna hai bhai.*' (Let's stop here.) 'Please, I don't want to talk anymore,' he said again. And yet, Salman will probably return to Jaipur, when the new leg wears out.

Struggles in Sickness

Amod Shah

This piece was written based on fieldwork undertaken with Saba Sharma at Yamuna Pushta, Delhi during 2012. The fieldwork was part of research on destitution amongst the homeless, an urban population that is not understood enough. The names of persons have been changed to protect their identities.

On a Tuesday afternoon in early September, about a month into our research with the homeless at Yamuna Pushta, we saw Manish hopping towards the Aman Biradari shelter. He was extremely dishevelled, with his unkempt beard, dirty t-shirt and trousers, and his left foot covered with a plastic bag. It was obvious that he was in a lot of pain, and when he removed the bag we realized why—half of his foot was missing, with maggots crawling all over the open wound. It was a shocking sight, unsettling even for the shelter's health staff who come across badly injured homeless people quite often. A crowd quickly gathered around Manish. Someone berated him for being irresponsible and not getting his leg attended to earlier, while another spoke about how terrible it is to lose a leg. The rest of us could not help but stare at the injured leg with a mixture of disgust and morbid curiosity. Manish himself looked dazed and unresponsive, repeatedly saying, *mera pair kaat do* (cut off my leg), to the person cleaning his wound.

Yamuna Pushta is a raised embankment on the Yamuna river, a short walk from the Kashmere Gate bus terminal in Old Delhi.

In 2004, slum settlements in the area were cleared as part of a city beautification drive, displacing about 3,00,000 residents. Many homeless men, however, continue to stay at the Pushta, particularly near the Nigambodh cremation ghat. Smoke from the ghat's funeral pyres often lends the area an inhospitable, almost ominous air. But perhaps this is also what makes it one of the few places in the city where the homeless do not compete for scarce space with the rest of Delhi's residents. Living at the Pushta offers other advantages, because of its proximity to many of the chowks where daily wage labourers are hired, and to temples and gurudwaras, which provide a source of food when work is hard to come by. In recent years, a few NGOs have set up temporary shelters here, providing housing and basic amenities like drinking water and toilets, besides a certain level of protection and support. At the Aman Biradari shelter, for instance, two large rooms made of tin and corrugated iron sheets sleep about a hundred homeless men each night. The shelter also provides basic medical care and referral services, and seriously ill or injured homeless men are a familiar sight on the cemented strip right outside the shelter.

Manish is a twenty-two-year-old from Ghazipur in eastern Uttar Pradesh. He has been in Delhi for a year and a half, earning money from odd jobs, like kabadi chunna (ragpicking) and dhakka lagana (work as a goods loader and porter). He told us that he injured his leg about ten days ago, but was vague about how exactly. He had come to the shelter a week earlier to get the wound dressed, but did not return for treatment until now, when his condition deteriorated and the pain became unbearable. Manish's situation follows a pattern similar to many homeless persons we interacted with at the Pushta, of serious medical conditions being left untreated, until they reach an advanced and chronic stage. In almost every case, the patient should be at a hospital, rather than receiving rudimentary treatment at a homeless shelter. In fact, there are at least three public hospitals within walking distance of the Pushta. Yet, for Manish and other critically ill or injured homeless persons, the shelters serve as their primary avenue for healthcare.

Such a situation would be unthinkable for the other residents of rapidly developing urban India. The public healthcare system, despite its highly dysfunctional nature, serves as a safety net for most of us, guaranteeing a certain minimal level of medical care. In other words, when faced with a major illness or medical emergency, we can count on receiving free or subsidized healthcare at public hospitals, though the quality of this treatment may at times be inferior to the private sector. For the homeless however, even such access is far from guaranteed. Vandana Prasad, in her work on healthcare access for the homeless in Delhi, documents a number of explicit and implicit barriers that prevent them from seeking medical care through the public healthcare system. Such barriers reflect the broader societal prejudices and discrimination that the homeless face in a number of other spheres.

Gordhan, a health worker with Aman Biradari, says that doctors often refuse to examine a 'dirty' homeless patient, telling them to clean themselves up and then come back. 'We have to go with them to push for them to be taken in', he says. 'If they go alone, the security guards will just turn them away'. Many of the homeless men we spoke to also reported rude behaviour and mistreatment by hospital staff. Setting aside the clearly unethical nature of these practices for a moment, there are practical considerations, such as the lack of a safe place to bathe and store belongings, which make it difficult for a homeless person, particularly one with a severe illness or injury, to clean up properly before seeking treatment.

Other peculiarities of the public healthcare system do not necessarily target the homeless, but nonetheless tend to disadvantage them disproportionately. Due to a shortage of staff, hospitals will refuse to admit a patient unless they are accompanied by an attendant, something that Prasad calls a 'uniquely Indian phenomenon'. Attendants are required to assist in a number of ways, including taking care of the patient, donating blood, purchasing medicines and supplies, following up on reports and other administrative tasks. Almost none of the homeless men we spoke to had a family member or friend who could accompany them as an attendant, effectively barring them from being hospitalized when needed. Moreover, the homeless typically lack any form of official identification, such as below-poverty-line or ration cards, which makes it easier for hospitals to turn them away or deny them free treatment. Raju, who had recently moved to the Pushta, recounted how, despite a serious leg injury, he was refused admission at two public hospitals because he had no one who could donate blood on his behalf. He was able to get some medication from the hospital out-patient department (OPD) once he got a little better, but the lack of adequate treatment has left him with a very prominent limp. Public hospital pharmacies are also notorious for being badly stocked, so medicines and even basic supplies like bandages and syringes usually have to be bought from the open market.

For all of these reasons, a visit to the hospital becomes an experience most homeless persons find extremely daunting and baffling, best avoided until doing so is no longer an option. NGOs working with the urban homeless have attempted to step in and help, through the provision of basic medical care and assistance to the seriously ill in accessing public hospitals.

At the Pushta, the Aman Biradari shelter has become somewhat of a halfway house for critically ill or injured homeless men. First, a patient has to be made 'admissible'; in Manish's case, another resident of the shelter shaves off his beard and hair completely, and helps him take a bath. Shelter staff then dress his injured foot and find him a clean set of clothes to wear. Gordhan says this is necessary to ensure that patients receive a proper examination by the doctor, rather than a quick, cursory look from a distance. After an initial evaluation by a medical team from St Stephen's Hospital, the nodal NGO designated by the Delhi government for interventions catering to the homeless, serious cases are referred to one of the public hospitals nearby. Those who do not necessarily require hospitalization stay at the shelter, and are taken by health workers to the hospital OPD for treatment. The health worker helps the patient navigate through the confusing procedures at the hospital, and as many homeless patients pointed out, improves his chances of being treated properly by hospital staff.

The sheer magnitude of the problem however easily overwhelms such efforts. Housing injured patients can prove to be a challenge in itself. Tuberculosis patients or those with badly infected wounds sleeping inside the shelter can pose a threat to the health of other residents and are therefore accommodated in a separate recovery room.

As cruel as it may seem, luck often plays a role. Urgent cases are taken to the hospital first, while the others must await their turn. At the time of Manish's arrival, shelter staff were dealing with two other seriously ill men—one appeared to have a severe urinary infection, and the other was experiencing extreme pain on the left side of his body. In the next few days, they were joined by a man with a severe case of tuberculosis, and a car accident victim in urgent need of surgery for his injured leg. While these patients were being attended to, Manish's leg was cleaned and dressed at the shelter; he finally went to the hospital the following week.

There are significant financial and personnel-related costs, which NGOs are ill-equipped to handle, given their limited budgets and the large number of cases. Usually a social worker or shelter resident has to act as the required hospital attendant, even for homeless patients admitted through the referral process mentioned above. Often, the expenses for medicines and supplies have to be borne by the NGO. In the current set-up, only the most critical cases can be referred to hospitals for proper treatment, while those with less serious symptoms have little by way of support. Medical camps at the homeless shelters do provide some help, but such treatment is largely focused on alleviating symptoms and cannot act as a substitute for the kind of medical care available at a hospital.

Resource constraints also limit the NGO's ability to reach out to the worst-off patients. Many of them are unable to even make it to the shelter, either because they are too ill or are unaware of the medical assistance available there. In our own experiences accompanying shelter staff on outreach visits to homeless people living under a bridge located less than 100 metres from the Aman Biradari shelter, we came across severely ill men in urgent need of hospitalisation on two separate occasions. In the first case, Bhaskar Nath had been lying there for about a week, too weak to move and seek help. He had not eaten during this time, surviving on water given to him by those nearby. By the time we met him, he was severely emaciated and barely able to speak. About a week later, we came across Vishal, lying close to the place where we had found Bhaskar and in a very similar condition to his. While NGO staff could call in an ambulance in both these instances, most such cases remain unattended, usually resulting in the death of the person.

Given the extremely challenging nature of life on the streets, it is perhaps not surprising to find a high prevalence of mental illness among the homeless. A recent report by the Technical Resource Group for National Urban Health Mission highlights the extremely high burden of mental illnesses like schizophrenia, psychosis and bipolar affective disorders, as well as substance abuse, among the homeless. Despite this, there is an almost complete absence of mental health facilities, in large part because the limited resources available are easily overwhelmed by the need to cater to physical ailments. The crisis is particularly acute for mentally ill men like Lokesh, a highly delusional and mentally disturbed young man whom we met often at the Pushta. Our conversations with him were often barely coherent; he was completely non-responsive to us sometimes, or at other times would ramble about a number of different topics. On a few rare occasions of clarity, he also talked to us about his family and how he had left home to come to Delhi. During our visits Lokesh was recovering from an accident which had left him with severe burns on his leg. Even though he was unable to walk properly, he remained extremely resistant to having the injury attended to. On each of the few times that he agreed to get the burns dressed, he had removed the bandages by the next day. For Lokesh and other homeless persons with serious mental illnesses, there is little possibility of getting the institutionalized care that they urgently need.

More generally, many homeless men, having lived on the streets for long years, suffer from less severe forms of mental illness, and require proper psychiatric diagnosis and medication to help them cope with their condition and prevent it from deteriorating. The mentally ill among the homeless are also particularly vulnerable, since they are easy targets of humour and derision for other homeless persons. Possibly as a consequence of such teasing, they tend to be extremely withdrawn, shunning social contact and harbouring a deep suspicion of others. The suspicion extends to shelter staff attempting to reach out to them, and so they are usually wary of staying in the shelter or visiting the medical camps when ill.

The healthcare crisis facing them has serious consequences for a homeless person's already precarious existence. The ability to work is crucial, since the homeless depend on informal, daily wage labour and lack assets or safety nets to fall back on in times of need. In this context, the inaccessible nature of the public healthcare system means that even treatable medical conditions often develop into permanent, debilitating physical impairments, a situation exemplified in Raju's case. When Raju first moved to Delhi from his village in Uttar Pradesh, he was not homeless. He had a job as a security guard and had been working there for more than a year when he suffered a serious leg injury. As mentioned earlier, the lack of proper treatment has left him with a prominent limp and unable to do hard manual labour. He is able to get some work for a few months each year during the 'party season', a period when many homeless men are hired as low-paid, daily wage labourers for weddings and other social functions. Even here, Raju is relegated to menial jobs like washing dishes, which he says are given to 'people like him'. The rest of the year he remains dependent on charity and undignified jobs like waste-picking to survive. Many of the worst-off men at the Pushta have similar stories, of medical conditions that result in partial disabilities, or leave the body severely weakened and unable to withstand heavy work. The cruel irony of homeless life is that the causality probably runs both ways, and years of rough living on the streets leave the homeless weaker and much more prone to ill health.

In other cases, the results are less visible but equally insidious. With Jagdish for instance, a prolonged illness coupled with a lack of proper treatment has created a deep distrust of the medical establishment. Jagdish left his village in Bihar to come to Delhi many years ago, working in a number of different places before his present job as a waste-picker. He fell severely ill in 2011 after getting wet in the rain, and initially sought treatment at the nearby Civil Lines hospital. Jokhan calls his illness *ole ki bimari*, literally, an illness of hail. He is convinced that he is unwell because there is a chill inside his body, and he will only get better if he eats hot food. '*Abhi sharir me thanda bhara hai, lekin woh dheere dheere nikal raha hai, garam khana khane se. Aur ab uske baad shareer naya banega, phir kuch theek hoga*', (Right now, my body is full of cold, but by eating hot food, the cold is slowly leaving. Only then will I get better.) Jagdish tells us. When we suggest that he visit the health camp at the Aman Biradari shelter, he refuses, saying that they distribute cheap and ineffective medicines there. The doctor at the hospital has said that medicines will be ineffective against his illness, he says. Jagdish is extremely adamant about this point, stating repeatedly that only eating hot food can cure him. Nothing we say can dent his deep conviction about the cause and cure for his illness.

For others, the lack of proper medical care has resulted in a state of intense fatalism, a complete loss of hope about the possibility of getting better. We meet Prakash under the bridge near the Pushta, where he has made himself a bed out of a used car seat cover thrown over two cement blocks. The area is very dirty, with garbage and broken cement blocks strewn all around, and the sound of cars passing by can be deafening at times. Prakash suffers from an unknown illness which has steadily weakened him over the past few years, while injuries on the soles of his feet cause him extreme pain when he walks. Over long, often frustrating conversations, we attempt to persuade him to come to the medical camp for treatment. However, he remains convinced that he cannot be cured, repeatedly telling us that his body has become weak. More than a distrust of the system, Prakash has developed an extremely deep-rooted fatalism about his condition, possibly as a result of being in this state for a prolonged period. By his own admission, living as he does, in a dirty, noisy place with no one to support him, will only worsen his illness. He also acknowledges that things are likely to be better at shelter. Yet, he is unconvinced that staying there will help him. *Shareer mein kamzori ho gayi hai* (my body has become weak), he tells us repeatedly, in response to almost everything we suggest.

Homelessness is more than simply the absence of a place to stay. As our conversations with homeless people repeatedly highlighted, it implies a whole range of debilitating circumstances—extremely harsh living conditions, the complete breakdown of family and social support networks, a constant struggle to maintain one's sense of dignity and severe societal discrimination, among others. Perhaps most crucially, it also involves an almost complete abandonment of the State's responsibilities towards one of its most marginalized and vulnerable populations. In the case of access to medical care, this is exemplified by the numerous explicit and implicit barriers that homeless persons face in their interaction with the public healthcare system. Such barriers make access to critical timely medical care very difficult, while at the same time deterring homeless people from seeking proper treatment when faced with an emergency. It is therefore hardly surprising that the homeless find it extremely difficult to 'bounce back to normal' from a serious injury or illness, like most of us are accustomed to. Even treatable medical problems often develop into chronic and debilitating conditions that threaten their ability to live an independent, dignified life.

It is particularly unfortunate that the response, of both society and government, to the crisis of medical care facing the homeless has generally been to blame the situation on the homeless themselves. A homeless person's unwillingness to seek timely medical treatment is generally viewed as a sign of laziness and neglect, rather than reflecting on the highly intimidating and exclusionary nature of the public healthcare system. The common refrain is, 'unless they are willing to help themselves, how can we help them?' Such a view is not uncommon, even among the homeless and people working with them.

It also ties into the larger narrative around homelessness, wherein the homeless are widely perceived to be lazy and undeserving. Their incorrect characterization as beggars, criminals, alcoholics and drug addicts, rather than legitimate and highly vulnerable members of society, effectively sanctions the neglectful, often hostile response of the State towards them. Even sympathetic views of the homeless, as people in need of charity, often serve to undermine their abilities and sense of self-worth. The lack of an empathetic and meaningful response to their condition is, in many ways, the biggest barrier faced by the homeless, in sickness and in health. Until this changes, Manish and others like him will remain a regular fixture at the shelters at the Pushta.

The Unknown Citizen

Anhad Imaan

The Yamuna Pushta, an area along the Yamuna river in Delhi, is home to several hundred homeless men. This piece emerged out of one of many visits made to the Yamuna Pushta as part of HAUSLA, Aman Biradari's Homeless Resource Team.

Once a residential space for several migrant workers and their families, the Yamuna Pushta is now home to many homeless single men, who seek shelter at the five shelters contracted to NGOs by the Delhi Urban Shelter Improvement Board, or sleep on a pavement adjacent to the Pushta under the open sky. The area is unknown to the few thousand middle-class citizens who pass by this place on the main road. Very few auto-rickshaw drivers ever know what you're talking about when you ask them to take you to the Pushta. Vendors at the cross-over bridge from ISBT, which is opposite the Pushta, pretend to not know the place, especially those that set up stalls for tourists, or next to the police.

Several gut-wrenching and appalling things happen at the Pushta. On one particular day, I happened to witness one such thing. A part of my job is to be in this area and capture these realities as they exist. Let me briefly pause here to provide the background for why I visit this place, and more importantly, why I was there that particular day.

The Delhi Urban Shelter Improvement Board is the nodal agency that sets up homeless shelters in Delhi. Two of these shelters at the

Pushta are contracted to the Centre for Equity Studies (CES), the organization I work with. In addition to monitoring and running the shelter, the team also works in programmes towards health care, livelihood support, primary and secondary life skill sessions for the residents, motivational sessions, psycho-social support and reintegration/repatriation of isolated cases over time. All our research work is closely wired to the work carried out in these programmes. Our studies and research are derived from these efforts by HAUSLA, the national resource team for the urban homeless at CES.

HAUSLA runs one of the shelters as a recovery shelter, a unique model that caters to the needs of those homeless men who are either severely ill and/or severely injured, and need a space for recovery upon leaving a hospital. The recovery shelter also helps men with fresh injuries or infectious diseases avail services at hospitals. It is not a hospital. It is a recovery home that exists to ensure that the homeless do not relapse in during or after the treatment for their injuries or diseases.

In addition to the recovery shelter, the health team also runs a mobile clinic for the homeless: The Street Medicine Programme. Every day, the Street Medicine team drives to fourteen different locations in five areas where substantial numbers of the homeless reside. Here, they provide free medication, on-the-spot diagnosis and first aid. Tsering, the nurse, can always be found after 9 p.m. in one of these fourteen locations bandaging a patient. The team is fun, ecstatic, committed and united. They work like machines after dark, especially on nights when the number of patients overshoots anyone's expectation.

Dr Pradeep, the most senior member of our team, is an energetic, intelligent and entertaining man. Despite working amongst the most deprived people in the country, he is always cheerful and never disturbed by the sight of blood, filth and destitution. Perhaps this is down to the fact that doctors are inured to, and so are not disgusted when they see human flesh, puke, sweat, debris and blood. Deepak, who wasn't there with us on the day, is the youngest. He's talkative and shares an organic, fun-filled relationship with our homeless residents and clients. Given these qualities, he is an outreach worker who brings patients to the doctor. Pratap Singh is the team's most treasured asset. He is the ambulance driver, though he also assists Deepak in mobilizing patients and giving out free meds. Phuntsok, a trained nurse, is a close friend and the coordinator of the Street Medicine Program. Every evening, when the sun's about to set, Tsering, with the help of health workers Lucky and Shabana, runs an evening clinic right outside the shelter.

I was at the Pushta that day as my colleague, Ashwin, and I had to understand a somewhat unclear source of work for the homeless men that we had been hearing about on our visits. While I looked out for Saroj, a man who I thought could enlighten me about it, another man began crying and howling in pain. This was not unusual at the Pushta.

'I hate all of you! How dare you hit me! I'm going away, I'm never coming back!' He screamed and looked up at me. I saw that he was bleeding from his nose. I hadn't seen anything happen, even though I stood right there.

The man tried his best to walk. Beneath the mud-splattered path from the tea shop behind the ISBT to the stretch at the Pushta there lie tiles, anonymously and casually installed, only in part. They reminded me of a painting left unfinished by a lethargic, modern aristocrat. Perhaps this was one of the PWD's masterpieces. The man fell flat a few hundred meters from the shelter. A few men who stood nearby picked him up and tried to talk to him.

The shelter looked much more festive than usual. Prem Babu, our homeless volunteer and cook, had trimmed a few of shrubs on the minute boundary of the flower bed that stretched along the shelters. Shamshad, our newly appointed health worker at the recovery shelter, had bought four hens that pecked anything they thought edible. Shamshad had also bought a few chicks along with these hens. They chirped in a symphony of destruction.

A large group of men sat outside the recovery shelter to see Dr Pradeep. The evening clinic had opened. Raj, Sahib, Chanderbhan, Khursheed and Honey Singh, the gang of five, all approximately the same age, are young homeless men who are also volunteers at CES. They love sports, and on that day, like all other days, played cricket at a field right at the back of the shelters. This field divides the main road from the Pushta.

Ramzan, one of our volunteers and formerly from one of the homes run by Dil Se, (Aman Biradari's project that works on street children) was in the middle of a motivational class at the recovery shelter. The shelter reminded me of a machine, and the men, its incongruous, yet indispensable parts. I felt like the only one not really doing anything. I remembered that I had to look for Saroj. I found him at the back of our second shelter and spent some time speaking to him about the work. It was 6:15 p.m.

'How difficult is it to get work?'

'At this time of the year it is not as easy, but we have contacts.'

'How does that help?'

'If you know someone who knows a contractor, or know someone who's pally with someone who knows the contractor, you just stay close, keep following up, and you will almost certainly be taken on board every labour trip that sets sail from here.'

'Who's the contractor here?'

'Umm… Anand…don't you know that, brother?'

'I see, I see. I am sorry, I had forgotten that'. I pretended to already know this. Anand (one needn't be surprised) is also a homeless man. He is a contractor for men who recruit labourers for 'shaadi party' work: labour required for cooking, placing tents, washing dishes, carrying tables, chairs, pots and pans in trucks from one location to the other for the marriage reception of two individuals these homeless men never meet. These are typically a few things that casual homeless labourers at the Pushta do for a living. Since Ashwin and I have been researching the lives of not just our patients at the shelter, but the reality of these men as a whole, it was important that I have this conversation with Saroj.

'So how do you and Anand get along?'

'We're ok, but I heard from Chanderbhan and others that in the last week he offered a few unknown men a better "party" than the one I and others had done.'

'What do you think of that?'

'Can't say. Could be that Chanderbhan is lying, but why would he do that with me? I am no threat to Anand or him. Could be that he's telling the truth and that Anand may have something in for him from those men. That's completely understandable. You see, I respect Anand because he's worked his way up the ladder faster than us. Besides, here, at the Pushta, it's each man for himself. Everyone does not believe in brotherhood you know.' Saroj instantly looked at the board outside the shelter that read 'Aman Biradari'. He kept quiet for a minute.

'Hmm. Tell me, Saroj, apart from getting better work, what other advantages do you enjoy if you know the contractor personally?'

'I don't know how it works in other parts of the city, but here, if Anand knows the monitoring staff on location, [the venue of the marriage reception], which he almost always does, he makes sure that those known to him get work that is less taxing. If I go with him, he ensures that I don't do work that's more difficult, such as putting up tents and cleaning. I get to arrange flowers, utensils, sometimes even serve wearing a fancy uniform!'

Saroj and I sat talking for about half an hour. He had never spoken about what he does for a living. Nobody had taken so much interest in his professional life. At that moment, I had completely forgotten about the evening clinic.

At that moment, one of the patients sitting in line to see the doctor howled and screamed. My Auden-inspired intuition began calling him 'The Unknown Citizen'. I am not trying to be clever or funny. This man was literally unknown. As we figured later, none of us, not the staff, not Dr Pradeep, not even the residents, had ever seen him before.

The man was short and bulky. The first time I noticed him, I could not see his face. The modest lighting at the entrance of the shelter wasn't enough for any of us to see what he looked like. I walked a little closer towards him. The man looked unkempt, unshaven and seriously ill. He had been sitting there a while, waiting for the doctor to see him. Before we could catch our breaths, he growled and moaned loudly. He fell sideways on the pavement immediately outside the recovery shelter. Sunilji, one of our community researchers and shelter managers at the Pushta caught him just in time and quickly called Tsering to have a look at him. It was the first time, I had seen Sunilji move with such urgency and force. Perhaps I had never witnessed an emergency at the Pushta till that point. It made me feel uninformed about the space.

'Doctor, his pupils! I cannot see any pupillary reflex.'

'Tsering, this man needs to be taken to the hospital, right now.'

What? I was in no man's land, momentarily. Less than a minute later, I was carrying this man along with Shiva, another health worker at the recovery shelter, and another volunteer into the van. I lost all contact with Saroj. I wasn't thinking about work, or the casual labour market any more. Shabanaji, who monitors medication at the recovery shelter, sat in front with the doctor, and we sped off towards the nearest hospital.

All of this happened really fast. I realized that I was a little lost in the midst of what was going on. I had not heard the doctor saying anything about what was happening to him, but I should have understood by Tsering's and the team's reaction. This man was, in actual fact, having a cardiac arrest.

It took us twenty minutes to reach. Pratapji drove fast, yet strategically, dodging traffic as if it were a large heap of mud and the ambulance a heavy-duty bulldozer. It was in these twenty minutes that my outlook on the nature of the subject I had engaged with was to change irreversibly.

The man lay on the only seat/stretcher placed on one side of the ambulance. Tsering, Shiva, the volunteer and I stood and sat around him. Seven minutes past seven. For the next few minutes I had a momentary yet extensive lapse of analysis, thought and rationale. I felt a rush of blood through my body, most of it to my head. My palms were sweaty, and I shivered from head to toe.

'Anhad, pass me some of those clothes!' said Tsering, pointing towards a pile of old clothes that had originally been brought for distribution. I did not even look at what I was passing on to him. He put two and a half pieces of winter wear underneath the man's head. The man was still breathing and his pulse indicated that he was ok. The volunteer, a tall lanky homeless youth who had just moved into the shelter, was holding the man's legs. I heard Tsering scream at the top of his voice, 'Bhai Saab! Bhai Saab!!'

How often do Dr Pradeep and Tsering have to witness something like this? Despite the anguish, urgency and worry, was this something that was now a part of their lives?

'Anhad! Quick, ask the doctor for his stethoscope!"

'What?'

'The stethoscope! Quick!'

I went towards the window that parted the driver's seat from the rest of the van. Panic. It struck me like an astringent poured on a five-second-old wound. It had taken me ten seconds to realize that Tsering wanted the stethoscope.

'Where in god's name are we?!' Tsering was frustrated that we were still not at the hospital. He tried to shake the man. Upon checking his carotid pulse (the pulse in the neck) he realized that there was no indication of blood supply to the man's head. Tsering began to perform CPR on him. I had only seen this in the movies.

We had reached the hospital. 7:20 p.m. I jumped off the back of the ambulance, and ran towards the entrance, where a number of stretchers lay on the right. It took me and the volunteer fifteen seconds to bring the stretcher. We put the man on the stretcher and rushed inside, ignoring the security guard who tried to assert his authority. 'Not more than two...'

'Move out of the way! Can't you see this is an emergency?' The security guard said no more.

The floor inside stretched for about a hundred feet in both directions. Contrary to how I had imagined Emergency Wards, there was nothing that evoked a sense of urgency. It was worrying to see how almost all activity inside this ward was gradual; all movement and almost all work was in slow motion. On the right was a counter where a man sat with an untouched register. At the rear end of the room were people (perhaps relatives) all sitting on chairs.

We took a left into the hallway, and put the man on a cot at right at the end. Less than a minute later, we were asked to put him on another cot. He was then put onto advanced cardiac life support. This entailed CPR, constant medication via injections and an endoscopy-like procedure, which I later learnt was called endotracheal intubation. A heavily bearded doctor placed a funnel-shaped structure on the man's mouth, inserting the narrow end into his oesophagus. Air was then blown into his system through this funnel. An assistant and a nurse were simultaneously involved in monitoring his injections and medicines.

'These men are taking too long! This entire procedure should be performed ten times faster! What is wrong with these men?' Tsering was clearly not happy.

The bearded doctor then prepared for shock therapy, something that even a medically uninformed audience would understand to be the last resort. A member of the hospital staff asked us to wait outside at this point. Dr Pradeep and I left for the ambulance while Shiva and Tsering stayed inside.

'The only reason that man still had a pulse on him was because of Tsering; because of the CPR in the ambulance.' Dr Pradeep remarked as we exited the building.

The morbidity of hospitals, the urgency and sheer baggage of trauma they carry for a lot of people came back to haunt me momentarily, as I noticed more than a dozen patients huddle right outside the entrance. From time to time, they rushed indoors, the moment there was some space to sit inside the building. An auto rickshaw crossed us, and a man with a terribly damaged knee was brought out of it. The doctor, not surprisingly, looked fairly composed.

On our way back, we continued attending to patients on the streets of Delhi. A gigantic clock hung outside AIIMS, indicating the current population of the country. It fluctuated by the minute, as we looked at it. I always knew that thousands die every minute, every second. I hadn't seen anyone die before. All of a sudden, someone's death was no longer just a number on a clock. The death of a stranger was, suddenly, a poignant and disturbing reality.

'This must not have been easy, Anhad. I understand.' The doctor by virtue of his profession made no big deal out of what happened. He tried to converse with me about other things to take my mind off the situation. For the next fifteen minutes, we sat and talked about politics. Almost half an hour later, Tsering came back to us.

'He's gone. They are wrapping up the body and the police has told us to not worry about this at all.'

An hour ago, a man was alive; a mass of biochemical reactions to a medical college, where many such bodies eventually land up, but a father, a son, a labourer; a human being to the doctor, Tsering and I.

On our ride back, Tsering sat in front with Pratapji. An unusual poignancy occupied the ambulance. It was a disturbing moment for me, and poignant one for Tsering, who sat quietly, highly distressed, despite us patting him on his shoulder. All of us knew that Tsering had done everything in his power to save the departed.

We had tried to search for some kind of ID for this man, but he did not have any on him. He was dead, and we didn't know him, and we didn't know where he came from. He was, however, a citizen; entitled to the same set of rights as the Prime Minister and the homeless volunteer who accompanied us; the same set of rights as Dr Pradeep and myself. The police assured us they would find out who he was. In the interim, he remained unknown.

I felt responsible. Not for his death, but for what must be done next. We drove past the Pushta. The residents had fallen asleep, surviving on the edge, not knowing whether they will be alive tomorrow. Perhaps they were all like him, unknown, yet human beings.

I could now pull myself together and think that if I ever had a chance, I would write about this man. I would write about what happened that night. I had to, for it would probably be the only way people could know of a man who, even towards the last half hour of his life, remained an unknown citizen. I would render it important.

I would like to think of this as a rightfully vivid epitaph; not of a famous, or even a known individual, but a man, like any other man, who breathed and walked this earth. 23rd December occupies a space in my cerebrum like no other. I know that this chapter will give readers only a snapshot of the man, of his life, of my experience that night. Nevertheless, it is vital to bear witness.

Shared Spaces

Annie Baxi

This essay reflects the researcher's confrontation with personal and ideological questions that emerged during interviews with Muslim tenants in Abul Fazal, an unauthorized, predominantly Muslim locality in South Delhi. The researcher resides in a neighbouring area, which is dramatically different in terms of its geographical, spatial, visual, social, political, economic and other cultural parameters. As she articulates her experiences of 'privilege' and attempts to build research with her participants rather than on or about them, the space shared by the researcher and the researched expands to include questions of personhood similar to both of them. Names have been changed in this account.

My research, as part of the 'Housing Discrimination Project', is a qualitative study of the experiences of Muslims tenants in the Delhi increasingly segregated housing rental market. The study has been formulated to understand the processes of the rental market and the networks within and outside Muslim-concentrated spaces that contribute to the creation and growth of segregated Muslim localities. The project included interviews with Muslim tenants residing in such localities. I worked in Abul Fazal, located within Jamia Nagar, which has been popularly called a 'Muslim ghetto' for several years. It has a dense Muslim population of mostly migrants from neighbouring states. The area suffers infrastructural challenges because of its unauthorized status, making its cramped streets and unregulated buildings starkly different from the posher areas that surround it.

A typical day during this phase started with meeting my friend and co-researcher at the community centre market of New Friends Colony (an upmarket authorized colony in New Delhi). We would take the Gramin Sewa to reach Abul Fazal for our interviews. Towards the end of the day, we would return to the market near the relatively posh area to discuss the day and our personal reflections on the research. We both belong to upper-middle-class backgrounds and Abul Fazal was dramatically different in aesthetics and spatial, visual and cultural aspects from where we stayed.

In one of these discussions, as a concluding comment, he said '*We cannot deny our privileges.*' In the silence following this statement, I considered the difficulties I experienced, as a young Sikh woman living in posh New Friends Colony area. Despite being brought up amid 'privileges', my life was marked by negotiations with my relatives about my decision to pursue the current research. This statement made me feel heavy, as if in the definitions of privilege, me and my challenges have little or no space, as issues 'bigger' than mine already exist within kilometres of my residence. Was I to feel guilty about the 'privilege'? Or was I 'supposed' to feel grateful? Are they really 'privileges'? Do they aid my life?

With these thoughts, I responded, '*You and I are occupants of a certain social position and also carriers of the baggage that the position thrusts on us, sometimes willingly and often unknowingly.*'

***

During my academic training, I would experience a split between what I read, and what I lived; a sense of alienation, as many of the accounts of 'marginality' I came across did not speak to my experiences of being side-lined. In the dominant narrative of 'marginality' there was little space for people like me who are visibly 'privileged'.

The embedded hierarchy in a study, with the researcher being the knowledge producer, cannot be denied. Such a paradigm often promotes a research position that is mostly 'on' and 'for' a particular group and rarely 'with' people. However, in the intimate sharing of the researcher and researched, the question that confronts me is how much of myself am I willing to bare; whether I am able to lie nude and embrace vulnerability in the attempt to understand the other.

This felt vulnerability became the site through which I related to the difficulties of others. I realized that an acknowledgment of my personhood, with its intimate vulnerabilities provided me with an enriched and more sensitive vocabulary to understand another. In the complexities of living, I cannot isolate my 'privilege' from my vulnerability: both feed the other. Thus, research became an activity of co-construction, where the researcher and the researched bond through touching their own and each others' vulnerability a mingling of their subjectivities and the possibilities of newer and more nuanced meanings about human experiences.

Shared Spaces Between the Researcher and the Researched

During the data collection phase of the study, I took the Gramin Sewa auto from my house to Abul Fazal. The ten-minute journey every morning in the loud traffic, with the dust and sewage smells was spent contemplating my daily difficulties in doing the research. As an upper-middle-class Sikh woman, working in a 'downtrodden' Muslim neighbourhood, it was a challenge to convince my parents about the importance and relevance of my work. I could not reveal to them the exact nature of my work, as I was apprehensive that their perceptions and resulting skepticism would be a hindrance to my commitment as a researcher. I am the first woman in generations of my family to go beyond a graduate degree, and the first to remain unmarried at the age of twenty-seven. My parents struggle with the lack of a template to understand me, as even though they empathize with their daughter, the 'unmarried researcher woman' troubles them immensely. I try to understand them, not without becoming emotionally drained myself.

I would and still often ask—can we divorce our personal life trajectories and social locations? To what extent do my mental categories 'misrepresent' the world to me? As I am, much to my annoyance, understood through fixed schemas of my family, am I offering a fluid schema of representation to the research participants? Do I allow the participants to challenge what I know about them and how much of what I already know do I thrust on them? How much of my family's and my perceptions of the Muslim ghetto are permeating the research? And with these questions, I realized my class and religion did play a role as I navigated through the lanes of Abul Fazal.

The data collection process opened up for me an arena of unanticipated abstract and empirical realities. Based on the research objectives, I was to explore through in-depth interviews with Muslim tenants the access to their current rental house, and the role of religious identity in the choices available to them and made by them. Thus, our study was an exploration of the 'house', but underneath lay the desire for a 'home'. A house signifies a physical structure of walls and roof, whereas a 'home' is the embodiment of identity, intimacy, belonging, rootedness, safety, comfort and the ease to merely 'be'. As I heard tenants narrating how they obtained these 'houses', I also heard faint reverberations of my own desires, dreams and ambitions of 'home'. The discourse between the 'house' and 'home' became one of the sites where bridges between two seemingly contrasting spaces were built via the shared identities and longings of the researcher and the researched.

Khursheeda Begum lived in a small home with her family members. Their house was visited three times by our team. In the first visit, we gathered some basic information regarding the procedural aspects of how they obtained their current housing. The second visit was denied, as it was made by two men and the house had only women members at that time. The third visit included me and another female colleague; most of the excerpts below are from this visit.

When we arrived, we spoke to her daughter, peeping through a window. She was uncomfortable and hesitant, but as we persisted, she allowed us in with a frown. It had initially seemed that we would be made to leave without clarity, but the conversations gradually took the form of catharsis and female bonding far beyond the research objective.

The entrance of the house has an iron gate with a clothesline above. The house had two rooms for nine members. The room in which we sat had two beds, one queen-sized and a single one. This room was shared by Khursheeda, her husband, and their three daughters. The other one was for Khursheeda's son, his wife and their two children. They had been living in this house for two-and-a-half years. I sat on the edge of the bed shared by Khursheeda and her two daughters. I could differentiate among the smells of three bodies as we sat on the bed. The moment felt morose and gloomy as I looked at the exhausted and irritated faces of the daughters and the curious gaze of Khursheeda Begum. I had one leg resting on the bed and the other swaying to avoid contact with the three rats I had noticed within seconds of my entry. The remaining portion of the bed had piles of clothes as winter clothes of nine family members were being locked away for the next season.

As they responded to my questions, the daughters' marriages emerged as the most essential factor in deciding their choice of housing. Sabina said: '*Intezaar mein jee rahe hain. Ache Pathan milna hi mushkil ho gaya hai. Jo aata hai dekhta hai, kissi ko chhoti ladki chahiye, kissiko zyaada ameer. Log aate hai dekhne, lekin umar zyaada hone se baat nahi ban rahi. Tees ka ho, to chalega.*' (We are living in an endless wait. It is difficult to find good Pathans. People visit us, but somebody wants a younger girl, others prefer a richer family. Nothing seems to proceed because of our age. We are looking for Pathans in their thirties.)

The reason they never vacated any house unless suggested by owner and continued to stay in Abul Fazal was because of their 'good' reputation and its importance in getting suitable proposals for their daughters. *'Hum ghar nahi chhorna chahte kyunki jab ladke waale aas paas poochenge, tab humaare baare mein acha bataane waale bahut honge, aas padhos mein.'* (We do not want to leave any house until we are asked to do so. We have built healthy relations with our neighbours and have a good reputation amongst the people residing close by. When families come to inquire about us in context of our daughters' marriage, there will be many neighbours who know us and can narrate good things about our family.) We also learnt that that they were uncomfortable with the last visit of two male researchers. *'Hum ladkon-padkon ko bulaate nahi. Bagal waale bolenge phir. Apne hath mein hai izzat banana aur mitana.'* (We don't entertain men. I do not want the neighbours to speak ill of my daughters. It is in our hands to maintain a good reputation.)

They were keen to know about my marital status. One of the daughters told me, *'Aapko toh aaraam se husband mil juyega. Aap ko kaam karna allowed hai, aap logon se milti hain'* (Finding a suitable husband will be easy enough for you as you are allowed to work and you meet many people.)

On most remarks about marriage, their words struck me and I was speechless despite my desperate desire to respond and give the conversation a sense of closure. I juggled with the sense of responsibility and the desire to share my grief and add to the collective cathartic moment. The responsibility was of the 'informed researcher' hoping to give a sense of closure and meaning as they shared and revealed their vulnerable and intimate life details. I wanted to hold their hands and tell them that even though we belonged to different social worlds, we suffer the same angst in particuliar ways. Yet, I found myself taking the position of an 'objective' outsider, stating that it was important to marry 'right' rather than simply marry. They saw me as an independent woman, embodying a life they perhaps desired. I, however, knew that my lived sense of this independence did not provide the escape or relief from the burdens they spoke about.

I wrote in my journal that evening, 'How different was my life from them? I am "educated" and have been "allowed" to work, but has it fundamentally changed anything about my choices or the way perceptions around me were built? At least the women knew that they were to wait, what was I supposed to do? Wait for my Pathan? Or should I be consolidating this imagery of an independent woman that on the surface is unperturbed by these questions?'

I live in a four-bedroom house in an affluent, upper-middle-class neighbourhood. I do not experience rats, open sewers and flooding in rains, yet I do not feel rooted. We (Khursheeda Begum's daughters and I) both had a 'house' but not a 'home'. Our non-marital status influenced our lives significantly, even though in different ways. If the presence of male researchers posed a threat to social reputation and marriage proposals for Khursheeda Begum, the very pursuit of my studies and research was antithetical to the ideal of womanhood upheld by my parents, which was crucially defined by marriage. It was our respective inability to fit into the ideal moulds that allowed us to share in and feel each other's mostly unacknowledged personhood.

Another experience took place with Nagma, whose current house is on one of the relatively broader and better built roads of Abul Fazal. In comparison to those of other participants, her house was bigger and closer to my house in terms of the number of rooms and certain interior structures, like the separation of a drawing room from the bedrooms. My male co-researcher and I came to her house during afternoon hours and there was some hesitation from her about opening the door to complete strangers. She first asked us to return at a time when her husband would be in the house, but for reasons unknown to us, opened the door as we turned away. I assumed that maybe, in a moment of trust, she allowed us to listen to her life.

She directed us to the common room, which had a sofa set, a table and a small bed. She served us tea and wanted to speak to us extensively but her three-year-old son demanded all her attention. I thought of sharing her motherly responsibilities, playing with him, maybe teaching some alphabets and numerals. The boy was restless, she said, as there was rarely any space to play in the area.

Originally from Varanasi, Nagma had shifted to Abul Fazal after her marriage. The house was a 'bachelor pad' for her husband and his cousins before the marriage. She obviously did not know much about how the decision to take this house was made. She did not like Abul Fazal, as there was no direct sunlight in her house and the roads were cramped. She could not even invite elderly relatives to her house as it is located in a elevator-less building on the fourth floor.

They were about to shift to a house they had had recently bought in Noida. The new house had open space, parks, easier road connectivity and good schools. She longed for her 'big Varanasi home', in a 'mixed locality'. It was a metaphor for the life she lived as an unmarried woman. She now had a house, but not a 'home'.

I understood her better during the second visit to her house to meet her husband, Aslam. He was stern, stiff and repeatedly underlined his choice to not share personal information with us. He rarely made eye contact with me and spoke mostly to my male co-researcher.

He was not sure whether he would shift to Noida soon as he preferred Abul Fazal due to easy availability of food and established familial networks. In an almost candid moment, he mentioned that the Noida house was Nagma's as *she* had paid most of the amount.

Aslam: *Noida ka ghar to Nagma ka hai. Aap inse pooch sakte hain.* (The house belongs to Nagma. You can confirm this with her.)

Nagma: *Aap aisa kyun keh rahe hain? Jo hai who humaara hai.* (Why are you saying this? The house is ours.)

Aslam: *Arre, jo sach hai woh sach hai. First installment to tumne hi di hai na.* (You gave the first installment. It's a fact.)

It seemed that he viewed the Noida house as an embodiment of Nagma's unfulfilled aspiration, and did not share her views. He told my male co-researcher, '*Aurton ki soch ghar ko lekar alag hoti hai. Unko chahiye aisa ghar jiske baare mein woh apne rishtedaaron ko bata sakein.*' (Women have their own ways of thinking and for them a house has a different meaning. They want the house that gives them social standing amongst their relatives.)

I looked at Nagma. She was silent and so was I. I was not only silent for myself, infuriated by his remark, but also for her, as I knew that his interpretation of the Noida house was not hers. This silence became intense, and we all could experience it growing among us.

In our first meeting, Nagma was a woman of longings, opinions and hope. In the second meeting, Nagma was silent. I felt she was hoping for her husband to validate what she had shared earlier. The 'home' is also a collective endeavour where its meaning is shared and embodied with others. We 'make a home' but the house is given. The nature of this collectivity demands negotiations with each other. I do not know whether and when Nagma will find her home, but in that silent moment, we shared our longing and its difficult pursuit.

***

The three of us—Khurhseeda Begum, Nagma and I—have different trajectories through lives governed by religion, class and marital status. I would be seen as 'privileged' on multiple fronts as I live in a 'big' house and have an individual room to myself. But in my mind, even though I stayed in an 'ideal' house, I longed for a home too: a place of comfort, acceptance, security, belonging and identity. In this shared quest for home, I experienced the stories the study's participants shared and had a connection with them. My privileges have made my life easier, but they have also caged me as an upholder of a tradition that I never chose. Thus, the participants and I are located, and we hold hands, in our personhood.

A Sense of Closure

I have imposed my personal reflections on the gathered transcripts, perhaps to make the narrative more cohesive. There always exists a gap between the realities as experienced and its description through the written word. It is in this gap, between the reality lived and the reality told, that art and literature strive to go beyond the said.

I will end with a poem 'Hatasha Se Ek Vyakti Baith Gaya Tha' by the acclaimed Hindi poet, Vinod Kumar Shukla, who paints an imagery of acknowledging personhood beyond the domains of the preordained categories of knowing. I dedicate this poem to Khursheeda Begum, her daughters, Nagma, Aslam and several others as we discovered togetherness, despite our obvious and subtle differences.

A man had sat down
Weakened by despair
I did not know him
I knew despair
I went to him
extended my hand
Taking it
He stood up
he did not know me
he knew me extending my hand
We started walking together
Both did not know each other
We knew 'walking together'.

To See and Be Seen

Saba Sharma

This piece was written based on fieldwork undertaken with Ankita Aggarwal in Raigarh, Chhattisgarh in March 2012. We visited Balsamund, a colony of former leprosy patients on the outskirts of the city, as part of a study on understanding destitution. Names have been changed in this account.

Today, Shobha is going to the hospital to have a cataract operation. After many weeks of waiting, it is an important event, and her neighbour Santoshi, one of six people who are going to accompany her (including two somewhat bemused researchers), has worn a bright new sari for the occasion, starched to crisp perfection. Her other neighbour, Savitri, has just returned from her bath in the nearby naala, where she complains the water stings the skin, because of chemicals. At 8.50 a.m., we are all camped outside Shobha's one-room house, waiting for the auto driver who has promised on the phone earlier this morning that he will ferry us to the hospital and Tulsi (known across the basti as Madam), the anganwadi worker who has been promising for many weeks that she will help them with the paperwork at the hospital.

An hour passes. The sun grows stronger. We are still waiting, chatting, but the tension is mounting—neither Madam nor the trusty tempo has made an appearance. Meanwhile, in the leprosy colony, as in any other basti across the country, the morning is proceeding. People are taking turns to bathe at one of the three common taps, and a few, like Savitri, risk the naala that separates the basti from the main road. A bridge over this naala, connecting the basti to the rest of the world, built after many years of requests, will collapse again the following monsoon, leaving people stranded before a shaky kachcha structure emerges again. An assortment of men are nursing hangovers from the day before, sitting quietly around the women. They are unrecognizable in the morning light, the drunken belligerence of the late afternoon having been replaced by the acquiescent silence of daybreak. Among them is Santoshi's husband, Bodhan, who, in his morning stupor, looks nothing like the man who picked up and carried Shobha through torrential rain when the entire basti was flooded last year.

The flood has left its mark all around the basti; houses continue to be in various states of disrepair, indicative both of the amount of compensation the government gives and the inability to build the houses up again. Some of the homes look almost like their old selves—kachcha mud walls, small, dingy rooms, but a roof over your head. And some are open to the sky, or only held together by sheets of plastic, their inhabitants either too old and weary to do much else, or choosing to live in half-broken houses and using the money to pay the children's school fees or medical bills instead. But broken or not, for most in the basti these houses are the culmination of a long, arduous journey from their initial expulsion from the villages to the indifferent footpaths and bridges under which they lived until they came here. The basti lacks any sanitation facilities, faces frequent power cuts, and according to one rumour that is passed on with relish, is haunted. But it is home.

The Balsamund leprosy colony is set in the heart of the district of Raigarh, and on the outskirts of the city itself, one among the many contradictions that characterize the basti. Its residents have come from the surrounding villages in Chhattisgarh and neighbouring Odisha. Over the course of more than twenty years, it has gone from being abandoned land on which trees and shrubs grew freely to the uneven rows of houses we see today. Progress has come slowly—from the makeshift huts and clusters that characterized it first, to the three pucca houses that stand out among the many kachcha ones, and the sporadic electrification which cannot protect against the long power cuts. Just outside it is an old-age home, whose inhabitants are also refugees from their homes in the nearby villages, but ones that are too old to take care of themselves. Some of Shobha's neighbours think she should be here too, but she is adamant about not going. If she does go, it will be to the mission, which is further away, but far more trusted than the home next door, about which suspicions exist among many old people in the basti. There are stories of ill treatment, inadequate care and worst of all, Savitri tells us, 'they take away your old age pension, and give you only forty rupees a month to spend on your own'. Her wrinkled face is disapproving when she adds, 'in my old age I am like a child, I want to spend money on silly things'.

It is a Tuesday, and this means many residents of the basti will go out into the city to beg for food, rice, money and sometimes the rotting vegetables discarded by others. You take what you get— as Savitri puts it, 'some people give, other people don't. And some people set their dogs on you'.

The older, more disabled people will go and sit at the bottom of the 500 steps to the nearby Pahar Mandir. Each devotee is greeted with a 'ram ram bai' or 'ram ram babu', and almost each leaves something behind—a piece of coconut, prasad, and occasionally some coins or a note. But it is rare to hear the greeting returned. The day's earnings will be split in accordance with age and relative disability. In the crudest terms, those with the most deformities take a greater share of the total, but only because the believers themselves favour them. Those who can walk will not sit at the mandir and instead walk into the city, roaming for hours on end under the burning sun. Another one of Prabha's neighbours, Jalmati, explains this, 'you don't feel right if you just sit and beg. It's better if you're walking, moving around'. Long walks culminate in door-to-door visits—many of the benefactors are regulars, and know when to expect their visitors, according to what day of the week is it. Occasionally, the party will, with unconcealed delight, reveal something special provided unexpectedly at one of the houses—a batch of idlis made on demand, or a cold glass of nimbu paani on a hot day. Sometimes the day's earnings are compared with the others', or eatables are shared.

Despite the seeming normalization of begging, the frankness with which it is discussed, the 'schedules' and 'rounds' that regularize it in the basti, it is still experienced and internalized as something to be ashamed of. '*Naraaz mat hona*' (don't be angry), Jalmati says to us once, smiling nervously and peeling the discarded beans she has received on that day's rounds. On another occasion, when we wake up uncharacteristically early in the morning to accompany a group on one such trip, we find that the embarrassment at this prospect has caused them to leave half an hour earlier than usual. After this, we abandon our 'participant observation' fervour, and the incident is only referred to obliquely, with sheepish looks on both sides.

Finally, it is 10 a.m., and Tulsi is running down the path to Shobha's house, clutching her small bag tightly to herself, loudly defending herself all the way for being late. People around us explode into a flurry of conversation, some supporting her, some getting angry. But there is no time for this, and there is still no sign of the auto. We call him—he is still half an hour away. Finally, we decide to hail an auto from outside the basti, into which the six of us jam ourselves. Shobha is old with a broken hip, and also almost completely blind; getting her into the auto turns out to be the most challenging. Pushing herself along with her hands, she manages to clamber onto the floor of the auto, and with some help, is finally sitting upright.

The rest of us squeeze in around her. We haggle with the auto driver, settling at Rs 150 for a distance which finally turns out to be less than 2 kilometres. It makes the basti, which is barely on the edge of the city, seem further away than it actually is.

At the district hospital, we stand in line to take a receipt for Shobha. Her age and disabilities convince the lady behind the counter that she deserves a free receipt, on which she is categorized, without a sense of irony, as a 'poor free Hindu'. She is unable to climb the stairs to see the eye specialist, who instead comes downstairs and examines her in a crowded waiting room, while she's sitting on the floor. Our entire crew is being stared at by everyone else present. We find an old, rickety wheelchair, on which Shobha is seated and manoeuvred with difficulty for various tests. The five of us take turns trying to keep the wheelchair steady on a variety of surfaces, finally giving up and asking some men standing nearby to help us out. It is decided that Shobha will have a cataract operation tomorrow, but there is no guarantee that she will be able to see, because leprosy and age have weakened her optic nerves substantially.

As she is leaving, the doctor adds, 'don't come too early in the morning. Leprosy patients are operated on last, in any case'. This statement is made in innocence, with the genuine concern of a doctor not wanting to take a risk with the rest of her patients. But it leaves us squirming uncomfortably nonetheless.

Leprosy has a long and uneasy history with stigma—an association that has long surpassed the medical advances made towards curing leprosy. Since the mid-twenthieth century, leprosy has been curable, and the erstwhile forced confinement of patients no longer exists. Medical knowledge aside, however, leprosy continues to be misunderstood in society, not least by law. The Bombay Prevention of Begging Act of 1959, for instance, separates leprosy patients as a distinct category of beggars, who can be removed to a 'leper asylum'.

The Hindu Marriage Act of 1955 lists leprosy as a ground for divorce, alongside adultery and bestiality.

Leprosy is treatable, ceases to be infectious once cured, is not hereditary, and is a disease for which most humans have a natural immunity. But leprosy patients in India continue to be expelled from their villages, setting up bastis like the one we visited. However marginalized they are from the urban space, the edge of a city is an improvement on the extreme discrimination faced in the villages. Most are thrown out of their houses, or hidden like a family secret. In an eerie parallel of the caste system, the most common experience that is retold among the basti's residents is of being denied access to village lakes, wells and hand pumps.

Some are in voluntary exile, like Sukanti, who says she will stay away until her children get married, so that their prospects are not affected by having her as a mother. Unlike many others, she speaks of a loving and supportive family, who send her money and take her home for visits. She is not here because anyone pushed her out, she insists, 'I came here on my own, out of shame'. Others in the basti also stay in touch with family members, sometimes being visited by them, and sometimes, as with Shobha's grandchildren, giving them money. 'Return' is a fuzzy concept; only a day or two is spent in the village before discomfort and the restlessness to leave sets in. Whatever bitterness or resentment may accompany expulsion from the village, its only public expression comes in the form of a guarded response when they are questioned about their original 'home'.

'I stay there for two days, and then I come away'. Why only two days? Why not stay longer? 'I just like to stay there for two days', is uttered with finality, and with a stoic look that clearly signals the end of the discussion.

Many remember being forced to leave their villages so as not to adversely affect the marriage prospects of the children—a parent or sibling afflicted with leprosy is too much of a liability (but Sukanti continues to insist that this is not the case with her, 'I chose to leave myself. I don't want my children to suffer'.) Those outside the community who transcend the apartheid caused by this kind of stigma are remembered fondly—and for a lifetime. 'The district collector who insisted on eating with us twenty years ago' is as vivid in their memories as Madam who, for all her tardiness, is still someone in an official position who does not discriminate and is not disgusted.

Political leaders and senior administrative officials are understood through two categories—not political ideology or corruption records, but Those Who Visited the Basti, and Those That Did Not. Most patients tend to regard the state with a certain wariness—its processes and logic seem confusing, if not altogether mysterious, and people have generally accepted the idea of a state that delivers occasionally, without an explanation or rationale. Many continue to vote for the Congress because they believe the last significant piece of legislation relating to leprosy came from Indira Gandhi, who decided to include leprosy patients under the category eligible to receive disability pensions. In recent times, however, accessing the pensions has become more difficult, as a lone official informs us from his vantage point in what looks from the outside like an abandoned cow shed, but is actually the nirashi (pensions) department. As the files disintegrate further in the dust, we are told that while inclusion in the disability pension scheme used to be automatic for leprosy patients, today they are expected to also be on the Below Poverty Line list, and prove with a doctor's certificate that they are '80 per cent disabled' (a requirement that is halved if you happen to be of school-going age).

Experiences of stigma, 'ghinna', are referred to with unconcealed bitterness. This is a sensitive topic in the basti, evoking many memories of trying unsuccessfully to hide one's hands and feet, feeling too ashamed to eat in public places for fear of being stared at, and worse—being denied entry altogether. The overt stigma has faded a great deal, we are told, especially in the cities. No one will hold their nose if you walk by, or prevent you from boarding a bus or a train. Certain privileges exist too, like a special compartment on trains, and (theoretically) free travel on public transport. But people still look at your hands and feet, and then at their own. Down the lane from Shobha's house, an old and widowed Malati evolves a karmic theory to account for this: 'those who do ghinna will contract leprosy themselves'. Other karmic models turn this around and question the self, 'what must I have done, in this life or another, to be afflicted like this? Could it be my own fault?'

The worst-affected leprosy patients in the basti tend to be older, while their children are either leprosy-free, or have had the opportunity to have the disease detected early and therefore treated in time. Nonetheless, children of leprosy patients, regardless of whether they are affected by the disease, continue to face certain forms of residual stigma. Most attend school in hostels run by the missionaries that work with leprosy patients, along with other children of leprosy patients. In one of his less inebriated moods, Bodhan tells us, 'what is the point of keeping children here out of love? So we give up love and send them away, so they can make something of their lives'.

Caste does not matter, but it is understood that children of leprosy patients will only marry other leprosy patients usually from other such bastis, and sometimes within the same basti. Our questions about why this rule is never broken is met with a gentle shaking of heads; we do not understand. Marriage is something of a final frontier, one that seems nearly impossible to transcend. We attend one such wedding while we are there, and, being in possession of a digital camera, are also made responsible for the photographic documentation of the event.

During the course of our visit to the hospital, Tulsi has subtly but unambiguously handed over escort duties to us. As an overworked anganwadi madam, she finds relief where she can get it. This is further complicated by the fact that the anganwadi workers of the district are supposed to be on strike this week. Although her official function is the overall running of the anganwadi, which she does with the help of her lethargic but pleasant helper, Indumati, as an educated, somewhat aware individual, she often serves as the basti's link to the outside world. It is she who is in charge of securing 'items' for the wedding, imploring officials and strangers alike for donations. In the end, she is successful at this, and the bride departs Balsamund with a large bed and a sturdy-looking almirah. After we leave, she will once again take charge of taking the sick to the hospital and writing out applications and complaints, making it difficult to grudge her the momentary relief that we perhaps provide. Despite our temporary brush with celebrity, she is the genuine star, taking up many responsibilities for little, and usually delayed pay.

The next day, when it is time for Shobha to go for her operation, word has spread that we have become de facto health workers, and other people begin to request that we go with them to the hospital as well, mostly to the eye specialist for cataracts. The refrain is always, 'if people like you don't go with us, the doctors don't treat us well'. And so we go, each time queuing up to get our 'poor free Hindu' receipts, standing in line to see the doctor, and perfecting the pre-surgery drill for cataract operations—blood sugar report, blood pressure measurement and 'don't come too early, because you will be last'. We become better at haggling with the autos, and manage to bring the price down to Rs 40. The staff at the hospital has begun to become curious, but also more affable, asking us what job we could possibly have, delivering sick patients from the leprosy colony every day? One doctor's assistant tells us irritably, 'why can't you bring all the leprosy patients on one day? After they come in the OT shuts down'.

Shobha's operation goes off without incident, but when the bandages come off, she still cannot see. The doctor tells her to wait—her sight may or may not come back, but it will take time. Radheshyam, the next patient, meets a similar fate, although he can see a little bit more than Shobha can.

But watching Shobha and Radheshyam is too much for Babu Lal, our third and most sceptical patient. He blames not the weakened optic nerves, or age, but the hospital. 'They don't operate properly at the district hospital. I'm going to wait until I go to the mission's hospital, and get my operation done there'. He is among the oldest in the basti, and almost completely blind. Finally he decides that it is, after all, too hot to have surgery. He will wait for the winter.

The mission is the first and often last place of refuge for leprosy patients. Their relationship with leprosy has by no means been uncomplicated or entirely benevolent. In their earliest avatars, as part of the colonial project, they were responsible for setting up leprosy asylums, places where residents, though provided with treatment and care, were essentially locked up. Nonetheless, the mission continues to be an important (and perhaps the most significant) point of reference in the basti. Their hospital, though far away, is considered vastly superior to both public and private healthcare options in the neighbourhood. It is a place of first contact for treatment, and of shelter when wounds and blisters become unmanageable, or when one is too old or otherwise incapable of taking care of oneself. The mission holds a place in the basti's life that the government has been unable, or unwilling to step into. Their loyalty towards the mission is expressed in terms such as Babu Lal's 'they do *good* operations there, not like in government hospitals'. At the mission, treatment is free and patients are fed and cared for while they recover. In the district hospital, after her surgery, Shobha has no option but to crawl to a corner of the general ward and urinate just outside the door. Babu Lal is responding as much to the dignity with which he and others report being treated with at the mission hospital as to the quality of the treatment.

In the run up to our departure from the basti, we check on each of our 'patients'. Radheshyam can see a little bit better, and seems to be satisfied with this much. Babu Lal continues to hold off on his treatment, hoping to go to the mission hospital. Shobha is the most desolate of the lot. Every day her neighbours ask us, 'when will Shobha be able to see?' Savitri echoes Babu Lal and insinuates that it must be the fault of the hospital. 'We should have taken her to the mission', she muses. Shobha is fed up of the routine—of waiting for other people to take care of her, cook her food and remind her to take her medicines. She and her neighbours have decided collectively that in a few weeks, she will go to the old-age home at the mission hospital, where she will be taken care of and where she will also be extremely lonely. No one is happy about this decision, but there are no alternatives. When we return to the basti a few weeks later, her house is locked, and Savitri tells us she is crying every day at the hospital—there is nothing to do, no one to talk to.

***

Months later, we get a call from one of the few cell-phone holders in the basti. We hear the updates—one of the most vulnerable women living in the colony has passed away, Santoshi has contracted some mysterious illness and gets thinner every day, new ration cards were made, and one of Shobha's neighbours is marrying her daughter off—will we come to the wedding? But the best news is yet to come. 'Shobha is back, she didn't want to stay at the mission anymore.' A pause for breath, a beat before the punch line. 'And she can see!'

Melting into the Foreground

Rhea John

Everyone expected a qualitative study on poor disabled women in rural India to be full of grim stories, and it is. Some people pointed out that it would be unhelpful for policy advocacy; the fact that we as a society give each of these demographics—the poor, women, the disabled and the rurally located—a bad deal is universally acknowledged, and old hat. Yet the people we met—a number of often isolated, but complex and resilient women, as little defined by their demographic descriptors as we researchers ought to be— confirmed the importance of bearing witness. What follows is an attempt to describe what our patchwork of transcripts, field notes and audio recordings cannot convey: the personalities and complex lives of these women, and the reality of what it means to have encountered them.

Panchami Devi has some form of autism, I hesitantly decide when I meet her. I am no expert—in fact I know little about the different forms of intellectual disability—but I feel the need to make some assessment, to enter in my Excel sheet under 'Type of Disability'. She isn't able to communicate much with us; she can't cook or clean the house or dress herself. She manages washing the dishes though, is very pleased with that contribution, and tells us that she hopes that when her daughter Pooja grows up, she will learn from Pooja how to cook.

Her husband looks weary when asked about his wife, but

explains that though he has thought of leaving in the past, now he doesn't bother anymore since the worst is over. Pooja helps with the cooking and is finishing school; his son attends college nearby. All this was possible with the support of the extended family and the thoughtful largesse of Panchami's well-off father. Panchami sits quietly on a charpai during this conversation, intermittently arguing with a neice over the use of her comb and watching us wide-eyed. Her daughter is embarrassed and reticent; her son, though at home, does not make himself known to us at all.

Panchami's husband wonders whether they will earn something for recounting their story. When he realizes this is not forthcoming, he loses interest. His home near Patna was washed away in the floods many years ago and his family has become dispersed, he says. They were poor farm labourers in any case, and his uncle, who lives nearby, brought him to Hazaribagh and recommended this marriage as a way to settle him well for life. He still objected to it quite a bit at the time.

My co-researcher said proudly as we left, 'See, the Bihari male is such a good and responsible type! He stayed and took care of her!' I laughed but agreed: according to the last census, the number of previously-married women is far higher among disabled than non-disabled women, which seems to confirm our mutual assumption that even a higher dowry and other 'perks' may not be considered sufficient reason for their husbands to stay with them.

At the same time, I wondered how a person could live so long and so closely with another, but continue to see her only as a liability, a thing to be dressed and fed, and perhaps disciplined. Of course, he may not have been willing to bare his soul to casual, data-gathering visitors. But during my brief visit, I fancied I could see Panchami's longing for the approval of her daughter, her slight fear of her son—whom she was proud of but did not approach—her desire to be helpful and to participate, her delight in having visitors of her own and people who wanted to listen to her. Does long familiarity reduce a person to their daily, mundane capacities (completely opposite to the romantic idea of marriage), or does the definition of disability do this? Various women listed to us the chores they do at home as reasons why they counted as members of the household—while revealing that, in fact they were not being counted, and their contributions were being overlooked. To ask a more sentimental question, are emotional bonds with others or the ability to do 'work' more significant in defining 'normal' personhood?

***

Perhaps the opposite of Panchami's situation is that of Masidhani Tigga, who lives in a kaccha house in a village where the tarred roads of Jharkhand do not reach. When she was younger, her father and then her elder brother would take her to town for treatment—at first for her fits, then her paralysis. After they both died, she could not ask anyone else to make the requisite sacrifice. It is also unlikely those around her would be able to—her elderly parents, older sister-in-law and younger brother's small children are the other official occupants of her household. On good days, when she can move a little, she is pushed to church in her (poorly designed, but benevolently donated) wheelchair by her younger sister-in-law's brother, who lives with them.

When I ask about what causes disability, or who suffers the most when they have it, or about gender or social group differences in the experience of it, Masidhani never says—as most others I interviewed do—that she doesn't know or hasn't thought about it. Perhaps all the researchers who keep visiting her have forced the reflection; however, I think that researchers return because she tells them more than they thought to ask. I certainly would return, if I could. When I ask, for instance, how her community treats her since she is confined to her house, she replies with a charming dirty grin. 'When I see people passing on the road, I call out and ask them to sit and talk. They usually do. Even Santhalis come and talk—I speak Santhal, though most of us Christians (Oraons) don't. But you have to—ahem—ask.' Then she treats me to a brief anthropological description of the practices of the Santhals, complete with witty and uncharitable othering, which I chuckle at before telling myself I really shouldn't.

At another point in the conversation, she soberly tells us of the failure of the disabled women's self-help group that she and a few others in the same village were part of. They were supposed to make and sell 'tribal handicrafts'. Linkages were the problem, she said, both backward, in procuring materials, as well as forward, in marketing their products. The only mobile person had a sight impairment, so she couldn't buy thread in the colours they needed for embroidery; in any case, embroidery is expensive and unfashionable, so it doesn't sell. Moreover, the state's tribal affairs department decided that the group's baskets made of date-palm leaves couldn't be marketed as 'tribal handicrafts' since they used plastic thread to tie them. 'How else are we supposed to tie them so as to be of any use?' Masidhani demands. I am sitting on the cool mud floor and she in her wheelchair. 'These people want to pretend tribal people live in the past.'

Meanwhile the NGOs, though they meant well, had gone and replaced her old wheelchair with a new one that was poorly balanced—too narrow and top-heavy, and with wheels positioned wrongly for this terrain—and built her a squatting toilet that she can't use. Still, it was better than the government toilet, the pit of which was too shallow. She is thinking of keeping pigs in it. She's heard of an NGO programme for pig-farming, though she personally thinks pigs are much more of a pain to rear than chickens. She reflects that perhaps they are cheaper to distribute. I think she's right. In fact, I spend most of our two-hour interview thinking about this, and nodding up at her with my notebook lying forgotten in my lap.

When we prepare to leave, she looks at me and says, 'People who get disabled later are much worse off. They feel the trauma, they relive their past life, they always wonder what happened and why. They can't stop thinking, even when it's of no use.' That link Masidhani draws through her experience, between the knowledge of how you became disabled and having to face that it could have been otherwise, was not made by most of the women I spoke to. Perhaps it was because they knew little about the medical processes that brought on their condition, or the alternative social circumstances that could have alleviated it. Or perhaps seeing their fate as random chance—or worse, as something wholly preventable—was too cruel a thought to face.

***

Four days before meeting Masidhani, I spent an afternoon with Soni, an adolescent girl. Her elder sister told us that they are quite sure it wasn't the evil eye that caused Soni's disability, because she has had it since birth. Soni is now twelve or thirteen (her mother and the researcher argue lightly about it, but nobody's sure), small in build and bewildered at the attention. 'She's always been like that, so no one could have caused it to happen', her sister repeats with conviction, giving her the once-over.

Soni's sister is married, with two toddlers, but lives with her natal family since her husband, who is a manual labourer in Ramgarh, is not particularly solvent (and I gather might have a drinking problem as well). Her children were noticeably cleaner than Soni, and had clothes that weren't visibly torn. They also prodded Soni while she brought water for the guests as instructed, which their mother explained as retaliation for the years when Soni used to rage at and slap them. Throughout the conversation, she first used the present tense to describe Soni's failings, before remembering that she's much better now and not like that anymore. At one point she suggested, after some thought, that the onset of Soni's period might have brought about the change—though she can't say how.

The anganwadi worker was altogether more positive about the change in Soni. She did not mention any specific past misbehaviour, instead remarking that Soni now comes in to the anganwadi early of her own accord and shares the workload of her mother, who is employed as the helper there.

'Earlier, when the village parents heard of this child being present, they would come to observe what was going on, and check whether their children were in any danger,' she said. 'They soon realized that Soni was playing with the children and helping look after them, and that when she did get angry she would go and sit with her mother in the corner quietly, not take it out on anybody. After all, it's not like she's an outsider here—we all know who she is and where she comes from. They know her mother and I are here, making sure everything's alright.'

Yet, when we first arrived, Soni was playing alone and unobserved at a public bus stop beside a main road, with torn and dusty clothes and matted hair, while her mother visited the health centre in the next village for flu medicines. The question that occurred to me was not who Soni took care of, and how well, but who cared for Soni. Even accounting for poverty of money, time and information—and all of these were gravely present—it seemed no one really did. Soni has Down's syndrome, you will want to know, and also that she is quite a champion at peethu—as I discovered when I joined her at the bus stop.

***

The ride back from Soni's village, Churheta, took forever. The roads till Churchu, the block headquarters and venue for the local weekly market, are pretty good, constructed under the Pradhan Mantri Gram Sadak Yojana (PMGSY). The trouble lay in finding autos, infrequent in themselves, and moreover, in getting one willing to be 'reserve' for the journey, rather than picking up other passengers along the way. Convincing our local partner to dispense with this superfluous elitism—no less than our due as guests from Delhi, in his view—was as complex as asking him not to interrupt when our respondents spoke to us. Issues of hospitality, his age, his eminent local position (as dispenser of key NGO funds and work), and his knowledge of the area all intrude into our carefully-considered research ethics. When we were not visiting participants, he showed us in his guestbook the names of various eminent people who have visited and lauded their work with local women and disabled people. During the auto ride he was unusually quiet, perhaps planning the next day's activities to take into account our odd whims.

When, to dispel the sad silence after the interview, I tried to ask our disabled researcher why she doesn't use her tricycle, her male (non-disabled) co-researcher laughed uncomfortably and spoke first, to confess he had broken its chain. 'A toddler from the village was playing with it and getting his fingers caught in it,' he said with his usual sheepish grin. 'It was dangerous for the child, so I broke it.'

She quickly chipped in: 'In any case it wasn't much use to me, since the streets in my part of the village are too narrow and bumpy, and of course it doesn't fit inside the house.'

I nodded and changed the subject, asking where she heard of the machine, which she was enthusiastically describing to Soni's mother, which is supposed to cure disabilities of many kinds if you simply lie down on it. It's cheaper than the treatment Soni's mother told us she will someday save up for, at a good hospital in Ranchi or something—this one only takes a one-time investment of Rs 300, the price of a bedsheet you might use. She told me all about it all the way home, relieved to shift the conversation to a less socially awkward medical appliance, her dusty hands waving animatedly through the air, bangles rattling their own story.

***

In the middle of a hot day a week later, we visit thirty-eight-year-old Tara Devi, confident from the transcript of her initial interview that she will have a more optimistic story to tell. When we ask for her, someone points out a tallish, straight-backed, perfunctorily veiled form amidst a rapt crowd watching a godman market some amulets.

Urged by the hawk-eyed anganwadi worker, she leads us into the dim back room of the anganwadi nearby, while goggle-eyed children are shooed out and try to hang back to peer through the door.

As we attempt to capture her attention for the interview with polite questions about the day's events, Tara frowns and dismisses as gullibility the very idea that amulets can protect you from anything. Just a plot to get money out of us poor people, she grumbles, but her eyes keep returning to the window and the bits of his sales pitch that drift in to us. She's impatient, telling us that she has no major problems except how to finance her three sons' education. Her family treats her fine, even helping her to fetch water sometimes when her leg hurts. Her husband does okay driving a trailer, though he isn't home often. Her limp doesn't bother her in her daily life, no. It wasn't a problem for her to get married. Tara doesn't even reiterate the slight animosity towards a sister-in-law that I'd noticed in the transcript of her initial interview. That baba must be some orator, I think peevishly.

Whizzing through the usual questions, we arrive at the one that marked her out in the first round of interviews—political participation.

'If you could contest in the panchayat elections, would you?' I ask her.

'No,' she says, 'I don't have the money.'

'What if you had the money?'

'No, that's for the big people.'

'But you said you would, when the last researchers came!' (Not expressed quite so plaintively at the time, I hope.)

'Did I?' she says idly, her eyes fixed on the barred window. The amulet-seller is nearing the end of his performance, now calling on volunteers from the agog audience. I say thanks and let her leave, thinking that she couldn't be more 'normal'—and that I didn't know how to interview her as a result.

***

Our final interview for that day couldn't have been further from Tara, in location as well as in content. Dumrawa village is many kilometers along a dusty mud-track at right angles to the highway; a vast dry river-bed runs bleakly beside us all the way. When we reach the village, we stop at a little grocery shop to ask the way to Meena's house and the disabled girl who runs the establishment tells us to sit and wait; she will fetch Meena, who won't be able to speak freely in her own home.

The girl's parents fill us in on various rumours about Meena while she makes her way here—a broken engagement, a malevolent immediate family, blighted hopes—interwoven with the plot of a recent movie to more clearly highlight the moral points, though causing some doubt in us as to which events belong to which story.

When Meena arrives, slowly and tiredly on her crutches, and sinks into a seat in a corner of the room near me, the luminescent eyes in her drawn, austere face tell me why people are reminded of grand tragedy when they think of her. Meena's brother doesn't evict her from their house because of the social backlash, but that is all she receives from him, or from her mother who also lives with them. She does most of the household work for which she receives scraps to eat, along with recriminations for being bad luck, and no appreciation. She would like to work, but has never been sent to school—with no opportunities for girls to work nearby, there seemed to be no point. She looks up at us only rarely, speaking quietly with jagged edges, confirming the bare facts of what we already know. A difficult silence lies in the wake of her words.

'What do you think would help your situation?' I ask her naively. She looks up and says, 'I have no hope anymore'; then nods to us in acknowledgement, and leaves.

The Earth Is Bound to Shake

Saba Sharma

This piece was written based on fieldwork undertaken with Ankita Aggarwal in Maruda block, Mayurbhanj, Orissa, in October 2012, for a study on destitution. Mayurbhanj district is home to a significant population of the Lodha denotified tribe. Names have been changed in this account.

It is a scorching October day in Maruda, Orissa, our first in the district of Mayurbhanj. It is lunchtime, and the earth is shaking violently. We are bewildered, and it shows on our faces. Meanwhile, the owner of the dhaba, its other patrons, and our translator, Ramkant, continue eating and working unperturbed. Once the shaking stops, we look around for an explanation. 'Bomb blast', the dhaba owner says casually, as he offers more rice to the men at the next table. This does not help. Finally, Ramkant looks up from his plate and says, 'they test missiles for nuclear weapons in Chandipur, which is close by. This happens every few days'. And as if nothing has happened, we resume the debate we were having about the Lodha community, one we will continue to have repeatedly, the gist of which basically boils down to this: are the Lodhas lazy, thieving drunkards, or could there be more to their story than that? We are trying to explain to Ramkant our interest the Lodhas, in studying their lives and livelihoods, and in trying to understand how they might be better served by public policy. He, on the other hand, is trying to explain that the problems of the Lodha community can be explained by alcohol and an unwillingness to work. So far, both parties are sceptical about each other's argument.

Ramkant is not the only person in Maruda with whom we will have this discussion in the days to come. During our study of the Lodhas, we come across various societal and political actors that form crucial parts of their lives and hold similar views about them. The Lodhas are a Denotified Tribe in Orissa, informally known as 'ex-criminal' tribes. The Criminal Tribes Act of 1871, enacted by the colonial government, listed as criminal offenders multiple nomadic and semi-nomadic or forest-dwelling tribes. Often these were communities that resisted the efforts of the colonial government to aggressively occupy the forests these tribes depended on for their livelihoods. It arose as part of the larger criminalization of anyone who opposed the colonial regime. The Act required all members of the 'notified' tribe to be registered with the local police station. Their 'criminal' status was revoked after Independence, but the original act was replaced with the Habitual Offenders Act of 1952 which, while denotifying the tribes listed in the Criminal Tribes Act, effectively perpetuated their persecution.

Despite the official denotification of the Lodhas as criminals, the idea of them as underperforming, unproductive members of society persists, if not in official discourse, then privately (and often openly) among those responsible for upholding the discourse. Barely two years ago, an article in the most widely read daily newspaper, explaining the history of the term 'criminal tribes', claimed that it was needed by the colonial government to identify the most 'bloodthirsty' of the nomadic criminals. The idea of labelling them, the piece further explained, was to help them uplift their socioeconomic status, and establish a permanent place of dwelling.

On every level of governance we encountered during our study on the Lodhas, there was an undercurrent of patronizing—if not contemptuous—disregard of their capabilities. Even among the officials assigned to a special development agency meant to protect the Lodhas against their specific historical and societal disadvantages, there is almost a sense of resignation, as if all the good done by the agency is being undone by the Lodhas themselves. Their stigmatized history gives rise to a tense equation between them and the government, one which plays out on many levels.

Common grouses heard in various government offices range from the officious 'they are not laborious' to the somewhat more fantastic 'they are 24/7 in a state of intoxication'. The latter is the most repeated explanation for why Lodhas are not able to move forward, a rationalization that surpasses historical oppression, criminalization, or present-day caste and political dynamics.

Alcohol is also Ramkant's favourite subject, one that in each interview is approached with a mixture of condescension and humour. Judgment permeates the silences in our conversations, especially when we ask questions about the consumption of handia (local liquor made from fermented rice). He, along with a gaggle of people that surround us, smile sheepishly when an impoverished old Lodha woman, Phoolmati, tells us frankly that she drinks handia every day to get a little strength for the three to four hours she will spend walking in the forest to pick dried leaves, and the hours she will spend stitching them together. She is a 'half mind', others inform us, with knowing smiles on their faces. Alcohol is serious business when we talk about the progress of the community, but funny when the old, especially women, confess to drinking it. But Phoolmati is unfazed by the derisive laughter, telling us that her hands and legs ache constantly, and she drinks even when she doesn't have money, taking credit from the liquor shop.

After our first day in the village, as we are on our way out, walking through lush paddy fields and forests, Ramkant leans in conspiratorially and says, 'they're all thieves, they rob other people's houses at night and that is why they don't work during the day.... But, of course, I couldn't have told you this in front of them, they would have been offended', he adds after some thought. Ramkant himself is a Mahto, from an upper-caste land-owning family in a neighbouring village. In addition to being our translator, he appoints himself our guide, taking it upon himself to tell us what things are *really* like. Often, this takes the form of him answering the questions we direct at the Lodhas, instead of translating. He seems genuinely befuddled that we insist that he ask the question directly to the person being interviewed, instead of just letting him answer. He is further perturbed that we choose to ask the same questions over and over to different people, often eliciting similar responses. The results range from comic to frustrating, and repeatedly reveal the inherent bias that arises from his social position relative to the Lodhas.

Matters between Lodhas and the other village groups are generally peaceful, though with the understanding that the Lodhas will be looked down upon. With other tribal groups, such as the neighbouring Santhals, there is an undercurrent of hostility—perhaps because they are seen as competing for resources and government benefits. In one of the villages, some Lodha children are dutifully produced to report that they regularly get into fights with Santhal children. With land-owning upper-caste groups like the Mahtos, the relationship is more one of patronage, for Mahtos are often employers, moneylenders and buyers of the forest produce that the Lodhas collect. But these relations are not free from their own sources of friction. In one village, the Lodhas report that their children are not fed at the local ICDS centre, which is run by an upper-caste Mahto anganwadi worker. In a fit of annoyance, one Lodha woman declares, 'it would be better if there were only Lodhas in the village, no Santhals, and no Mahtos'.

In one particularly heated discussion at a village, Ramkant claims there is more prosperity among Mahtos as a result of their drinking less, to which a young Lodha man responds curtly by asking him how much land the Mahtos have in comparison to the Lodhas. Everybody drinks, but how many goats and hens do the Mahtos have, and how do their bank balances correspond to the amount of land they own? In the mixed villages, where Lodhas and other tribal and non-tribal groups live together, this kind of tense interaction is not uncommon. In one village, Lambodhar Bhakta, who says he is 110 years old, is sceptical of idea that the Lodhas' behaviour and drinking habits justify their poverty. In his century-old existence, he recalls everything from being forced to work on tea plantations in Assam by the British and having land grabbed by the Mahtos, to earning a daily wage that did not buy even a kilo of rice. He does not drink handia, which prompts Ramkant to triumphantly hypothesize that this must be the reason for his health and long years, until the old man reveals that he drank regularly until a few years ago.

'I wonder if we will live as long as him', muses Ramkant before concluding, 'probably not'.

'Because of handia', I want to say, to beat him to the punch line.

'Pesticides', he says sadly, and shakes his head.

Despite his wariness about Ramkant's analysis ('Lodhas are not in the mood to work'), Lambodhar is mindful of the improvement in their situation, and of the relative security of being able to take rice from the ration shop, as opposed to eating wild potatoes from the jungle. Many Lodhas reiterate this sentiment: 'ever since we have started getting grains from the public distribution system, life is a lot less hard'. Lambodhar Bhakta knows the situation has improved, but not enough: wages are up from before, but still very low; people are not constantly hungry, but his family runs out of rations and has to eat rice with salt a few days in a month. In general however, the Lodhas, while generally an impoverished and deprived community, do not suffer the levels of abject and dehumanizing poverty that is sometimes seen among the most neglected or on the streets of urban India. Despite their relative disadvantage, being automatically included in the public distribution system and being able to access subsidized grains has prevented them from facing extreme hunger, the way they did before.

While the Lodhas see government-subsidized grains as a means of sustenance, it is perceived by other castes and government officials as a catalyst to the inherent Lodha laziness, encouraging them further not to work, to make and drink handia, even to sell their rations in the open market at higher prices. It is near impossible to argue with the assertion that the Lodhas are unwilling to work, and always looking for an easy way out. The fact that it takes three or four hours, and sometimes a whole day's worth of walking through the forest to collect leaves or other forest produce, which are sold for paltry amounts at local markets (also a substantial distance away), still does not qualify the labour done by the Lodhas as 'work'. A local chemist we meet at the development agency's office informs us that 'agriculture is not their traditional occupation; stealing is. They're used to foraging from forests, living from one day to the next.'

The curious dichotomy in official discourse is to both berate the Lodhas for not wanting to work hard, and to perpetuate a complete lack of recognition of their current occupations as requiring intense physical labour, often for very little remuneration. Stacks of 1,000 pattals made out of sal leaves, which take days to pick out, dry and stitch together, sell for as little as Rs 120, and prices become lower the further a village is from the block headquarters. For the government, however, the collection of forest produce constitutes illegality, despite the Lodhas having done so for years. In modern environmental terms, it is spoken of as if the Lodhas collecting dry wood from neighbouring forests create a greater ecological imbalance than all the mining companies in Orissa put together. As if the Lodhas, once infamous for stealing from people, are now stealing from nature instead.

We meet Budhi Bhakta at the panchayat office, just on the outskirts of the village, an eighty-something man who, it is revealed, sleeps not at his own house, but in the panchayat office. 'We have only one small room in the house, so I let my son and his wife sleep there'.

Until recently, he would sleep at the house of his Mahto employer, whose cattle he took out grazing. For this service, they paid him Rs 500 every six months, three meals a day and a verandah to sleep on. Of late, he reveals, he has become too unwell to work, and his shoulder hurts from when he fell down, who can remember how many months ago? These days he goes home for meals, and also deposits his meagre pension of Rs 300 with his son, worried that he might lose it.

A small crowd of men from the village has gathered, a regular audience that we encounter when we interview those that are vulnerable, intoxicated, or in Budhi's case, somewhat senile with age. Like Phoolmati, he is unabashed about telling us that he takes one or two rupees every day from his son to drink handia. When he can't find the money, the owner of the handia shop gives him credit, interest-free, which sends the crowd into fits of giggles. They begin to speculate whether Budhi's shoulder injury was because he got drunk and lost his balance, at which point the suppressed giggling turns into peals of laughter, which Budhi barely registers.

That day, when we are walking back from the village, we are back to the original debate: is liquor and laziness the problem; do the Lodhas really want nothing but to spend their days in an inebriated stupor, looking for ways to avoid work? In a sudden moment of sympathy, Ramkant admits that handia is sometimes drunk out of hunger, and sometimes it's the cheapest thing to fill your stomach with. We do some calculations, and realize that it is cheaper to drink 700 ml of handia for Rs 5, than to buy rice in the open market at Rs 15 a kilo. Ramkant looks thoughtful as he adds that even if it provides a degree of intoxication, there is more to the drinking of handia than laziness or inability to be good towards oneself.

During the course of our interactions with the Lodhas, Ramkant gradually evolves from being dismissive of their answers, to being actively interested in asking the questions. Becoming familiar with our pattern, he now asks the questions himself, and even manages to follow up with questions of his own, showing a slow building of interest in the subject matter himself.

While it is seen as acceptable to accuse the Lodhas of being drunk and lazy, there is more ambiguity surrounding their original 'profession', stealing. Some, like the chemist, do not beat around the bush. One government official speculated that stealing was a sort of hobby for the Lodhas, a task undertaken for pleasure. Others, particularly those in the government, either acknowledge that it is not true that all Lodhas are thieves, or are careful about not saying so bluntly. Some may be a bit more sympathetic and concede that they are not thieves *anymore*, but for a Lodha there is no getting away from an outlaw past. The line from erstwhile professional robbery to present-day irresponsibility is drawn frequently, in a way that almost pities the Lodhas for an unfortunate past, one that makes them unable to think as the rest of society does.

One government official speculates that another reason the Lodhas are so backward is because they don't mix enough with the 'general caste'. The Lodhas are often compared unfavourably to other tribal communities (ones which do not have a history of being criminalized), or to upper-caste Hindus that cohabit with them in some of the settlements. Another official claims that there is hope for the next generation, but only if they mingle more and go to study in hostels away from Lodha villages. At the special hostel for Lodha girls, only three of the teachers are Lodhas. Nobody is qualified enough, the official adds with regret.

At the school, the teachers reiterate these views. We sit in the room of the only Lodha teacher who stays on the premises, in a little box-like structure near the gate that resembles a security guard's room, with his shirts hanging from a hook on the wall, his toothbrush in a corner. He sits quietly as one of the other teachers explains why it is important for Lodha children to study away from their families. The village school is underfunded; there is not enough emphasis on studying; and how is a parent who is permanently high expected to ensure that their child goes to school every day? Here you have facilities—food, clothes, books and 'cosmetics'. It is often reiterated that the Lodhas have no vision of the future, and that unlike other castes, they are not able to plan ahead, either for themselves or for their children. This is another reason that all government officials, and many outside of government, believe that it is essential for the children to stay away from the villages and get jobs as clerks and peons in small blocks like Maruda.

Towards the end of our stay, as his investment in the process intensifies, Ramkant also takes upon himself the task of giving advice. To Samali Bhakta, an old widow who is afraid of eating three meals a day because she is afraid the food will run short if she does, he elaborates on the advantages of eating regularly, especially for the aged. (Nonetheless, when she says she has to pay her nephew Rs 10 every month to go and fetch her rations, he reflexively responds, 'must be spending it on handia'). In the same breath, he also directly tells off one of her distant relatives, sitting close by and listening in, for not doing his bit in taking care of her, since she is alone. At first, Samali insists that even if she runs short of money, she never asks her relatives for a loan, a situation that led to her husband's death from an illness when they didn't have money for treatment. Later on, she admits that she has asked several relatives and her son, but none of them will give her any money. Instead, it is she who has lent her son Rs 500. 'What if you fall ill', is the logical next question, 'will you ask for money then?' A pause. 'Probably not, I will sell one of my goats.'

With Ramkant, we start to have deeper, more compassionate conversations about the Lodhas, and in particular he is interested in the insinuation of corruption within the development agency, an allegation that seems to resonate across villages. In one village, a woman complains of being thrown out of her job as a cleaner at the Lodha hostel for girls because she refused to pay a commission. This leads Ramkant to go so far as to boldly ask one of the Santhal teachers at the girls' hostel if she paid her way through to the job. She looks at him coldly, responds with a curt 'no', and ignores him for the rest of the conversation.

Corruption is one facet of the inherent mistrust between the Lodhas and the government, as if neither can be completely sure of the other's intentions. The Lodhas are often cynical of the government's efforts, with many complaining that the authorities favour other tribal groups, like the Santhals. Others astutely observe that Lodhas are not part of their own development process—none of the employees in the development agency are Lodhas themselves. Several Lodhas complained that even to get a job as cleaning or maintenance staff in the school, bribes need to be paid, while getting one's rights (such as the house they are entitled to from the development agency) involves the lining of several pockets.

The Lodhas have a complicated relationship with the government, which perhaps has its roots in the historical state-sponsored oppression and stigmatization of 'criminal tribes'. Despite the disdain, officials are acutely aware of the need for special programmes and provisions for the Lodhas, though sometimes this is interspersed with a snide reference to how jealous other communities are that the Lodhas have everything handed to them on a platter. One of the officers at the development agency, after a long rant about the moral depravity of Lodhas, still ended the conversation by saying of his work, 'I am not satisfied. But I hope to see progress in another eight to ten years'. Despite the patronizing and sometimes downright offensive views of government officials towards Lodhas, many of them still seem genuinely invested in seeing an improvement in their situation.

Lodhas, equally, are well aware of the power of government services. When we tried to enquire about the poorest of the poor, the most vulnerable in the community, we were repeatedly faced with the same realization—while Lodhas as a community are stigmatized and often dismissed by the government, their inclusion in the state's development agenda means that with some exceptions, a certain abject level of poverty was avoided. As they say themselves, while they are still not entirely food secure, a basic level of sustenance exists that did not before, thanks to their automatic inclusion in the public distribution system and pension schemes. Moreover, the development agency has also built houses for the Lodhas in the entire block of Maruda. Some other, less effective schemes exist as well, with regard to irrigation and other forms of agricultural support. For all of their ideological inconsistencies, the hostels for Lodha children are also generally considered to be of good quality, and parents are usually keen to send their children there.

On our last day in Maruda, we have a meeting at a block-level office, to discuss our findings and general impressions. We take Ramkant along, and for much of the meeting he sits on the side, nodding along, his translation duties no longer required. He has come more to watch than to participate, and the officials are as curious about his presence there as he is about them. The meeting goes as expected—we give an overview of what we have seen, and they in turn call the Lodhas lazy, thieving drunks. In addition to everything we have already been told before, we are also informed that the rural employment guarantee scheme, the NREGA, does not function here because the Lodhas find the work too hard, and would prefer to collect leaves from the forest instead (which, they say solemnly, is not very difficult).

When we finally approach the issue of corruption in the development agency, we find ourselves in an uncomfortable position. It is something we want to speak about, but involves the naming of individuals that may later get into trouble. We skirt around the issue until Ramkant, as if on cue, and with merely a nod in our direction, launches into a long tirade about corruption in the development agency and its adverse impact on the Lodhas. He makes the case effectively and with perhaps more credibility than two outsiders could have. The bureaucrats are squirming, but the subject of the conversation has officially changed. For a brief while, and indeed for the first time since we began conversing, none of us are arguing about the consumption of alcohol, the nature of hard work or the inherent drive to steal (in fact, in the ultimate irony, it is the Lodhas that are being stolen from in this case).

Ramkant speaks with clarity and restraint about bribes and commissions, names are written down and promises are made that no one is sure will be kept. They nod vigorously, and insist that action will be taken, while trying subtly to steer the conversation elsewhere. But Ramkant is not in the mood to be manoeuvred. He is holding forth, speaking firmly and with justified relish. The earth may not be shaking, but something has slowly moved.

A Tale of Two Villages

Ashwin Parulkar

This story is based on fieldwork conducted with Kanchan Gandhi in Narauli Sen and Doomri villages of Muzaffarpur district, Bihar, during the months of September and October 2012, for a study on destitution.

Imagine a road in Northern Bihar that cuts through hamlets and villages. It is October. On either side of the road are yellow and green fields. Beyond the crops lie floodplains and swamps. Beyond the floodplains, a river. And between fields of crops and marshland by the river, ponds, where herders lead water buffaloes to bathe. Dirt hills line the road leading from village to village. Stray dogs sit there and look out over the fields. There are fields past the water that look as though they stretch to the Nepali border. There are hamlets beneath the hills where labourers live in huts. It is unclear to you where the jurisdiction of each village begins or ends. But what you'll need to know for now is that you will enter this picture, you will walk along this road in the Musahari block of Bihar's Muzaffarpur district.

With a population of 5,996 people, the majority of the people in Musahari block are Dalit agricultural labourers. Most are landless. Of all the Dalit families, nearly all who belong to a group of people known as the Musahars have lived and worked on the landowners' land for generations. In comparison to other Dalit groups, they rank far lower on all social indicators—literacy, maternal and child mortality and the ratio of agricultural labourers to the rest of the population. You will meet the Musahari people in the villages of Narauli Sen and Doomri.

It is potato and turmeric season. Labourers will be working the fields from seven in the morning until sunset for the harvest, until next month. Each of the villages has hamlets demarcated by caste. The lower castes—Rams, Paswans and Dhobis—live on the fringes of the village, in huts or half-constructed homes. The higher castes—Yadavs, Bhumihars, Rajputs, Srivastavas and Brahmins—live in houses that overlook acres of fields where various crops grow, depending on the season.

The Musahars are on the same rung as other Dalit castes on the Hindu hierarchy but the practice of untouchability exists even between Dalits. It is common for other Dalit groups to consider and treat the Musahars as inferior to all. The layout of the hamlets indicates as much. People from all Dalit groups work for landlords in the fields but Musahars are the only group to exclusively live on the dry areas of the landlord's plots and, until recently, have worked only on the land through a feudal, semi-bonded relationship. It is unclear where one village ends or another begins, but it is clear where the divisions between the hamlets lie.

Before you make your way to Narauli Sen and Doomri, you read about the Musahars to gain some understanding of why the nearly 2.1 million people who belong to this group in India are, arguably, one of the poorest in the country.

Sajjad Hassan[8] visited Nairoli Sen and Doomri months before you walk the road into those villages. You read in his account that the Musahars are descendents of Kol tribal people who lived in the

8. Sajjad Hassan, a colleague at the Centre for Equity, conducted a separate field study of the Musahars shortly before our visit. He provided us valuable background reading, including his own work, later published in the 2013-2014 Indian Exclusion Report as a chapter entitled, 'Musahars—What Keeps Musahars Entrapped in Poverty.'

north-eastern hills of Jharkhand and migrated to the plains in the twelfth century. They were brought into the Hindu caste structure and identified as the lowest, or untouchable. You read disputed accounts of how the group was named—it is certain that the name was given to them—but find that most scholars agree that Musahar means either rat or flesh eating people. You learn that a characteristic that has defined the life of this community for generations is their relationship of bonded labour to their landlords, known as the 'kamiauti' system. For generations, a select groups of landowners—sometimes the same family—has dictated the terms and conditions of farm work for the Musahars.

You read in government documents and field surveys that the Musahars are one of twenty-two Dalit groups in Bihar that the state government has identified as Mahadalits, a select group considered more vulnerable to chronic and endemic poverty in relation to other Dalits. The literacy rate of Mushar children, for instance, is only 9 per cent compared to the All-India Dalit level of 54.7 per cent, while nearly all of their people—93 per cent—are agricultural labourers, as compared to the 46 per cent of Dalits nationwide.[9] Mahadalits comprise 31 per cent of Bihar's population and there has been no improvement in the extreme deprivations that Musahars face—malnutrition, landlessness, illiteracy, and infant and maternal mortality—since the time that social activists and academics first identified the severity of these problems decades ago.

You read that social movements that began in the 1970s in the very villages you will visit led the government to initiate a series of nationwide schemes meant to address rural poverty associated with landlessness and hunger. The Whole Village Development Plan in the Fifth Five Year Plan, for instance, included a system of credit access and job creation for the rural poor and was implemented in over fifty villages in India—nearly half of them in Musahari block.

9. These figures were compiled by a 2007 Mahadalit Ayog report, and cited in 'Musahars—What Keeps Musahars Trapped in Poverty'.

Over time, marginal improvements in access to education and more diverse forms of rural employment improved the condition of other Dalit communities, but the daily realities of the Musahars are much the same as they were in the 1970s and before.

You ask yourself how social movements in the past tried to address poverty in this region and find books on the recent history of labour and land reform movements in Bihar. You read that widespread landlessness and starvation of the labouring poor in Bihar led to social upheaval in Musahari block in the mid to late 1960s. The majority of the population were landless Dalit agricultural labourers—Rams, Bhuiyas and Musahars—and the land they worked on was owned by, and the conditions of their work were dictated by middle and higher caste Kaashtas, Bhumihars and Brahmins. Land reforms did not take place in the 1950s after the abolishment of the zamindari system made way for the Bihar Land Reforms Act.

In 1968, Naxalites mobilized landless peasants in Musahari to take the lands they worked from the landlords by force. Violence ensued. Naxalite-led peasants killed six landlords in Ganjapur village and retaliatory violence claimed the lives of peasant leaders. The atmosphere of aggression, disquiet and violence paralyzed the new state government—a non-Congress-led coalition was elected for the first time in the state's history in 1967. Divergent ideologies arose between Naxalites, Gandhians and political leaders across the spectrum on how to address extreme poverty induced by long-standing economic inequality and predicated on generations of caste-based feudalism.

Unrest amongst Dalit agricultural labourers was also brewing in other areas of the country. In rural Andhra Pradesh and West Bengal, Naxalite-led violence was also underway, but there was something different about Musahari block. This small region had proved an essential support base fifty years earlier, for Gandhi's

Champaran Satyagraha. A social activist and leader of the Gandhi-inspired Sarvodaya Movement decided to intervene. His name was Jayaprakash Narayan and he came to the Musahari block in June 1970—a decision he said was 'spontaneous'—around the time that Naxalites murdered four people and issued death threats to two of Narayan's Sarvodaya volunteers. The spilling over of violence from against landlords to against people in disagreement with violence as a means toward social change proved that not only was the fate of the current social and economic relations in Bihar at stake, but also that of peace.

Narayan was astonished by the poverty he saw in the nearly 200 villages he visited. 'My first experience on coming face to face with the reality of Musahari,' he wrote, 'was to realize how remote and unreal were the brave pronouncements of Delhi or Patna from the actuality on the ground.'[10] He viewed the violence, unsettling as it was, as an outcome of the unchecked injustices that determined the quality of life for Dalits in the area. He believed that the chaos had resulted from large landowners not complying with the Land Ceiling Act; the people of powerful castes illegally taking seizure of government land; the role of money lenders in facilitating the diversion of land from the poor; and from corrupt politicians and bureaucrats who benefited from the power imbalances in the villages.

Narayan constructed a 'Musahari Plan', which was to consist of Gram Sabhas (village councils), Gram Koshes (village treasuries) and Gram Shanti Senas (village peace forces). He also engaged with local officials to establish the Muzaffarpur Development Authority to achieve these goals. They instituted and oversaw village councils, wage programs, rural credit systems and education programmes. 'When we started work in Musahari there were ten volunteers, of which most were from Bihar,' he wrote. 'Now there are twenty-five, most still from Bihar. Some volunteers stayed with me while

10. Narayan, Jayaprakash. *Face To Face*. Navchetna Prakashan, Varansi, 1970.

others worked in nearby villages—still others went to other far away villages. This was very intense work. Volunteers had to go house to house, usually more than once. I went to each little village, each village council meeting, and sometimes I would meet small groups of people in their homes. People from the villages would come to meet me and tell me of their problems.'

You also read that while Narayan's efforts were a major victory in stemming the kinds of mass poverty-related violence that occurred before his arrival, and spread in the 1980s and early 1990s to other parts of Bihar, the Musahars still remain amongst the poorest and most alienated people in the country.

Now you are on the road that leads into the villages where Musahars live. The road begins as a turn off the main highway that leads south–north into the district town. It is paved and you will travel by car until you reach the first house that marks the entrance of the village of Narauli Sen. From the back seat, you will marvel at the foliage around you. It is seven in the morning. The sun is out, the landscape in full view. Green, yellow, bright red, orange. It is all around you. Nature has endowed this land, you think. Numerous crops grow in abundance: corn, wheat, cucumber, rice, turmeric, eggplant, potatoes, red and green chilies. There are also too many local crops for you to know by name. You will eat one every day. Parval: your favourite. Farmers harvest this green vegetable on every patch of land. Some families stash them in baskets that line the open courtyards and kitchens of their homes.

Then you see the people who live on the fringes of these lands. You do not get the same feeling from seeing the people that you do from seeing the land. You see people and you forget about the land. Small ladies, young and old, under the weight of bundles of firewood on their backs, as they walk to their huts from the forests. A small girl sitting alone in front of one of broken hut rocking a baby goat in her lap. You see a woman named Murti Devi squatting over a stack of pots and pans to boil more chai. Hers is one of the many dirt-floored wood shacks on that road. And later, when you walk that road in the dark you'll mark her home as a landmark to get your bearings. Murti Devi's home by the tree whose trunk is shaped like the neck of a brontosaurus. Her grandchildren are there too. Standing by the door-less opening, smoke billowing out. You cannot tell their gender. Hair cut too short. They're small. Ragged shorts, no shirt. Runny noses. Malnourished.

Murti Devi's hut is the local chai stall. She sells chai, cigarettes and pakoras for a rupee each to thin men in dhotis, like Bharat Pasman and Santnarayan Pasman, who make chillums with their fists and talk through smoke about work, unpaid wages, their sons who've gone to Delhi to work in the factories. Every morning, the same discussion. Food, work, water.

And if you were to walk that road every morning you'd see the old widow Dukhi Devi too, wrapped in cold-weather shawls, her baby goat always trailing. She shouts at it. Kicks it when it chews at people. Sometimes she scoops it up in her arms and scurries off to her hut when the men tell her to stop complaining. But she's complaining about the same things they are: she hasn't received her benefits for the rural housing program, hasn't found work on the public works program for two years, hasn't got her pensions. When she gets work, she gets paid the woman's wage—Rs 50 a day.

Only she's got more fight in her, it seems, compared to most. She went to the Gram Sabha. Complained. Went to the mukhiya's house. Complained. About the public works program, nothing. About the rural housing program, they said they'd activate the benefits for a bribe: Rs 1,000, in cash.

When she stomps down the road with her goat, you'll say 'If it happens to everyone, have you ever thought about forming a group and talking to these officials together?' And Bharat Pasman will laugh and say, 'They know we're poor and weak so they can do what they want.' And Santnarayan Pasman will say, 'I don't give any thought to that.'

You'll stay with one of the families who do not have to worry about food, work, housing and school. They're one of the landlords of Narauli Sen. Some members of this family are working with the people of the villages in Mushari block who do have to worry about food, work, housing and school, by monitoring and implementing social programmes to get them access to such services on a regular basis. Their house has an open courtyard in the centre with a hand pump, a hearth and a wooden stairway that leads to an open roof where the oldest daughter, Nishi, gives tuition lessons to children from poor families who come in the mornings before school.

People call the owner of the house Master Ji. He is a kind man in his eighties who sits in the same chair facing the trees each day, chewing tobacco, talking to men in the village who come to see him and chat. He used to teach English and history in the district town until 1988, when he retired. And his daughter-in-law, Kiran, is a social worker for the Muzaffarpur Development Authority who works on issues of women's empowerment: credit access, training sessions on how to deal with domestic abuse and the alcoholism destroying the men. Nights there is no electricity. The younger children of the house study by candlelight before dinner is served.

After having your breakfast, you'll make your way to one of the Musahar tolas. You'll pass by other tolas. At the beginning of the road, before it curves outward, the landlord's houses: Bhumihars, Rajputs. Large houses, like Master Ji's. The curve fattens as you walk towards the tip of the blade where the Musahars live. More houses, fewer amenities. The roads are dirt, lined with stones. Barefoot goat herders. Buffaloes. Stray dogs. Toddlers walking solo. Kids collecting reeds and grass in bundles to feed their cows and goats. There are bright spots. Boys playing stick-ball cricket. Girls climbing trees.

You pass a lane of potters making bowls and inkwells from mounds of clay. A lane of bright blue houses. They are small but clean. You feel good watching them. One woman holds up a bowl to your face. 'We make 1,000 bowls a day,' she says.

It takes one hour to get to the Musahar tola. You feel thirsty. The hand pumps in the hamlets on the way look just like the one near Master Ji's house. But when you fill your bottle up, the water turns yellow with dregs at the bottom. You take a swig. It tastes like blood.

The road ends. There is a path forward. It is dirt. You smell animals and waste. Black and green liquid meld with the dirt and wild leaves. Children stand by the reeds. You see mud huts, a charpai, women and more children. You have entered the Musahar tola of Narauli Sen. It is still morning. Many adults have left for the fields. Jagdish Manjhi is sitting shirtless on a charpai on the edge of the path. He is the ration dealer of the local grain shop. He is sixty years old. Each month, a truck comes to the hamlet to offload 25 quintals of grain for the 370 families in the area so they can buy 10 kilogrammes of rice and 15 kilogrammes of wheat for cheap. The shop is a wood shed on the other side of the path.

'There are twelve people in my house. But I'm lucky. I have three grandsons and one son. Each of them earns,' he says.

Each year at least one of the men leaves the village for months at a time to find work. In August, there is no farm work. This year, his twenty-year-old grandson, Ramesh, went to Gujarat with five other young men to work in a plywood factory. Every summer, a contractor takes the young men to Gujarat and gives families Rs 6,000 as an advance for a month's salary. The advance helps to buy food to feed the rest of the family. His family also has an Antyodaya Anna Yojana (AAY) card, which allows them to buy their grains at Rs 3–4 a kilogramme. This year, Ramesh will return to Narauli Sen by Durga Pooja. Jagdish Manjhi says there are families in the hamlet who aren't so lucky. All Muslims, Rams and Musahars should hold AAY cards, but most of the people in the tola have been given BPL cards. Families who do not have multiple members who can earn suffer most. It is common for people to have more than one person in the family who is ill. There is a group of women standing around both of you as you talk. He looks at one of the women in a green dupatta, both arms around her two little boys. He says, 'Like her. She is the poorest woman in the village.'

Pavitri Devi is forty years old. She lives in one of the houses that you can see down the winding path. A few are half-brick, half-hay. A few are mud huts. Pavitri Devi was born in Bhirpur, a village in Kauti block. Her father, Shijdoth, was a bricklayer and her mother, Jalsi Devi, was a farm worker. They lived and worked on the fields of the landowner in the village. She started working in the fields with her parents when she was ten years old. Her three sisters and one brother also worked in the fields. They earned Rs 10 a day. In those days, she said, the landowner built small houses for the families who worked the land. There was no school in the village, but she wouldn't have been able to attend in any case, because the Musahars were forbidden from attending school. 'When we work in the malik's fields, there is no untouchability,' she says. 'But when we enter their courtyards, we're untouchables.' She was poor when she was a child, but people would support each other through tough times.

She didn't stay in her village for long. She was married to Punit Manjhi when she was fifteen years old and moved to Narauli Sen. In the early days, she and her husband worked as labourers in the landlord's field together. She gave birth to her first child, a girl, twenty years ago and when you meet her, her youngest is about a year old. Together, they had four girls and a boy. A few years ago, Punit Manjhi contracted tuberculosis. He died two years before your visit. Since his death, life has been very hard. She has still not received her widow's pension. She received Rs 5,000 of the Rs 10,000 due from the National Family Benefit Scheme, provided to below-poverty-line families upon the death of a main income earner. She works in the fields and earns about Rs 50 a day. When she's not working, she collects wood from the forest for the day's cooking.

You visit her home. There are puddles of dirty water on the floor, numerous sticks, a winnowing basket and plates overflowing with mud. There are two cows in the front yard. You see oyster shells piled in the corners. 'When the rains come, the shells wash up in the river and we sift them out to eat.' She says life was better when her husband was alive. Today, she and her kids eat a small portion of rice twice daily. When times are bad, they eat once.

You will see Pavitri Devi again, at a dharna protesting the sale of alcohol pouches in the area. In the days that you stay in the village there will be reports of violence against women by men who sell and consume these pouches and the women's groups will decide that it is time to demand that the local government ban them for their protection. For now, you will make your way on to the next nearest Musahar tola, in the village of Doomri, about 3 kilometres away.

You meet Sheila Devi outside her hut. Her husband, Ashok Manjhi, left for the fields that morning. Sheila Devi is home with her children and she tells you that the people have to work as much as they can this month to stock up for the winter. Work dries up in December. Come January through March, the planting season will begin, but the wages they're paid aren't enough to live on because the landlord gives food for wages only during harvest season. So they'll have to supplement the winter farm work with trips into Muzaffarpur to work on construction sites. Other young men go to Punjab or Delhi. At this time, transportation into the district takes an hour or more and the fares cut into the day's wages. But it's better than July and August, when there is no farm work at all.

She tells you people can't rely on the ration dealer because the shop is open only two to three times a year. Cheap grain helps. Dal is too expensive—about Rs 70 a kilogramme. Still, even when the ration shop is open, their wages aren't enough to pay the subsidized rate of Rs 120 for 25 kilogrammes of rice and 10 kilogrammes of wheat. So, families in the tola take a loan from the dealer and pay him back when they earn enough money. It takes months to shave off the debt. They have never been free of debt. Eight children surround Sheila Devi while she talks to you. Four are her own—Ruby Kumari (12), Anjali Kumari (5), Khushbu Kumari (2.5) and Ravi (1).

You see Shivji Manjhi, Ashok's brother, laying on a charpai outside their hut. He is ill. You walk over to him. His mouth is open and trembling. He tells you his wife died of diarrhea a few months ago. Her name was Meena Devi. One of the children sits with him. Other children are playing in the dirt. Their private parts are dragging along the dirt and stones on the ground. The boy's name is Ravi. He stumbles over to you. He just stands there looking at your pen and pad. His curly orange hair is all over the place.

Sheila Devi, his mother opens her arms out, laughing. 'Come! Come!' He starts laughing too. He walks over to her, falls into her lap while she smothers his face with these rapid hard kisses. She opens her sari and he feeds while she talks to you. One of her girls starts crying. There is a patch of haldi behind you and a dog limping by the hut with a broken leg. The child keeps crying and the sound gets inside you. You have never heard a child cry like this. You look behind the haldi patch, through some leafless trees; there is another hut. There is a man holding a baby in his arms. He is small, wearing a dhoti. He is very old. His head is shaved, just white stubble. There are large black blemishes on the baby's face. You ask Sheila Devi: 'Who is that?'

His name is Vijay Manjhi. You walk over to his hut. Vijay Manjhi is only fifty-five years old. He looks at least twenty years older. You see that his granddaughter's face is maligned with black pustules and yellowish white discharge is running out of them. Her name is Neesha. She is two years old. She is not crying any more. Vijay is rubbing her soiled head. He is disabled. He suffered kala azar when he was a boy and has had trouble walking for forty years. His brother died of the disease when they were children and his parents died when he was a teenager. Malti Devi comes out of the hut holding a favda in her hand, wiping the sweat from her face with her dupatta. She is Vijay Manjhi's wife. She has just come back from the fields and will return after spending time with her granddaughter. Neesha is their oldest daughter's daughter. Each of their daughters— Sunita (30), Rita (27), Sita (25) and Nageena (18)—is married and lives in a nearby village with her in-laws.

'What is wrong with the baby', you ask.

She has a skin disease. They are trying to keep up with the treatment. They borrow Rs 2000–3000 every one to two months. The baby is on a schedule of allopathic medicines that cost Rs 550 every eight days. It is pushing them further into debt and the treatment hasn't worked. Malti Devi and Vikas Manjhi took her to the public hospital where treatment is supposed to be free, but the doctor asked them to pay for medicines.

People say that this family is the poorest of the fifty or so families in the tola. They have an AAY card, but the couple says that they do not get grains every month. Malti Devi tells you that she received one month's work building wells on the NREGA program, but no one got their wages. This makes things difficult. Vijay Manjhi doesn't earn money. He has not been able to get a disability pension. Each time he has tried to apply for one with the panchayat he was asked for a doctor's certificate. The hospital where he has found out he could get one is near the railway station in the city. His disability makes it too far for him to travel. He gets grain from time to time from the landlord for watching the fields for animals and thieves who may ruin or steal crops. You will go with him one day. He crouches down with his cane in the reeds and watches. Buffaloes and their herders pass by. Boys send the animals into the water to bathe and jump on their backs, diving into the water off their humps. All you can see is open fields, floodplain, the sky. Vikas Manjhi, kneeling in the reeds, says 'I am good at what I do.'

When he is not watching the master's fields, he collects forest wood for the hearth at home. It takes the whole day. Malti Devi earns Rs 50 a day in the fields, which enables one meal a day. Usually just a bit of rice. 'Right now,' she tells you, 'I can still earn, but when my health doesn't allow it, I have to beg.' The couple says that, in one way, there is less stress on them since they got their daughters married. Still, they tell you, their economic situation is worse because they're still paying off loans they had to take for the marriage—Rs 3000–5000 in instalments, at 10 per cent interest. Other expenses include medical care for their granddaughter and themselves. They both fall ill routinely. Malti Devi has bouts with malaria often, she says, and on a later visit you will visit her when she is down with a fever, unable to work.

One of their daughters happens to be there during a later visit. Sita Devi is twenty-five years old and lives in a nearby village named Dhali Sakan with her husband, Ranjeet. She worked in the fields with her mother when she was a child to help feed the family. When you asked her if life has changed much since she was a child, she tells you that generations of people have worked the fields for generations of the same landowner. The landowners are a family known as the Thakurs. On the one hand, wages have always been low. Today men earn Rs 70 a day, women Rs 50. On the other, Sita Devi tells you, the landlords have, through the years, provided some support: they will give out vegetables when the harvest is good or will pay for a medical expense when a labourer is too debilitated to work. When her father needed medical attention for an appendix ailment, the landlord helped out with Rs 1,000, to help cover the Rs 4,000 bill.

On a later visit, Malti Devi tells you how it was when she was growing up. She grew up in a village in Muzaffurpur district called Kirdpa. Her parents were also farm labourers for a Rajput landowner. They earned about Rs 20 a day and when she got married to Vijay Manjhi at the age of ten or twelve she moved to the Musahar tola of his village.

About eighty or ninety years ago, she tells you, the Musahars in this tola used to live in a village called Pushtaria, where one of the older Thakurs owned land. You learn that different groups of Musahars were bonded to select members of the landowning family. When the farmland was divided up, the male member who was granted farmland in Doomri took the ancestors of these Musahars with him and they have lived in this plot of land where these mud huts were built and have stood ever since.

When Malti Devi was young, she told you, she was not allowed to go to school. She lived with four sisters and two brothers. Her parents died when she was a small child. 'When they were alive,' she tells you, 'we had enough to eat. But when they died we had much trouble feeding ourselves.' Today, only two of her sisters are alive. But she does not know much about them, she says, because she hasn't been in contact with them for years. She tells you that she and her husband are doing the best they can to keep their granddaughter alive. But she expresses uncertainty in the future because she does not know how long her health will hold up. She tells this to you on a day that she is sick.

Over time, you become aware of the lack of faith people in the tola have in public programmes. None work. Officials responsible for the wage programme have not paid wages. The ration dealer does not open the grain shop regularly or sell grains to the most impoverished AAY cardholders. No anganwadi centre exists. Farm work pays very little and some months there is no work at all. You observed that a Gram Sabha was held on 2 October in the neighbouring panchayat. No such meeting occurred for the panchayat in which Doomri is located. Many people say 'we eat once a day'. One man says 'if we don't get NREGA work, we'll die of hunger.'

One day you speak to the landlord at his home. His name is Sudhir Thakur. He and his brothers have inherited their shares of land from their father, Bhola Thakur. He lives in a nice cement bungalow. Labourers are working on the house as you visit. He has a garage with a truck and an SUV. But before you see this, you walk through rows of vegetable patches to get to this house. On the way, you spot Malti Devi, picking potatoes and putting them into a sack across her shoulder. She asks you what you are doing there. You sense the concern in her face and wonder if speaking to him is a good idea. Perhaps it is not. You ask her if she is okay with this. She has a worried look. You are worried now. She says as long as you do not tell him that you spoke to her personally it is okay. You say yes, you understand. On your way to meet him you feel guilty. Naïve. You tell yourself to merely ask general questions. Draw information out of him. Do not press hard. It could have consequences.

You approach the front of his house. He is outside talking to someone. He sees you. He welcomes you. He tells one of the workers to bring you a chair. He tells another worker to bring tea. He offers you his time. You tell him that you are researching the lives of the Musahars. He tells you a number of reasons why the community suffers. It is true that the Musahars are an almost wholly illiterate people, he acknowledges. They do not have the competency for or the interest in school, he tells you. It is true that they are ill and hungry much of their lives, he also says. But he also willingly gives out broken pieces of vegetables that cannot be sold in the market. And when workers steal from the land, he doesn't take action because he knows they are hungry and poor.

But there is also something else to take note. The community has always been desperately poor, yes. He also agrees the wages he gives are very low. But he wants you to understand that the factors driving these people into poverty are different today than what they may have been twenty to thirty years ago.

What are those factors, you ask.

He tells you that agriculture is stagnating throughout the country. You do not know how much land he owns. But he wants to disabuse you of the notion you may have that only the small farmer is struggling. Large and small farmers, he says, are finding it increasingly difficult to get government support for inputs required to grow adequate amounts of various food. 'The truth is,' he tells you, 'it is getting costlier to produce adequate yields.' He says that this has an impact on his ability to pay decent wages. The problems in agriculture, he tells you, produce another problem.

What is that problem, you ask.

He tells you to take a good look at him. Does he look like a farmer? He is wearing a white polo shirt tucked into jeans and white tennis shoes. You think no, he does not look like a farmer. He tells you that is because he is not one. He does not live on the land twelve months a year. He has a house in the city where he lives with his wife and kids. Two of his brothers who also have land shares live in Bombay. The days when the landowners lived on their lands year round and threw themselves into farming as a way of life are over, he tells you. As he speaks, you try to guess his age. About forty-five, you think. He says that his generation was the first to seize opportunities in more lucrative kinds of work. And this was aided by the increased access to education. He himself has a bachelor's degree in Chemistry.

More and more land-owning families, he tells you, are selling their lands. Not merely because they are finding better opportunities elsewhere, but there are other pressures as well. For instance, everyone in Bihar is shackled by the customs of dowry. Many land-owning families who have left farming also have to pay exorbitant dowry rates to get their daughters married. To do this, they sell their lands. He tells you that this change has also affected the lives of people like the Musahars who are dependent on working the land for their survival.

You visit the Musahar people many more times. Your conversation with the landlord and the understanding that each of the major food, wage, and work programmes are defunct makes you wonder if people migrate out of the village for work and food. People tell you that they are not allowed to leave, because there is a court case against them, which originated out of a land dispute. You ask, what is the nature of the land dispute?

There had been land disputes in the area before, you have read, between disgruntled peasants and landlords. But you come to find out from the people that the land dispute in Doomri originated between Bhola Thakur's remaining brothers, Amrinder Thakur and Pappu Thakur. Since Bhola died, the land that the Musahars live on is legally in Amrinder Thakur's name. Pappu Thakur believes that this land and the surrounding farmland belong to him. The two are currently in a legal dispute over the ownership of the land.

But things became complicated when you learn that Pappu Thakur hired one of the Mushars in the tola to manage his fields. He pays Chandrasekhar Manjhi Rs 300, more than four times the wages paid to men in the fields. The higher wage was one source of angst amongst the community.

Trouble also started to brew when Chandrasekhar Manjhi, responsible for reporting the activities of the workers to his boss, disclosed that his neighbours were periodically stealing food from the field. Pappu Thakur came to the tola and told the people that cases would be filed against them for stealing.

One day, a fight erupted between Chandrasekhar Manjhi and a few others of the tola on the dirt road leading into the village. You hear several accounts of how and why the fight started. Everyone in the village agrees that no one was badly hurt. But the conflict gave reason for Chandrasekhar Manjhi to file a case through Pappu Thakur's stewardship in the courts. During your visit you come to know that sixteen people in the tola have had cases of rape and theft against them. The rape cases, the people say, are false. Most of the accused are women. The court, you learned, has prevented any of the Musahars from leaving the village. It is believed that Pappu Thakur is backing Chandrasekhar Manjhi in the case with hopes that the incident will help the initial land dispute case with his brother over the Musahar plot to legally transfer the land under his name.

You think there are levels that you can understand and levels you cannot. You understood what you read before you came here. You understand the bits of stories people tell you, but you cannot put them together as you could the neat synopses you had read before you arrived. Before you leave, you see Malti Devi and Vijay Manjhi crouched down, looking at the fields over a hill. They're looking at the fields that stretch to Nepal. You're looking at another world. What do you see?

About the Authors

Amod Shah is a PhD candidate at the International Institute of Social Studies in the Hague, the Netherlands, focusing on land-acquisition-related conflict in India. He was previously a researcher with the S.R. Sankaran Unit on Hunger and Social Exclusion at the Centre for Equity Studies.

Anhad Imaan is a Delhi-based policy and action researcher, musician, film score designer and sports blogger. He is currently in charge of operations and research at YouRTI, an online service and social enterprise that helps the citizens of India file RTI queries to the government conveniently and anonymously. Previously, he worked with Yugantar, a think-tank, as a project consultant. He was a researcher and program coordinator at CES from August 2013 to January 2015. Anhad is a guest blogger for Eventraveler, a sports and music promotional start-up, and is also the founder member of Mellowghost, an instrumental quartet with whom he has designed background scores for documentary films.

Annie Baxi is a doctoral scholar in Psychology and trained counsellor. She is a part of the Housing Discrimination Project affiliated with Centre for Equity Studies. Her academic interests include gender studies, issues of marginality, mental health and qualitative methods. In her work, she attempts to listen to silent aspects of human experiences and is always keen to hear/read stories of others and narrate her own.

Ashwin Parulkar is a Senior Researcher at Centre for Policy Research in New Delhi. He was previously with Centre for Equity Studies.

Harsh Mander is a writer, human rights worker, columnist, researcher and teacher; he works with survivors of mass violence and hunger as well as with homeless persons and street children. His books include *Looking*

Away: Inequality, Prejudice and Indifference in New India, *Fatal Accidents of Birth: Stories of Suffering, Oppression and Resistance*, *Unheard Voices: Stories of Forgotten Lives*, *The Ripped Chest: Public Policy and the Poor in India*, *Fear and Forgiveness: The Aftermath of Massacre*, *Fractured Freedom: Chronicles from India's Margins*, *Untouchability in Rural India* (coauthored) and *Living with Hunger and Ash in the Belly: India's Unfinished Battle against Hunger*. He regularly writes columns for *The Hindu*, *Hindustan Times* and *Mint*, and contributes frequently to scholarly journals. His stories have been adapted for films, such as Shyam Benegal's *Samar* and Mallika Sarabhai's dance drama *Unsuni*.

Rhea John is a student at the Institute of Development Studies, Sussex and formerly a researcher with the Centre for Equity Studies, New Delhi.

Saba Sharma is currently a PhD student in the Department of Geography at the University of Cambridge, studying the state and ethnic conflict in Assam. She was a former research associate at the Centre for Equity Studies, New Delhi.

Shikha Sethia is a masters student in Development Studies at the International Institute of Social Studies, the Hague. She was previously a researcher with the S.R. Sankaran Unit on Hunger and Social Exclusion at the Centre for Equity Studies.